VOLUME 486　　　　　　　　　　　　　　　　　　　　　　　　JULY 1986

THE ANNALS

of The American Academy *of* Political
and Social Science

RICHARD D. LAMBERT, *Editor*
ALAN W. HESTON, *Associate Editor*

REGULATING CAMPAIGN FINANCE

Special Editors of this Volume

LLOYD N. CUTLER
LOUIS R. COHEN
ROGER M. WITTEN

Ⓢ SAGE PUBLICATIONS　　*Beverly Hills / London / Newbury Park / New Delhi*

MARTHA S. GRAFTON LIBRARY
MARY BALDWIN COLLEGE

THE ANNALS
© 1986 by The American Academy of Political and Social Science

ERICA GINSBURG, Assistant Editor

All rights reserved. No part of this volume may be reproduced or utilized in any form or by any means, electronic or mechanical, including photocopying, recording or by any information storage and retrieval system, without permission in writing from the publisher.

Editorial Office: 3937 Chestnut Street, Philadelphia, Pennsylvania 19104.

For information about membership* (individuals only) and subscriptions (institutions), address:

SAGE PUBLICATIONS, INC.
275 South Beverly Drive
Beverly Hills, CA 90212 USA

From India and South Asia, write to:
SAGE PUBLICATIONS INDIA Pvt. Ltd.
P.O. Box 4215
New Delhi 110 048
INDIA

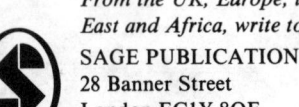

From the UK, Europe, the Middle East and Africa, write to:
SAGE PUBLICATIONS LTD
28 Banner Street
London EC1Y 8QE
ENGLAND

SAGE Production Editor: JACQUELINE SYROP

**Please note that members of The Academy receive THE ANNALS with their membership.*

Library of Congress Catalog Card Number 85-072102
International Standard Serial Number ISSN 0002-7162
International Standard Book Number ISBN 0-8039-2543-3 (Vol. 486, 1986 paper)
International Standard Book Number ISBN 0-8039-2542-5 (Vol. 486, 1986 cloth)
Manufactured in the United States of America. First printing, July 1986.

The articles appearing in THE ANNALS are indexed in *Book Review Index; Public Affairs Information Service Bulletin; Social Sciences Index; Monthly Periodical Index; Current Contents; Behavioral, Social Management Sciences;* and *Combined Retrospective Index Sets.* They are also abstracted and indexed in *ABC Pol Sci, Historical Abstracts, Human Resources Abstracts, Social Sciences Citation Index, United States Political Science Documents, Social Work Research & Abstracts, Peace Research Reviews, Sage Urban Studies Abstracts, International Political Science Abstracts, America: History and Life,* and/or *Family Resources Database.*

Information about membership rates, institutional subscriptions, and back issue prices may be found on the facing page.

Advertising. Current rates and specifications may be obtained by writing to THE ANNALS Advertising and Promotion Manager at the Beverly Hills office (address above).

Claims. Claims for undelivered copies must be made no later than three months following month of publication. The publisher will supply missing copies when losses have been sustained in transit and when the reserve stock will permit.

Change of Address. Six weeks' advance notice must be given when notifying of change of address to insure proper identification. Please specify name of journal. Send change of address to: THE ANNALS, c/o Sage Publications, Inc., 275 South Beverly Drive, Beverly Hills, CA 90212.

SEP 1 5 1986

The American Academy of Political and Social Science

3937 Chestnut Street Philadelphia, Pennsylvania 19104

Board of Directors

ELMER B. STAATS
MARVIN E. WOLFGANG
LEE BENSON
RICHARD D. LAMBERT
THOMAS L. HUGHES
LLOYD N. CUTLER

RANDALL M. WHALEY
HENRY W. SAWYER, III
WILLIAM T. COLEMAN, Jr.
ANTHONY J. SCIRICA
FREDERICK HELDRING

Officers

President
MARVIN E. WOLFGANG

Vice-Presidents
RICHARD D. LAMBERT, First Vice-President
STEPHEN B. SWEENEY, First Vice-President Emeritus

Secretary	*Treasurer*	*Counsel*
RANDALL M. WHALEY	ELMER B. STAATS	HENRY W. SAWYER, III

Editors, THE ANNALS

RICHARD D. LAMBERT, *Editor* ALAN W. HESTON, *Associate Editor*

THORSTEN SELLIN, *Editor Emeritus*

Assistant to the President
MARY E. HARRIS

Origin and Purpose. The Academy was organized December 14, 1889, to promote the progress of political and social science, especially through publications and meetings. The Academy does not take sides in controverted questions, but seeks to gather and present reliable information to assist the public in forming an intelligent and accurate judgment.

Meetings. The Academy holds an annual meeting in the spring extending over two days.

Publications. THE ANNALS is the bimonthly publication of The Academy. Each issue contains articles on some prominent social or political problem, written at the invitation of the editors. Also, monographs are published from time to time, numbers of which are distributed to pertinent professional organizations. These volumes constitute important reference works on the topics with which they deal, and they are extensively cited by authorities through-out the United States and abroad. The papers presented at the meetings of The Academy are included in THE ANNALS.

Membership. Each member of The Academy receives THE ANNALS and may attend the meetings of The Academy. Membership is open only to individuals. Annual dues: $26.00 for the regular paperbound edition (clothbound, $39.00). Add $9.00 per year for membership outside the U.S.A. Members may also purchase single issues of THE ANNALS for $6.95 each (clothbound, $10.00).

Subscriptions. THE ANNALS (ISSN 0002-7162) is published six times annually—in January, March, May, July, September, and November. Institutions may subscribe to THE ANNALS at the annual rate: $50.00 (clothbound, $66.00). Add $9.00 per year for subscriptions outside the U.S.A. Institutional rates for single issues: $10.00 each (clothbound, $15.00).

Second class postage paid at Philadelphia, Pennsylvania, and at additional mailing offices.

Single issues of THE ANNALS may be obtained by individuals who are not members of The Academy for $7.95 each (clothbound, $15.00). Single issues of THE ANNALS have proven to be excellent supplementary texts for classroom use. Direct inquiries regarding adoptions to THE ANNALS c/o Sage Publications (address below).

All correspondence concerning membership in The Academy, dues renewals, inquiries about membership status, and/or purchase of single issues of THE ANNALS should be sent to THE ANNALS c/o Sage Publications, Inc., 275 South Beverly Drive, Beverly Hills, CA 90212. *Please note that orders under $20 must be prepaid.* Sage affiliates in London and India will assist institutional subscribers abroad with regard to orders, claims, and inquiries for both subscriptions and single issues.

THE ANNALS

of The American Academy *of* Political *and* Social Science

RICHARD D. LAMBERT, *Editor*
ALAN W. HESTON, *Associate Editor*

──────── FORTHCOMING ────────

IMMIGRATION AND AMERICAN PUBLIC POLICY
Special Editor: Rita J. Simon

Volume 487   September 1986

REVITALIZING THE INDUSTRIAL CITY
Special Editors: Ralph R. Widner and Marvin E. Wolfgang
Includes the edited proceedings of the 1986 Annual Meeting
of The American Academy of Political and Social Science

Volume 488   November 1986

INTERNATIONAL AFFAIRS IN AFRICA
Special Editor: Gerald J. Bender

Volume 489   January 1987

See page 3 for information on Academy membership and
purchase of single volumes of **The Annals**.

CONTENTS

PREFACE .... *Lloyd N. Cutler and Roger M. Witten*	9
THE NEW FACES OF AMERICAN POLITICS .... *David Adamany*	12
POLITICAL FINANCING AND THE CONSTITUTION .... *Ralph K. Winter*	34
POLITICAL FINANCE IN THE LIBERAL REPUBLIC: REPRESENTATION, EQUALITY, AND DEREGULATION .... *Stephen Harder*	49
SHOULD THERE BE PUBLIC FINANCING OF CONGRESSIONAL CAMPAIGNS? .... *Charles McC. Mathias, Jr.*	64
MONEY IN POLITICS .... *Richard Bolling*	76
CAMPAIGN FINANCE REFORM: THE UNFINISHED AGENDA .... *Fred Wertheimer*	86
DEMOCRACY OR PLUTOCRACY? THE CASE FOR A CONSTITUTIONAL AMENDMENT TO OVERTURN *BUCKLEY* v. *VALEO* .... *Jonathan Bingham*	103
CAN THE PARTIES REGULATE CAMPAIGN FINANCING?............................... *Lloyd N. Cutler*	115
LIVING WITH THE FECA: CONFESSIONS OF A SOMETIME CAMPAIGN TREASURER .... *Michael S. Berman*	121
OF PHILOSOPHERS, FOXES, AND FINANCES: CAN THE FEDERAL ELECTION COMMISSION EVER DO AN ADEQUATE JOB? .... *William C. Oldaker*	132
PUTTING ON THE CANDIDATES: THE USE OF TELEVISION IN PRESIDENTIAL ELECTIONS .... *Newton N. Minow and Lee M. Mitchell*	146
CAMPAIGN FINANCE: THE SYSTEM WE HAVE .... *Michael Barone*	158
BOOK DEPARTMENT...	163
INDEX	193

BOOK DEPARTMENT CONTENTS

INTERNATIONAL RELATIONS AND POLITICS

CLARKSON, STEPHEN. *Canada and the Reagan Challenge.* Craig McCaughrin 163

KEGLEY, CHARLES W., Jr. and EUGENE R. WITTKOPF, eds. *The Nuclear Reader: Strategy, Weapons, War*;
HUDSON, GEORGE E. and JOSEPH KRUZEL, eds. *American Defense Annual 1985-1986.* Roy M. Melbourne 164

SAMPSON, GEOFFREY. *An End to Allegiance: Individual Freedom and the New Politics.* Charles T. Barber 166

VAN DYKE, VERNON. *Human Rights, Ethnicity and Discrimination.* Allen Ballard 167

AFRICA, ASIA, AND LATIN AMERICA

BANERJEE, SANJOY. *Dominant Classes and the State in Development: Theory and the Case of India*;
BENNER, JEFFREY. *The Indian Foreign Policy Bureaucracy.* Craig Baxter 168

CALLAGHY, THOMAS M. *The State-Society Struggle: Zaire in Comparative Perspective.* James A. Casada 169

DAVIS, NATHANIEL. *The Last Two Years of Salvador Allende.* David M. Billikopf 169

HUSSAIN, ASAF. *Islamic Iran: Revolution and Counter-Revolution*;
MARR, PHEBE. *The Modern History of Iraq.* Karl K. Barbir 170

TEVETH, SHABTAI. *Ben Gurion and the Palestinian Arabs: From Peace to War*;
REICH, WALTER. *A Stranger in My House: Jews and Arabs in the West Bank.* Louay Bahry 171

EUROPE

SNYDER, LOUIS L. *Diplomacy in Iron: The Life of Herbert von Bismarck.* Franklin B. Wickwire 172

UNITED STATES

KREISBERG, PAUL H. et al. *American Hostages in Iran: The Conduct of a Crisis.* Edward Weisband 172

LAMBRIGHT, W. HENRY. *Presidential Management of Science and Technology.* Nicholas O. Berry 173

McCOY, DONALD R. *The Presidency of Harry S. Truman.* Jacques Szaluta 174

PERNICK, MARTIN S. *A Calculus of Suffering: Pain, Professionalism, and Anesthesia in Nineteenth-Century America.* Vaughn Davis Bornet 175

PINCKNEY, ALPHONSO. *The Myth of Black Progress*;
JONES, JACQUELINE. *Labor of Love, Labor of Sorrow.* Fred Rotondaro 176

WESTON, JACK. *The Real American Cowboy.* Kurt W. Back 176

SOCIOLOGY

ADLER, PATRICIA A. *Wheeling and Dealing: An Ethnography of an Upper-Level Drug Dealing and Smuggling Community.* Leonard Blumberg 177

BECKSTROM, JOHN H. *Sociobiology and the Law: The Biology of Altruism in the Courtroom of the Future.* Alvin Boskoff 178

CARNOY, MARTIN and HENRY M. LEVIN. *Schooling and Work in the Democratic State.* Edward R. Beauchamp 179

GOODIN, ROBERT E. *Protecting the Vulnerable: A Reanalysis of Our Social Responsibilities.* Janet Carter 180

McCLELLAN, JAMES E., III. *Science Reorganized: Scientific Societies in the Eighteenth Century.* Carl B. Backman 181

NELSON, BARBARA J. *Making an Issue of Child Abuse: Political Agenda Setting for Social Problems.* William R. Beer 182

PFEFFER, LEO. *Religion, State and the Burger Court.* Robert J. Sickels 183

ZOLLAR, ANN CREIGHTON. *A Member of the Family: Strategies for Black Family Continuity.* Marie Richmond-Abbott 184

ECONOMICS

LEAMER, EDWARD E. *Sources of International Comparative Advantage.* Michael D. Bradley 185

MINTZ, BETH and MICHAEL SCHWARTZ. *The Power Structure of American Business.* John C. Beyer 186

TAYLOR, SERGE. *Making Bureaucracies Think: The Environmental Impact Statement Strategy of Administrative Reform.* Anthony T. Bouscaren 187

PREFACE

Elections to federal office are central to our constitutional form of government, and money has become central to those elections. Campaign finance regulation is therefore an important issue of political and social science.

While agreement can easily be reached on the foregoing propositions, it is exceedingly difficult to find consensus on any other aspect of the subject. Some argue on constitutional and policy grounds that the government should not regulate campaign finance at all, or should only prohibit grossly antidemocratic behavior such as bribery. Others argue that broad campaign finance regulation is necessary to protect the electoral system from actual and apparent corruption and to restore the electorate's confidence in the integrity of elected officials. Supporters of campaign finance regulation often differ widely, however, on the appropriate means for achieving objectives they hold in common.

The debate about campaign finance regulation is not conducted solely at lofty legal and political science levels. The issue is redolent of realpolitik. Incumbent officeholders consider the crucial effect of legislative changes on their relative strength vis-à-vis challengers. Democrats and Republicans consider how regulatory changes might affect their relative strength. Party officials worry about the distribution of power between them and the party's candidates. Interest groups worry about access to officeholders. Business worries about labor and vice versa.

The debate about campaign finance regulation is dominated by legal considerations as well. The First Amendment, of course, protects freedom of speech and association from unjustified governmental intrusion. This protection has its most vital application in the context of federal elections, but all campaign finance regulation affects speech and association in federal campaigns. This produces an inexorable tension between First Amendment values and campaign finance regulations, which the courts have not been successful in resolving in a consistent manner.

This volume presents articles on campaign finance regulation by a distinguished and diverse group of authors. They include practicing politicians, a lobbyist, a judge, an academic, a journalist, and lawyers who practice in the field. The authors attack the issues at all levels—theoretical, practical, and legal—and from widely disparate perspectives.

The first article is by David Adamany, now the chancellor of Wayne State University, who has published widely on the subject of campaign finance. His article, entitled "The New Faces of American Politics," analyzes the impact of campaign finance regulation on American politics and, in particular, on the major parties and political action committees (PACs). Mr. Adamany finds that American politics have become more professionalized, bureaucratized, centralized, and nationalized and that financial constituencies have gained strength at the expense of voting constituencies. Mr. Adamany attributes these changes to factors other than campaign finance laws, however. His fact-filled article sets the stage for the ensuing articles.

The volume next presents two articles that cogently state the case against campaign finance regulation. In "Political Financing and the Constitution," Judge Ralph K. Winter concludes, principally on constitutional grounds, that there is no compelling justification for regulating the use of money in federal campaigns and, accordingly, that most such regulation violates the First Amendment. Judge Winter, currently a member of the United States Court of Appeals for the Second Circuit, has been an articulate critic of campaign finance regulation both as a law professor at Yale and as a lawyer in landmark campaign finance cases.

Stephen Harder complements Judge Winter's approach in his article, "Political Finance in the Liberal Republic: Representation, Equality, and Deregulation." Mr. Harder is a former political science student and is now a practicing lawyer. He argues, principally from a policy perspective, that the private market for political finance, left unregulated, should consistently deny any group the market power necessary to influence either elections or legislators significantly.

The volume next presents a series of articles that take issue with the viewpoints expressed by Judge Winter and Mr. Harder. The first four argue forcefully that additional campaign finance reform legislation is needed to cure current abuses, including the rise of PACs, and to protect the body politic.

In an article entitled "Should There Be Public Financing of Congressional Campaigns?" Senator Charles McC. Mathias recounts disturbing trends in the use of money in elections, based on his experience in the Senate. These observations lead him to advocate the adoption of public financing for congressional elections as a workable solution to these problems.

Former Congressman Richard Bolling, a member of Congress from 1949 until 1982, shares many of the concerns expressed by Senator Mathias. Congressman Bolling concludes that special interest money, in the form of contributions, honoraria, and lobbying efforts, threatens to destroy Congress. He proposes limits on PAC contributions and a radically different form of public financing that would be given to the opponent of a PAC beneficiary in amounts equal to the PAC's contribution.

The president of Common Cause, Fred Wertheimer, next recommends a comprehensive package of legislative reforms that he believes are necessary to cure shortcomings in the current laws. His article, "Campaign Finance Reform: The Unfinished Agenda," focuses on means to control PAC contributions, provide alternative public funding through tax credits or other mechanisms, and curb abuses relating to independent expenditures and soft money.

Two other authors, former Congressman Jonathan Bingham and Lloyd N. Cutler, agree that additional campaign finance reform measures are necessary. They question, however, the efficacy of legislative solutions such as those endorsed by Senator Mathias, Congressman Bolling, and Mr. Wertheimer.

Congressman Bingham proposes an amendment to the Constitution to increase Congress's power to regulate federal election campaigns, notwithstanding the First Amendment. His article, entitled "Democracy or Plutocracy?" argues that a constitutional amendment is needed because Supreme Court decisions too narrowly confine Congress's power to curb campaign finance abuses. Congressman Bingham does not believe public financing for congressional elections is a practical solution.

Mr. Cutler, who served as counsel to President Carter and has been involved as a lawyer in several significant campaign finance cases, takes a different tack. In his article, entitled "Can the Parties Regulate Campaign Financing?" Mr. Cutler argues that the parties have the legal power to bind their candidates to comply with comprehensive campaign finance rules, including expenditure limits that Congress cannot constitutionally impose. His article sketches a model set of party rules on this subject.

Michael S. Berman's article, "Living with the FECA: Confessions of a Sometime Campaign Treasurer," provides a counterpoint to the views of those who advocate increased regulation. From his vantage point as treasurer in the 1984 Mondale campaign and his experience in other campaigns, Mr. Berman pinpoints numerous deficiencies in the current regulatory scheme and the onerous burdens it imposes. These observations lead Mr. Berman to question the overall efficacy of those laws, notwithstanding his endorsement of their objectives.

William C. Oldaker addresses another issue: the performance of the Federal Election Commission in fulfilling its regulatory responsibilities. Mr. Oldaker served as general counsel of the commission. In his article, entitled "Of Philosophers, Foxes, and Finances: Can the Federal Election Commission Ever Do an Adequate Job?" he identifies weaknesses inherent in the commission's structure and deficiencies in the commission's performance of its enforcement responsibilities.

Newton N. Minow and Lee M. Mitchell contribute their insights on an issue that is intertwined with that of campaign finance regulation—the role of television in federal election campaigns. Mr. Minow was chairman of the Federal Communications Commission and is now a lawyer in private practice. Mr. Mitchell is president of The Field Corporation. Their article, "Putting on the Candidates: The Use of Television in Presidential Elections," makes several concrete suggestions for changes that would improve the way candidates use television in campaigns.

Finally, Michael Barone, a journalist for the *Washington Post,* contributes his overview of the state of campaign finance regulation in an article entitled "Campaign Finance: The System We Have." He comments on the patchwork, or custom-crafted, quality of the regulatory landscape and how such custom crafting inevitably leaves the job unfinished. Mr. Barone cites the phenomenon of soft money as an example of a problem that should have been and was thought to have been resolved by current law.

As these fine articles demonstrate, campaign finance regulation is a difficult public policy issue. It provokes strong and conflicting views. Answers that can command a consensus are elusive. These articles will help to inform the ongoing public debate.

LLOYD N. CUTLER
ROGER M. WITTEN

The New Faces of American Politics

By DAVID ADAMANY

ABSTRACT: Dramatic changes have occurred in American politics and campaign finance during the past decade. Many attribute these changes to the Federal Election Campaign Act, but modern campaign and fundraising technology have played a larger role. Together, they may have strengthened national political parties, but they have even more dramatically strengthened political action committees. Politics has also become more professionalized, bureaucratized, centralized, and nationalized. The financial constituency of politics has become more influential; the voting constituency has become increasingly removed from all aspects of politics—except casting ballots—that influence the outcomes of elections and shape national policy. These developments challenge deeply rooted beliefs about the preeminent role of voters in controlling democratic elections and government.

David Adamany is a graduate of Harvard College and the Harvard Law School. He also holds M.S. and Ph.D. degrees in political science from the University of Wisconsin, Madison, where he served as professor of political science. He is now president and professor of law and political science at Wayne State University. Adamany has had extensive experience in public affairs as a member of the Wisconsin Public Service Commission, chairman of the Wisconsin State Elections Board, and other posts. He is the author of many articles and books on constitutional law, the judicial process, American politics, and campaign finance.

SINCE the enactment of the Federal Election Campaign Act (FECA) of 1971,[1] many observers have sighted dramatic shifts in political power, influence, advantage, and access. Some have attributed these changes to campaign finance laws and current methods of financing politics.

Political parties have been weakened or strengthened in the new world of political money, depending on one's perspective. Political action committees (PACs) have become stronger and influential. Broader citizen participation in politics has been stimulated. The large contributors of yore have disappeared. A new class of money brokers who can raise many contributions in sums of $1000 or $5000 has emerged. Finally, politics has become more centralized, nationalized, and bureaucratized—or so it is said.

THE CONDITION OF POLITICAL PARTIES

An early criticism of the FECA was its purported hostility to political parties. This criticism was part of a broader commentary that American political parties were in precipitous decline.[2]

Second thoughts and changes in the law have produced a substantially revised view. The most exuberant is surely Xandra Kayden's: "The biggest winner under the new rules are the two major political parties."[3] A more cautious second thought has been expressed by Michael Malbin: "For the most part, the [FECA] has neither helped nor hurt the parties; it has simply stayed out of their way."[4]

In my view, the FECA was never as hostile to political parties as its critics suggested.[5] Furthermore, the 1979 amendments to the act expanded the role of political parties in campaign finance. From the outset, political parties received favorable treatment by the FECA's contribution and expenditure limits. For example, they may receive $20,000 contributions annually from individuals while nonparty committees may receive only $5000.

Similarly, parties may make substantially greater contributions to candidates than the $1000 allowed to individuals and $5000 permitted for nonparty committees. Under complex rules, national party and congressional campaign committees can each contribute $5000 to House candidates in both the primary

---

1. Federal Election Campaign Act of 1971, Pub. L. No. 92-225, 86 Stat. 3 (1972); Revenue Act of 1971, Pub. L. No. 92-178, 85 Stat. 497, as amended, 87 Stat. 138 (1973); Federal Election Campaign Act Amendments of 1974, Pub. L. No. 93-443, 88 Stat. 1263; Federal Election Campaign Act Amendments of 1976, Pub. L. No. 94-283, 90 Stat. 475; and Federal Election Campaign Act Amendments of 1979, Pub. L. No. 96-187, 93 Stat. 1339.

2. See, for instance, William J. Crotty and Gary C. Jacobson, *American Parties in Decline* (Boston: Little, Brown, 1980); Jeane J. Kirkpatrick, *Dismantling the Parties* (Washington, DC: American Enterprise Institute, 1978); Austin Ranney, "Political Parties: Reform and Decline," in *The New American Political System*, ed. Anthony King (Washington, DC: American Enterprise Institute, 1979), pp. 213-48.

3. Xandra Kayden, "Effects of the Present System of Campaign Financing on Special Interest Groups" (Paper delivered at the Conference on Presidential Primaries, Gerald R. Ford Library, University of Michigan, Ann Arbor, MI, 24-26 Apr. 1985), p. 2.

4. Michael Malbin, "What Should Be Done about Independent Campaign Expenditures?" *Regulation*, 6:41, 45 (1982).

5. David Adamany, "Political Finance and the American Political Parties," *Hastings Constitutional Law Quarterly*, 10:463, 525-30, 562-65 (Spring 1983); idem, "Financing Political Parties in the United States," in *Parties and Democracy in Britain and America*, ed. Vernon Bogdanor (New York: Praeger, 1984), pp. 153, 169-74, 178-79.

and the general election, for a total of $20,000. State party committees and their local units can each add $5000 in each election. Under a 1981 Supreme Court decision, the national party can act as an agent for the state party, thus allowing the national party—which may have greater resources—to spend the full $20,000. Both national and state political parties can also collaborate with candidates to spend—as what are called coordinated expenditures—up to $20,200 in 1984 dollars; the figure is indexed for inflation.

In Senate campaigns, national parties can give an aggregate of $17,500 while state party committees and their local units can contribute $10,000—$5000 in both the primary and general elections. Vastly more important are the coordinated spending provisions in Senate contests: national party committees can contribute the greater of $20,000 or $.02 per person of voting age within the state, and these limits are adjusted for inflation. State and local committees can spend similar amounts, and the national party can again act as an agent for them. In 1984, coordinated expenditure limits ranged from $40,400 in the smallest states to $752,409 in California. These amounts are doubled when both the national and state parties—or the national parties acting as state party agents—spend up to the limit.

Public financing of presidential campaigns was initially controversial because it appeared to exclude parties from their traditional role. But each national party can make coordinated expenditures of $.02 per voting-age person, adjusted for inflation. These came to $6.9 million in 1984. The parties may also help candidates raise amounts equal to 20 percent of their expenditure limit, to pay fundraising costs, and whatever additional private funds are necessary to comply with the FECA. Since the FECA excludes all contributions from individuals and nonparty committees to publicly funded presidential candidates in the general election, the parties have become special players in presidential campaigns.

The 1979 amendments to the FECA opened another broad avenue for party expenditures. State and local party committees are permitted to spend unlimited amounts for grass-roots activity on behalf of both congressional and presidential candidates. In addition, they can spend unlimited amounts for registration and get-out-the-vote activities on behalf of presidential candidates; parties may make unlimited expenditures for party-building and voter-mobilization activities that do not directly advocate the election of federal candidates. Such funds—called soft money—surely have a strong, favorable impact on party candidates by strengthening overall party efforts and getting committed partisans to the polls.

The usefulness of state and local party activities under the 1979 amendments and of their soft-money campaigning is evidenced by the sums spent and by the vigor with which national party leaders have urged contributors to channel money to state and local parties for these purposes. In 1980, Republican state and local party committees apparently spent $15 million for these activities, while Democratic groups spent only $4 million.[6] Preliminary estimates for 1984 suggest that Republicans raised about $10.6 million while Democrats amassed either $9.4 million or $5 million, depending on whether one credits

6. Herbert E. Alexander, *Financing the 1980 Election* (Lexington, MA: Lexington Books, 1983), pp. 113-14.

official Democratic National Committee reports or the private estimates of campaign officials.[7]

It has also been suggested that public funding of presidential prenomination campaigns has weakened the role of party leaders and organizations, by removing their candidates' financial reliance on them. Prenomination public funding is awarded under complex rules that provide for governmental matching of individual contributions up to $250. The FECA does not bar party leaders or party organizations from raising or contributing funds to candidates during the prenomination campaigns. Indeed, the matching-fund provision might make party activists more important, since each candidate must seek a broad base of small contributions and the party leadership is presumably already organized for such fund-raising. In any case, party organizations themselves—except for a few traditional political machines, such as those in Chicago or Pittsburgh—have not generally been deeply involved in prenomination campaigns in the post-World War II era.

A somewhat more plausible complaint might be that the public funding provisions have encouraged states to adopt the primary system of selecting national convention delegates, thus shifting influence from party leaders and activists to voters at large. It is doubtful whether there is much public sympathy for this complaint. In any case, the trend toward primaries was already very strong before the advent of public financing.[8]

One additional aspect of the FECA bears strongly and favorably on political parties: the public funding of national nominating conventions. In 1984 the FECA allowed each party $8.1 million, a sum that is adjusted for inflation. This grant reduces reliance on private contributors and allows parties to use their campaign funds for direct political action, which strengthens their ability to engage in campaign activities that strengthen their links to both the electorate and the party's candidates.

Perhaps the proof of the FECA's impact on parties is in their spending. Table 1 shows the net disbursements of national, state, and local party committees that are required to report to the Federal Election Commission. Many state and local parties do not report, and soft-money activities that benefit national campaigns are not included.

The increase in party spending from $112.8 million to $384.1 million in eight years easily outdistances increases in the consumer price index, which increased by 59 percent from 1978 through June 1984, and in congressional campaign receipts, which increased by 100 percent.[9] The political parties' finances appear, indeed, to signal their robust good health.

If parties have grown financially stronger, however, it appears largely unrelated to the FECA. The central fact of party finance is new technology, especially mass-mail appeals. The Republicans especially have become masters of

---

7. Herbert E. Alexander, "American Presidential Elections since Public Funding, 1976-1984" (Paper delivered at the Twelfth World Congress of the International Political Science Association, Paris, France, 15-20 July 1985, revised Mar. 1985), pp. 29-31.

8. A majority of the delegates to the national conventions of both major political parties were already being elected in primaries in 1972, before the public financing provisions of the FECA took effect in 1976. See Ranney, "Political Parties: Reform and Decline," p. 218.

9. Reports of receipts and expenditures by political parties, candidates, and political action committees throughout this article are derived from standard reports by the Federal Election Commission unless otherwise noted.

TABLE 1
EXPENDITURES BY NATIONAL, STATE, AND LOCAL
POLITICAL PARTY COMMITTEES, 1978-84 (Millions of dollars)

	1977-78	1979-80*	1981-82	1983-84*
Republicans				
Amount	$85.9	$156.4	$213.9	$295.0
Percentage	76.2%	83.4%	84.2%	76.8%
Democrats				
Amount	$26.9	$31.2	$40.0	$89.1† ($76.2)‡
Percentage	23.8%	16.6%	15.8%	23.2%
Total	$112.8	$187.6	$253.9	$384.1
Disparity†	$59.0	$125.2	$173.9	$205.9 ($218.8)‡

SOURCE: "FEC Reports Democrats Narrowed the Financial Gap in 1984 Party Activity" (Press release, Federal Election Commission, 7 May 1985).
*Omits party expenditures of federal subsidies for the operation of party conventions.
†Includes $12.9 million of loan repayments.
‡Excludes Democratic loan repayments from Democratic expenditure totals.

modern fund-raising technology. The Republican National Committee reported that in 1984 it received $1.6 million in contributions from 920,000 contributors whose average gift was $37.50.[10] Democratic fund-raising lags well behind, because Democratic incumbency in the White House and Congress until 1980 sapped the Democratic national party's determination to employ new fund-raising techniques. In 1981, the Democratic national party's contributor list numbered only 25,000, and the party had raised only $2.5 million—of its $15.1 million total—from direct mail.[11] In 1984, the Democrats claimed about 550,000 direct-mail donors.[12]

10. Republican National Committee, *1984 Chairman's Report: Leadership That's Working* (Washington, DC: Republican National Committee, n.d.), p. 8.
11. David Adamany, "Political Parties in the 1980s," in *Money and Politics in the United States*, ed. Michael Malbin (Chatham, NJ: Chatham House, 1984), pp. 70, 77-78.
12. Democratic National Committee, *The Democratic National Committee, 1981-1985: Building for the Future* (Washington, DC: Democratic National Committee, 1984), p. 30.

The emphasis on small gifts has not, of course, precluded either party from seeking financial support in larger sums.[13] Both parties have a wide array of donor groups, such as the President's Club, for the Republicans, and the Business Council, for the Democrats.

The dramatic increase in the financial prowess of political parties has been highly uneven, however. The Republicans have moved toward financial strength in giant steps; the Democrats only by half paces. Table 1 shows that Republican Party committees outspent their Democratic foes by margins of between three to one and four to one in the four elections listed. The dollar margin of Republican Party spending may be an even better measure of GOP dominance. The Republicans outspent the Democrats by $59 million in 1978; the GOP spending advantage rose to $218.8 million in 1984, omitting loans from the Democratic total.

Table 2 shows that parties have also been active in funding congressional

13. Adamany, "Political Parties in the 1980s," pp. 76-78.

TABLE 2
DIRECT PARTY FINANCIAL SUPPORT FOR CONGRESSIONAL CANDIDATES (Millions of dollars)

	1980	1982	1984
Democrats			
House			
Party support*	$1.3	$1.7	$3.1
Percentage of total†	2.1%	1.9%	3.1%
Senate			
Party support*	$1.6	$2.9	$4.7
Percentage of total†	3.9%	4.6%	6.5%
Republicans			
House			
Party support*	$5.7	$9.9	$10.5
Percentage of total†	9.4%	10.7%	11.7%
Senate			
Party support*	$6.1	$9.3	$7.5
Percentage of total†	15.1%	14.9%	8.8%

SOURCES: For 1980, "FEC Releases Final Statistics on 1979-80 Congressional Races" (press release, Federal Election Commission, 7 Mar. 1982); for 1982, "FEC Releases Data on 1981-82 Congressional Spending" (press release, Federal Election Commission, 2 May 1983); for 1984, "FEC Releases Report on 1984 Congressional Races" (press release, Federal Election Commission, 16 May 1985).
NOTE: General election candidates only.
*Direct party contributions to candidates plus coordinated party expenditures to advocate their election.
†Percentage of the sum of total candidate expenditures plus party expenditures to advocate the candidates' election.

candidates. On the other hand, the percentage of campaign support provided directly by political parties is still smaller than the portion provided by individuals or PACs.[14]

Beyond direct financial support is a wide array of other party activities. Republicans have recruited candidates, provided extensive training for candidates and their campaign staffs, developed media spots and news releases, supplied research on issues, fielded staff advisers and political consultants, and assisted through an impressive variety of other imaginative campaign efforts.[15]

14. Gary C. Jacobson, "Money in the 1980 and 1982 Congressional Elections," in *Money and Politics in the United States*, ed. Malbin, pp. 38, 39.

15. Adamany, "Political Parties in the 1980s," pp. 78-85, 97-101.

The Republican National Committee has reported that in 1984 it employed direct mail, door-to-door canvassing, and telephone contact to enroll 4 million new Republican voters and to reach 15 million households by telephone to get out the vote; it brought the GOP message to 10 million households by mail and 4.5 million by door-to-door canvassing. In addition, national Republican committees purchased institutional or generic advertising on behalf of the Republican cause costing $11.8 million. An additional $850,000 was spent for advertising in conjunction with state and local party units. Republicans staffed eight regional offices that gave technical assistance to party organizations and candidates.[16]

16. Republican National Committee, *1984 Chairman's Report*, pp. 6, 12, 16, 18, 20.

Democratic national party activity has tended to follow the pattern of Republican efforts, but on a much smaller scale.[17] After losing the presidency and the Senate, the Democrats made substantial new efforts to expand their contributor base and their financial resources. They also made renewed efforts to build up their party organization and to assist candidates. Training programs for candidates and campaign managers reached about 5000 Democrats between 1981 and 1984. The Democratic National Committee has also sponsored generic advertising critical of the Republican administration. There were Democratic efforts to identify and register voters, but they were hampered in 1984 by a shortage of early money.[18]

Extensive appraisals of state and local party organizations also showed little decline in overall vitality from the 1960s to 1980.[19] The number of state party organizations with professional staff increased, for example. So did state party fund-raising. At the local level, basic party structures appeared intact. Moreover, local parties reported considerable activity in recruiting candidates, circulating literature, advertising, getting out the vote, and other traditional campaign efforts.[20] Local party structures and activities showed no decline, and perhaps slight improvement, between 1980 and 1984, despite the rush of both parties at the national level toward centralized party operations and technology.[21]

In short, it is not evident that the FECA has undermined political parties. Changing campaign technology has dramatically altered the environment within which political parties operate. For their part, however, the parties have shown a capacity to employ new technologies to raise money, and they have found new roles to play in assisting candidates, promoting party issues, and mobilizing voters. American parties—never organizationally strong in the post-World War II period—are probably no weaker today than two decades ago. Moreover, some commentators believe they are more vigorous now, having adapted to significant changes in political technology and in society. In any case, their present weaknesses are not new, nor can their condition be easily connected to changes in campaign finance regulations.

THE EMERGENCE OF PACs

If the FECA has had relatively little effect on political parties, it has chartered and stimulated PACs. The number of PACs, their financial strength, and their role in campaigns have grown dramatically during the past decade.

There have, in fact, been two different factors in PAC growth. The FECA is one. Modern fund-raising technology—especially mass-mail appeals—is the other. The impact of these factors has been very different for different kinds of PACs.

The FECA is a charter for institutional, or connected, PACs. These are

17. Adamany, "Political Parties in the 1980s," pp. 85-93, 96-101.
18. Democratic National Committee, *Democratic National Committee, 1981-1985*, p. 34; Thomas B. Edsall, "Flush with Cash, GOP Looks to High-Tech Races in 1986," *Washington Post*, 8 May 1985.
19. Cornelius P. Cotter et al., *Party Organizations in American Politics* (New York: Praeger, 1984), chaps. 2, 3.
20. Ibid., p. 45.

21. James L. Gibson et al., "Party Dynamics in the 1980s: Changes in County Party Organizational Strength 1980-1984" (Paper delivered at the Annual Meeting of the Midwest Political Science Association, Chicago, IL, 17-20 Apr. 1985).

the PACs associated with corporations, labor unions, and other entities. In 1971, the FECA authorized such entities to use their own treasury funds to establish and administer, as well as to solicit funds for, "separate segregated funds"—that is, PACs. Most large unions and corporations, which held government contracts, were freed to create PACs when, in 1974, the FECA was amended to abolish the restriction that government contractors, including unions and corporations, could not form separate segregated political funds. One commentator has argued that these provisions of the FECA added legitimacy to corporate political participation, which had become suspect both to the public and to corporate leaders in the aftermath of Watergate-related convictions of corporations and their officers.[22]

The FECA specifies complex procedures for connected PACs to raise money. While these rules do not prohibit connected PACs from soliciting the general public, this is rarely done. Instead, connected PACs raise money from members of labor unions, management personnel of corporations, or other people formally associated with the parent entity.

By contrast, public appeals are the principal vehicle for fund-raising by nonconnected, or independent, PACs. They were legally free to operate even in the absence of the FECA, although the applicable limits on their contributions to candidates were different. The critical factor in the development of independent PACs was not the FECA, as it was for connected PACs, but rather the development of computer-based, mass-mail appeals for money. Their major charter for political action comes not from the FECA's authorization to make campaign contributions, which always were legally authorized. Instead, it derives from the Supreme Court's decision that no restrictions can be imposed on PAC spending on behalf of a candidate—even though they can be imposed on contributions—as long as those independent expenditures were not made in cooperation with the candidate.[23]

Despite the difference between connected and nonconnected PACs, their fund-raising techniques and profiles are remarkably similar. All, except organized-labor PACs, use direct-mail appeals more than any other fund-raising method. The next most preferred method is personal solicitation. For unions, the preference for these techniques is reversed.[24]

Although PACs can receive contributions of up to $5000, all PACs rely principally on small contributions. A 1982 survey of 399 PACs showed that the average donation for all types of PACs was $100, ranging from $160 for corporate PACs to $14 for labor PACs.[25] Participation rates for individual PACs vary widely; one study reports rates as low as 10 percent and as high as 90 percent.[26] Several corporate studies indicate responses to fund appeals in the

22. Edwin M. Epstein, "Business and Labor under the Federal Election Campaign Act of 1971," in *Parties, Interest Groups, and Campaign Finance Laws,* ed. Michael Malbin (Washington, DC: American Enterprise Institute, 1979), pp. 107, 146-47.

23. *Buckley* v. *Valeo,* 424 U.S. 1, 54-59 (1976); *Federal Election Commission* v. *National Conservative Political Action Committee,* 53 U.S.L.W. 4293 (1985).

24. Larry Sabato, *PAC Power* (New York: W. W. Norton, 1984), p. 54.

25. Ibid., p. 59.

26. Frank J. Sorauf, "Political Action Committees in American Politics: An Overview," in *What Price PACs?* (New York: Twentieth Century Fund, 1983), pp. 28, 70.

30 percent range.[27] Institutional PACs of all kinds report participation rates of 25 to 32 percent, but nonconnected PACs, which engage in large-scale mass-mail appeals, have received support from only about 3 percent of those solicited.[28]

The dramatic surge of PAC power is demonstrated on one dimension by the gross characteristics of the PAC world. Table 3 shows that the number of PACs increased from 608 in 1974 to 4009 by the end of 1984. Table 4 reports an 1162 percent increase in PAC disbursements during the same decade, from $21 million to $265 million. Reported PAC disbursements do not include expenditures from treasury funds by unions and corporations to operate and administer their PACs; in 1980, Herbert Alexander estimated these expenditures at $30 million.[29]

A different dimension of PAC growth is political contributions and activity. Table 5 shows that total PAC contributions to general election candidates increased from $8.5 million in 1972 to $102.3 million in 1984 and from 13.7 percent of total general election candidate receipts to 28.9 percent. These contribution figures do not include independent expenditures. In 1983-84, $23.4 million was spent independently, with PACs making more than 90 percent of those expenditures. The contribution figures also do not include communication costs by unions and corporations advocating the election or defeat of candidates; very preliminary estimates by the staff of the Federal Election Commission in May 1985 set these expenditures at $4.4 million.

Finally, political contributions do not reveal the large sums spent for nonpartisan registration and get-out-the-vote drives or for political education materials that do not explicitly endorse or oppose candidates.

The PAC share of total contributions tends to understate the full impact of PAC support for candidates. Although the pattern of PAC contributions is enormously complex, it is clear that PACs generally support safe incumbents and that, in hotly contested races pitting a promising challenger against an incumbent or in districts where there is no incumbent, PACs generally support candidates whose party or ideology they share.[30] Hence, Frank Sorauf has shown that between 60 and 68 percent of PAC contributions in House races went to incumbents in the 1978, 1980, and 1982 elections. Between 48 and 64 percent of PAC gifts in Senate campaigns also went to incumbents.[31] This pattern repeats itself in 1984, when incumbent senators received 62.9 percent of the PAC contributions to general election candidates, while incumbent members of the House received 67.6 percent of the PAC general election gifts.

Consequently, the share of incumbents' contributions derived from PACs is very high. While PACs accounted for 18.8 percent of the receipts of Senate general election candidates, they were the sources of 28.9 percent of the receipts of Democratic incumbents and 21.6 percent of the funds of Republican incumbents. These patterns are even more pronounced in the House. In 1984, PAC funds constituted 36.5 percent of all House general election contributions. For incumbents, however, they

27. Ibid., p. 70.
28. Sabato, *PAC Power*, p. 59.
29. Alexander, *Financing the 1980 Election*, p. 131.

30. Sabato, *PAC Power*, pp. 73-78.
31. Sorauf, "Political Action Committees in American Politics," p. 45.

TABLE 3
GROWTH OF POLITICAL ACTION COMMITTEES SINCE 1974 BY TYPE

Type	1974	1976	1978	1980	1982	1984
Corporate	89	433	785	1,206	1,469	1,682
Labor	201	224	217	297	380	394
Trade, membership, or health	318*	489*	453	576	649	698
Nonconnected			162	374	723	1,053
Cooperative			12	42	47	52
Nonstock corporation			24	56	103	130
Total	608	1,146	1,653	2,551	3,371	4,009

SOURCE: "FEC Says PACs Top 4,000 for 1984" (Release, Federal Election Commission, 28 Jan. 1985).
NOTE: Number of committees is tallied as of 31 December of the years shown.
*Includes all categories of political action committees except corporate and union groups.

accounted for 46 percent of Democratic and 37.4 percent of Republican campaign treasuries. The Democratic Study Group has reported that while 40 House incumbents received more than half their campaign funds from PACs in 1976, in 1984, 166 House incumbents, or 41 percent, did so.[32] Moreover, in House races, small individual contributions of under $200, which constituted 50 percent of the general election campaign funds in 1974, had slipped to 22 percent in 1984 and were greatly overshadowed by PACs, which accounted for 36 percent of all receipts.[33]

A third dimension of PAC expansion is the sharp difference in growth rates in various PAC sectors. The growth of corporate, association, and nonconnected PACs has greatly reduced the preeminent role that labor played until the mid-1970s. Labor PACs accounted for more than half of all PAC disbursements in 1974, and they were just about a third of all PACs. (See Tables 3 and 4.)

32. U.S., Congress, House, Democratic Study Group, "Troubling Trends in Election Financing ... Grassroots Money Shrinks as PAC Money Grows" (Washington, DC: Democratic Study Group, 1985), p. 3.
33. Ibid., p. 31.

In 1984, they constituted less than 10 percent of the PACs and spent only 17.9 percent of total PAC outlays. Nonconnected PACs, corporate PACs, and association PACs all became larger in both numbers and dollars than union PACs. In 1984, labor PACs made only 23.2 percent of contributions to candidates, or $26.3 million, following corporate PACs, with $38.9 million, and association PACs, with $28.2 million. If independent expenditures are included with contributions, labor would be outdistanced also by nonconnected PACs. At the same time, labor's massive voter-mobilization efforts are not reported, so that labor's role in American campaigns tends to be understated by these measures of political action.

PACs will almost certainly continue to grow in numbers and resources. This growth is likely to continue to be strongest in the corporate sector, which has already experienced the largest growth in numbers since 1974, is the second-largest source of PAC disbursements, and supplies more financial support for candidates than any other sector. Studies show that PAC formation is most likely in firms that are large, subject to extensive governmental regulation, and union-

TABLE 4
TOTAL PAC DISBURSEMENTS BY TYPE OF PAC, 1974-84 (Millions of dollars)

Type	1974* Amount	1974* Percentage	1976* Amount	1976* Percentage	1978 Amount	1978 Percentage	1980 Amount	1980 Percentage	1982 Amount	1982 Percentage	1984 Amount	1984 Percentage
Labor	$11.0	52.4%	$17.5	33.1%	$18.6	24.0%	$25.1	19.1%	$35.0	18.4%	$47.4	17.9%
Corporate	} 8.1	} 38.6%	5.8	11.0%	15.2	19.6%	31.4	24.0%	43.2	22.7%	59.0	22.3%
Health, trade, or medical					23.8	30.7%	32.0	24.4%	41.7	21.9%	53.9	20.3%
Nonconnected	0.8	3.8%			17.4	22.5%	38.6	29.4%	64.6	33.9%	95.9	36.2%
Other	1.1	5.2%	29.6*	56.0%	2.4	3.1%	4.0	3.1%	5.8	3.0%	8.8	3.3%
Total	$21.0	100.0%	$52.9	100.1%	$77.4	99.9%	$131.1	100.0%	$190.3	99.9%	$265.0	100.0%

SOURCES: For 1974, 1976, and 1978, Joseph E. Cantor, *Political Action Committees: Their Evaluation and Growth and Their Implications for the Political System* (Washington, DC: Congressional Research Service, 1981), p. 83; for 1980, "FEC Releases Final PAC Report for 1979-80 Election Cycle" (Release, Federal Election Commission, 21 Feb. 1982); for 1982, "1981-82 PAC Giving up 51%" (Release, Federal Election Commission, 29 Apr. 1983); for 1984, "PAC Support for Incumbents Increases in '84 Elections" (Release, Federal Election Commission, 19 May 1985).

*Includes all types of PACs except labor and corporate groups.

TABLE 5
PAC CONTRIBUTIONS FOR GENERAL ELECTION CANDIDATES,
1974-84 (Millions of dollars)

	Candidate receipts	PAC contributions	PAC contributions as percentage of candidate receipts
1972	$ 62.2	$ 8.5	13.7%
1974	$ 73.9	$ 11.6	15.7%
1976	$104.8	$ 20.5	19.6%
1978	$158.2	$ 31.8	20.1%
1980	$201.6	$ 51.9	25.7%
1982	$302.2	$ 79.3	26.2%
1984	$353.6	$102.3	28.9%

SOURCES: For 1972, 1974, 1976, and 1978, Cantor, *Political Action Committees: Their Evaluation and Growth and Their Implications*, p. 74; for 1980, "FEC Releases Final PAC Report"; for 1982, "1981-82 PAC Giving up 51%"; for 1984, "PAC Support for Incumbents."

ized.[34] Many of the nation's largest firms do not yet have PACs. For example, more than 40 percent of the *Fortune* 500 still did not have PACs on the eve of the 1984 election year.[35] It is the largest firms—where there is still room for substantial PAC growth—that make the largest corporate contributions. Corporate PACs on the various *Fortune* lists accounted for 75 percent of corporate PAC gifts in 1982, even though only about 34 percent of those corporations had PACs and their PACs constituted only 31 percent of all corporate PACs.[36]

The growth of labor PACs may have reached a plateau. Nonconnected ideological PACs have also shown signs of weakness because contributors have been saturated with mass-mail appeals and because the costs of mass-mail fundraising have escalated dramatically.[37]

THE EXPANDING CONTRIBUTOR BASE

As already indicated, a theme that characterizes both the new condition of party politics and the emergence of PACs is their foundation in a broad base of small contributors. There is not yet much information about these new givers. Herbert Alexander has shown that from the first Eisenhower election in 1952 until 1980, the percentage of Americans who have made political contributions during presidential election years varied only within a narrow range of 8 to 13 percent.[38] It is estimated that participation in the national income tax checkoff that provides public funds to subsidize presidential campaigns and national party conventions has generally been between 32 and 35 percent of

34. Gary J. Andres, "Business Involvement in Campaign Finance: Factors Influencing the Decision to Form a Corporate PAC," *PS*, 18: 213, 215-19 (Spring 1985); Marick F. Masters and Gerald D. Keim, "Determinants of PAC Participation among Large Corporations," *Journal of Politics*, 47:1159-73 (Nov. 1985).

35. Andres, "Business Involvement," p. 213; Masters and Keim, "Determinants of PAC Participation," p. 1163; Sabato, *PAC Power*, p. 164.

36. Masters and Keim, "Determinants of PAC Participation," p. 1168.

37. Ronald Brownstein, "On Paper, Conservative PACs Were Tigers in 1984—but Look Again," *National Journal*, 29 June 1985, pp. 1504, 1509.

38. Alexander, *Financing the 1980 Election*, p. 422.

eligible taxpayers.[39] Another study suggested that 38 percent of the adult population made contributions, including those made via the checkoff, in 1980.[40] On the other hand, only about 13.4 percent indicated they had made direct contributions to candidates, parties, or PACs. Hence, in 1980 the funding appeals of parties and PACs raised the participation level only slightly above the long-term average.

Among these direct contributors, 7 percent gave to candidates, 7 percent to PACs, and 4 percent to political parties. Only 3 percent gave through more than one of these channels. A separate study of state-level campaign contributors showed that most giving was to candidates, followed by parties, and then to issue groups—presumably PACs—and nonpartisan groups.[41]

While the checkoff greatly broadens participation in campaign funding, those who contribute only in this way are not otherwise especially politically active or concerned.[42] They very closely resemble the economic and social profile of the population as a whole.[43] While their participation is quite passive, they do provide a campaign finance constituency that has very little economic class bias.

By contrast, organizational contributors—givers to candidates, parties, and PACs—tend to be better educated and better off financially than the population at large.[44] They are more ideological, much more interested in politics, and vastly more active in political affairs.

Within the total group of organizational contributors, however, there were important differences. Party givers tended to be older and financially more comfortable, while candidate and PAC contributors were somewhat younger and were drawn more heavily from middle-income groups. In this respect, modern candidate-centered campaigning and the newly emerging PACs have broadened financial participation among those who are not attracted to the traditional party system. The ideological differences are similar: party givers are disproportionately Republican and conservative, while givers to candidates and PACs—especially labor union PACs—tend more nearly to reflect the general population's ideological and party divisions.

A departure from these patterns emerges, however, on measures of political concern and political activity. Here PAC givers are less interested in and concerned about campaigns, have a lower sense of civic duty, and do not engage in as much other political activity as do party and candidate givers. So, while PACs have broadened participation, they—like the checkoff—have not substantially heightened political attention or activity.

One characteristic of PAC donors does come through clearly, however. They are highly issue oriented, and their preferences on issues conform to the

39. Kim Quaile Hill, "Taxpayer Support for the Presidential Election Campaign Fund," *Social Science Quarterly*, 62:767-71 (Dec. 1981).
40. Ruth S. Jones and Warren E. Miller, "Financing Campaigns: Macro Level Innovation and Micro Level Response," *Western Political Quarterly*, 38:193 (June 1985).
41. Ruth S. Jones and Anne H. Hopkins, "State Campaign Fund Raising: Targets and Response," *Journal of Politics*, 47:427, 441 (May 1985).
42. Jones and Miller, "Financing Campaigns," pp. 195-99.
43. Ibid.; Hill, "Taxpayer Support," p. 770; David Adamany, "The Failure of Tax Incentives for Political Giving," *Tax Notes*, 7:3-5 (July 1978).

44. Jones and Miller, "Financing Campaigns," pp. 195-99.

political slant of the PACs to which they give.[45] This is true also, but to a lesser extent, of party givers. A national survey of about 2000 givers to parties and PACs showed a very strong overlap between Republicanism and conservatism among contributors and a fairly strong overlap between Democratic affiliation and liberal political outlook. The emergence of PACs has tended, in short, to mobilize ideological givers, to increase the congruence between political money and ideology, and to heighten the division between the resource-providing constituencies of candidates and officeholders of different parties and of different ideological persuasions.

POLITICAL MONEY AND
PUBLIC POLICY

Are recent increases in campaign contributions and direct political spending driving public policy? Perhaps no question excites more debate or produces more contradictory evidence.

There is not much evidence, for instance, that party voting in Congress has declined dramatically in recent years.[46] If special interest campaign contributions are driving policy decisions, party-line voting should falter. Indeed, one commentator has said: "Events over which the parties themselves have no control now bring the promise that the two major parties may shortly be—if they are not already—more ideologically united than they have been for more than a hundred years."[47]

In addition, the substantial growth in party resources, especially money, may wed members of Congress more closely to their parties. The executive director of the National Republican Campaign Committee has suggested that the ability of the Republican Party to provide campaign support to its candidates has produced "a degree of loyalty to the party structure" and a measure of party "discipline."[48] As yet without substantial party financial resources, the Democrats might be expected to have a more difficult time organizationally in stimulating cohesion on public policy issues.

It will be difficult, in any case, for legislative cohesion produced by party campaign resources to offset the sweeping diffusion of power that has occurred in Congress in recent years. This change in the distribution of power is evidenced in the overthrow of the seniority system, the dispersion of power to hundreds of subcommittees, the periodic use of the party caucus to depose party leaders, the media orientation of so many younger members, and the decline of traditional patterns of deference to the leadership. In such a legislative environment PACs may well have substantial influence on policymaking.

One strand of evidence of PAC influence is the statements of members of Congress themselves.[49] Senator Robert

45. Joan C. Green and James L. Guth, "Partisans and Ideologues: A Profile of Contributors to Party and Ideological PACs" (Paper delivered at the Annual Meeting of the Southern Political Science Association, Birmingham, AL, 3-6 Nov. 1983), pp. 11-15.

46. Adamany, "Political Finance and the American Political Parties," pp. 508-11.

47. James L. Sundquist, "Party Decay and the Capacity to Govern," in *The Future of American Political Parties,* ed. Joel L. Fleishman (Englewood Cliffs, NJ: Prentice-Hall, 1982), p. 57.

48. Herbert E. Alexander and Brian Haggerty, *PACs and Parties: Relationships and Interrelationships* (Los Angeles: Citizens' Research Foundation at the University of Southern California, 1984), p. 65.

49. Elizabeth Drew, *Politics and Money: The New Road to Corruption* (New York: Macmillan, 1983), pp. 78-79, 89-90, 95-96; Sabato, *PAC Power,* pp. 126-27; David Adamany, "Political Action Committees and Democratic Politics," *Detroit College of Law Review,* 1983:1013 (1983);

Dole's expression of concern is typical: "When these political action committees give money, they expect something in return other than good government."[50]

This impressionistic evidence has been reinforced by journalistic and public interest group tabulations showing that incumbents, members of key committees, and congressional leaders are favored by PAC giving. For instance, Common Cause reported that 20 of 27 party leaders and committee chairs in the House of Representatives received 50 percent or more of their campaign funds from PACs.[51] Similarly, it reported that business PACs had given more than $11 million to the tax-writing committees in the House and Senate, and that all PACs had given these committee members about $17 million.[52] During the 1984 election, Common Cause issued a report pointing out that 111 of the 119 members of the four House and Senate committees that have jurisdiction over legislation of interest to the National Association of Realtors had received campaign contributions from the association in recent years.[53]

Several scholars have reached similar conclusions using statistical techniques.

One such study showed a positive connection between contributions made by Rockwell International and congressional votes on the B-1 bomber.[54] Another reported a significant relationship between contributions from labor unions in 1978 and congressional votes on various issues of interest to labor, including wage and price controls.[55] A study that examined party, ideology, and constituency variables as well as campaign funds concluded that contributions from the American Transportation Association were closely related to votes on the Motor Carriers Act of 1980 by senators up for election that year, but not to the votes of senators whose terms did not expire until 1982 or 1984.[56] A study of voting on dairy price supports shows that congressmen who had received contributions from the American Dairy Association were more likely to vote for higher supports and that the association, in turn, was more likely to contribute to those congressmen.[57]

Other evidence tends to cast some doubt on these findings. The focus of both business and labor PAC contributions is on other factors, according to this evidence. Contributions by affected PACs occurred at election time rather than close to key legislative votes on the Davis-Bacon Act in the Labor and Edu-

---

Paul Taylor, "Efforts to Revise Campaign Laws Aim at PACs," *Washington Post*, 28 Feb. 1983.

50. Taylor, "Efforts to Revise Campaign Laws."

51. "House Incumbents Get 44¢ of Every Campaign Dollar From PACs in 1984 Election" (News release, Common Cause, 12 Apr. 1985), p. 5.

52. "Business PACs Gave $11 Million to Congressional Tax-Writers" (News release, Common Cause, 16 July 1985), p. 1; "PACs Contribute Nearly $17 Million to Members of House and Senate Tax Writing Committees" (News release, Common Cause, 14 Feb. 1985), p. 1.

53. *A Common Cause Study of National Association of Realtors Political Action Committee Contributions* (Washington, DC: Common Cause, n.d.).

54. Henry Chappell, Jr., "Campaign Contributions and Congressional Voting," *Review of Economics and Statistics*, 62:77-83 (1982).

55. James Kau and Paul Rubin, "The Impact of Labor Unions on the Passage of Economic Legislation," *Journal of Labor Research*, 2:133-45 (1981).

56. John Frendreis and Richard Waterman, "PAC Contributions and Legislative Behavior: Senate Voting on Trucking Deregulation," *Social Science Quarterly*, 66:401-12 (June 1985).

57. W. P. Welch, "Campaign Contributions and Legislative Voting: Milk Money and Dairy Price Supports," *Western Political Quarterly*, 35:478-95 (1982).

cation Committee of the House of Representatives, according to one such study.[58] Another found some evidence that overall congressional voting records and membership on key legislative committees were importantly related to PAC contributions by oil, automobile, defense, and labor PACs; but it also found that a congressman's general ideological position and whether his home district was in the state where one of the industries was located were also important.[59]

Overall roll-call voting records of congressmen, rather than influence on specific legislative issues, were found to influence contributions by business, trade association, and labor PACs.[60] When party, ideology, support for the president, and constituency characteristics were also considered in another study, campaign contributions were found to have very little impact on roll-call votes of concern to five major business PACs.[61]

Even high correlations between campaign contributions and roll-call votes do not prove that money caused congressmen to take certain issue positions, of course. But when such other considerations as party affiliation, ideology, and constituency variables are held constant and a relationship between money and voting still occurs, there is certainly an inference that contributions influence policymaking. Moreover, it seems unlikely that members of Congress would come forward to describe the increasing impact of PAC campaign contributions on the workings of the legislative process if this were not true. It is difficult to ignore the forceful common sense of Congressman Barney Frank's protest that officeholders "are the only human beings in the world who are expected to take thousands of dollars from perfect strangers on important matters and not be affected by it."[62]

It is surely possible to agree with Larry Sabato's summary judgment that "it is ludicrously naive to contend that PAC money never influences congressmen's decisions, but it is irredeemably cynical to believe that PACs always, or even usually, push the voting buttons in Congress."[63] One need not dispute the view that constituency, party, and ideology are also important factors in how congressmen make public policy.

At the same time, if campaign funds from PACs are independently working an influence on policy, such influence may well be at odds with democratic expectations. The studies generally concede that contributors obtain access to decision makers,[64] and a number of them show that contributions are related to roll-call voting in Congress.

Contributors can also substantially influence who gets elected. This is, of course, not corruption in any traditional sense. It does, however, raise the two-constituency problem.[65] Those who give money become a constituency separate

---

58. Dickinson McGaw and Richard McCleary, "PAC Spending, Electioneering & Lobbying: A Vector ARIMA Time Series Analysis," *Polity*, 17: 574-85 (1985).

59. J. David Gopoian, "What Makes PACs Tick?" *American Journal of Political Science*, 28:259-81 (May 1984).

60. W. P. Welch, "Patterns of Contributions: Economic Interest and Ideological Groups," in *Political Finance*, ed. Herbert E. Alexander (Beverly Hills, CA: Sage, 1979), pp. 199-216.

61. John R. Wright, "PACs, Contributions, and Roll Calls: An Organizational Perspective," *American Political Science Review*, 79:400, 406-12 (June 1985).

62. Sabato, *PAC Power*, p. 126.
63. Ibid., p. 140.
64. Ibid., pp. 126-28.
65. David Adamany, "PACs and the Democratic Financing of Politics," *Arizona Law Review*, 22:569, 594-96 (1980).

and distinct from those who are constitutionally enfranchised to elect members of Congress. In modern campaigns, driven by expensive technology and conducted through expensive mass-media appeals, the contributor constituency has an enormous influence on who gets elected. Studies plainly show that the amount of money raised by challengers is a critical variable in whether the incumbent or the challenger is elected.[66] When money becomes a threshold for election, those making substantial contributions that advance candidates who share their views influence policymaking by shaping the outcome of elections.

In an era when PACs are becoming the dominant force in financing campaigns, public policy may well be affected by campaign money. This influence of money represents a substantial shift in the American political process. It also runs counter to many expectations about how a democratic political system—based on the equality of citizens' votes—ought to work.

CHANGING PATTERNS OF POLITICS

Concern has been expressed, first, about the professionalization and bureaucratization of American politics that have followed from the enactment of the FECA. There is no doubt that the campaign finance laws have contributed to those trends. The laws' disclosure provisions, contribution limits, and spending ceilings require that both candidates and parties keep a tight rein on all finance-related aspects of their activities.[67] The Federal Election Commission's enforcement of the laws involves audits, hearings, civil suits, and occasionally a criminal prosecution. The sweep of the laws invites parties and candidates to litigate, sometimes for tactical reasons.[68] Under these circumstances, lawyers, accountants, and paid campaign staff assume a major role in politics.

It is not the FECA alone, however, that accounts for this trend. Both parties and PACs now raise most of their funds by direct mail. Substantial bureaucracies—sometimes within these political organizations, sometimes operating as professional consulting firms—are necessary to identify and winnow the list of potential contributors, to store and retrieve contributor information, to draft, address, and mail vast numbers of letters, and to tabulate and record hundreds of millions of dollars raised in small sums. The new fund-raising technology, with its attendant bureaucracy, would eventually have occurred even without the FECA.

Similarly, changing campaign methods require professionalization of politics. Polling, media advertising, telephone banks, voter identification projects, research on issues, and similar activities have become very sophisticated.[69] The

---

66. Gary C. Jacobson, *Money in Congressional Elections* (New Haven, CT: Yale University Press, 1980); idem, "Money in the 1980 and 1982 Congressional Elections," pp. 61-65.

67. See Michael S. Berman, "Living with the FECA: Confessions of a Sometime Campaign Treasurer," this issue of *The Annals* of the American Academy of Political and Social Science; Xandra Kayden, "The Nationalizing of the Party System," in *Parties, Interest Groups, and Campaign Finance Laws*, ed. Malbin, pp. 264-65; Richard B. Cheney, "The Law's Impact on Presidential and Congressional Election Campaigns," in ibid., pp. 239-40, 247.

68. David Ifshin and Roger Warin, "Litigating the 1980 Presidential Election,," *American University Law Review*, 31:487-89, 535-36 (1982).

69. For descriptions of the modern campaign techniques employed by political parties during campaigns, see Larry Sabato, "Parties, PACs, and Independent Groups," in *The American Elections of 1982*, ed. Thomas Mann and Norman Ornstein (Washington, DC: American Enterprise Institute, 1983), pp. 73-86; F. Christopher Arterton, "Polit-

spread of these techniques has spurred the creation of professional staffs.

Nationalization

Second, there has been a substantial nationalization of American politics. The Supreme Court has held that national political parties have final authority to regulate delegate selection for national party conventions, thus depriving local and state parties as well as state governments of the power to structure local party processes.[70] The Court's decision that national political parties may act as "agents" for state parties in making coordinated expenditures on behalf of federal-office candidates has certainly shifted influence in those campaigns from the state to the national level.[71]

Beyond these legal changes, however, are the substantial disparities in funding at the national and state levels. National Democratic Party committees reporting to the Federal Election Committee received $71.7 million in 1983-84, while state and local party committees had receipts of $16.8 million. National Republican committees received $246.1 million; state and local GOP committees received $45.4 million. These figures do not, of course, include state and local party receipts for nonfederal campaign purposes, and there is no effective measure of those funds. It seems unlikely that state and local party financial resources are significant, however, in light of reports that the median nonelection-year budget of a sample of state parties was $340,000 and that average state party contributions to gubernatorial candidates were $39,000.[72]

Indeed, it appears that the national party committees are so dominant in funding that they not only assume state party funding authorizations under the FECA but they also provide funds to gubernatorial and state legislative candidates and for the development of local and state party organizations.[73] They also channel money to state and local parties for grass-roots campaigning, under the 1979 amendments, and for soft-money activities, thus making state and local parties dependent on the national party organizations.

A similar argument has been advanced that PACs have nationalized American politics.[74] It has been suggested that while many small contributors provide the funding for PACs, a relatively few people—PAC staff and executive committees—determine the distribution of the vast sums of money that PACs raise. In 1983-84, just 50 of the nation's 4000 PACs raised $116.7 million, 40.5 percent of the total PAC receipts of $287.8 million.

There is mounting evidence that PACs run in packs. Such organizations as the Business/Industry PAC and the U.S. Chamber of Commerce guide the contributions of many corporate and trade association PACs.[75] There are also informal networks of PAC operatives who meet to exchange information and develop consensus views about which

---

ical Money and Party Strength," in *Future of American Politics,* ed. Fleishman, pp. 104-16, 121-34; Adamany, "Political Parties in the 1980s," pp. 78-100.

70. *Democratic Party* v. *Wisconsin,* 450 U.S. 107 (1981); *Cousins* v. *Wigoda,* 419 U.S. 477 (1975).

71. *Federal Election Commission* v. *Democratic Senatorial Campaign Committee,* 454 U.S. 27 (1981).

72. Cotter et al., *Party Organizations,* pp. 16, 110.

73. Adamany, "Political Parties in the 1980s," pp. 80-81, 100.

74. Drew, *Politics and Money,* pp. 28-37; Adamany, "PACs and the Democratic Financing of Politics," p. 596.

75. Sabato, *PAC Power,* pp. 44-49; Drew, *Politics and Money,* pp. 28-32.

candidates to support. Political parties, especially the Republican Party, have also worked to channel the contributions of many PACs into key races.

In 1982, Washington-based PACs contributed $28.2 million to candidates for the House of Representatives, while non-Washington PACs contributed $31.4 million.[76] That represents substantial centralization of nationwide financial resources in Washington. Thus, while the PAC world is neither monolithic nor fully concentrated in Washington, the financial resources of large PACs, Washington PACs, and networked PACs certainly tend to both concentrate and nationalize political funds.

Institutionalization

Third, the growth of PACs, whether national or local, has changed American politics by establishing PACs as institutional competitors of political parties. In 1983-84, all national, state, and local political parties reporting to the Federal Election Commission had receipts of $397 million, including more than $16.9 million in federal subsidies for the national party conventions. PAC receipts came to almost $288 milion. While the party advantage of $109 million is impressive, it should be remembered that parties were virtually the only institutional players in the campaign world just a decade before. Moreover, the $109 million disparity was artificially inflated in 1983-84 by nearly $13 million in repayable Democratic loans;

76. These figures are based on a recalculation of information provided in Theodore Eismeier and Philip Pollock III, "The Geopolitics of PACs" (Paper delivered at the Annual Meeting of the Midwest Political Science Association, Chicago, IL, 17-20 Apr. 1985). Eismeier and Pollock, however, interpret their data as a sign of the decentralization and localism of PACs, which is at odds with the perspective presented here.

it should be discounted further by the more than $30 million in treasury funds spent by institutional PACs for operations, administration, and solicitation. In the end, political parties—rooted in history and long the preeminent institutions in American politics—probably had a funding advantage of no more than $60 million.

In direct support for candidates, PACs have surpassed political parties in all recent campaigns. (See Tables 2 and 5.) In 1983-84, political party contributions and coordinated expenditures for candidates were $36.4 million; PAC contributions were $102.3 million. Parties, of course, provide substantial services to candidates; they apparently channel about $20 million to state and local parties for grass-roots campaigning and soft money activities. But PACs also render some direct campaign services, including labor's vast expenditures to register and get out the vote. Moreover, PACs spent at least $4.4 million for internal communications advocating the election or defeat of candidates. Furthermore, while political parties have recently made substantial expenditures for institutional advertising promoting party slates—but not specific candidates—or attacking the opposing party, PACs made independent expenditures of $23.4 million in 1983-84 to advocate the election or defeat of specific candidates directly. This increased role for institutions whose goals are more narrowly focused on specific policies surely changes the character of both American campaigns and the American policymaking process.

Disparity

Fourth, the dramatic growth in Republican financial prowess has created a significant disparity between the two major parties, shifting the balance of party power in American politics. The Republican financial advantage is not new, of course.[77] But, as Table 1 shows, in recent years the Republican spending advantage has been between three to one and four to one. This spending base is due not to differential candidate fund-raising, as was formerly true, but to the financial strength of the Republican Party organization.

It is not clear whether this Republican financial hegemony will be permanent. The Democrats have begun to build a base of small contributors through mass-mail appeals, but they remain well behind. Since the GOP continues to have a strong lead among the American middle class, which makes most campaign contributions, the Democrats may not have the potential to catch up. Finally, of course, if corporate PACs continue to gain strength and maintain their present preference for the Republicans, their growing contributions and expenditures will increase the present overall Republican financial advantage.

Accountability

Fifth, there is concern that the new patterns of political finance have substantially reduced accountability. The greatest accountability undoubtedly continues to attach to candidates and political parties. The candidate and his or her party label appear on the ballot. If the public disagrees with campaign-funding practices, they can vote against a candidate or against a party ticket.[78] Within the parties, however, there may be some shift in accountability. The party leadership—the national committees and national chairmen—continue to be elected, of course. When local party leaders and organizations played a major role in party fund-raising, they had some additional influence in party affairs. But now that most party funds are raised directly through mass-mail appeals managed by national party bureaucracies in Washington, the national parties may operate quite independently of local party activists and organizations. Indeed, as previously noted, they may be gaining influence over local parties by making subventions of cash and technical assistance. Nonetheless, the degree of accountability in political party structures remains reasonably high, both to voters and to the party activists.

The accountability of institutional PACs is considerably less. Only in the minority of PACs where donors earmark their contributions for particular candidates or parties is there substantial accountability to contributors. Frank Sorauf has pointed out that "in formal terms the contributors to a PAC—the donors, or 'members,' as some PACs call them—do not participate in PAC governance. They do not choose the PAC's trustees, and they only rarely sit on its important committees."[79] In addition, PACs, of course, are not subject to direct electoral accountability; the candi-

77. The Republicans have outspent the Democrats in every presidential election campaign in this century, except for the contests of 1912, 1916, and 1960. In 1976 and 1980, however, the two parties were closely matched, largely because the FECA's expenditure limits held down Republican expenditures while its presidential campaign subsidies provided Democrats with the same funding base as the Republicans. Heard, *The Costs of Democracy* (Chapel Hill: University of North Carolina Press, 1960), pp. 16-20; Herbert Alexander, *Financing the 1976 Election* (Washington, DC: Congressional Quarterly, 1980), pp. 5-6; idem, *Financing the 1980 Election,* p. 109.

78. David Adamany and George Agree, *Political Money* (Baltimore, MD: Johns Hopkins University Press, 1975), pp. 103-15.

79. Frank Sorauf, "Accountability in Political Action Committees," *Political Science Quarterly,* 99:591, 595 (Winter 1984-85).

dates they support do not appear on the ballot under PAC labels for voter consideration.[80]

On the other hand, PAC donors can refuse to continue their financial support if they disapprove of PAC activities. There is also evidence that most institutional PACs seek donor opinion about PAC operations as well as about candidates and parties. Moreover, the leadership of institutional PACs is restrained by the anticipation that officeholders or voters might strike back if PAC behavior is so blatantly offensive that it engenders public controversy or becomes a campaign issue.

Nonconnected PACs have the smallest degree of accountability. Their donors may exit if they dislike the PACs' activities, of course. But the governance of such PACs is not derived from established institutions, such as corporations, associations, or unions. Rather, most nonconnected PACs are run by their staffs and perhaps a group of self-perpetuating insiders who constitute an executive committee. Moreover, because nonconnected PACs generally use the largest share of their campaign funds for independent expenditures, candidates cannot impose accountability by refusing their contributions. Nor do voters have mechanisms to chasten such PACs. It makes little sense for voters to strike back at the candidates supported by nonconnected PACs, when those PACs' independent expenditures are made without the direction or control of the candidates.

Finally, while PACs have been praised for vastly expanding participation in American politics, it is clear from the surveys of donors that the new participants are not likely to be aggressive in holding their PACs accountable. PAC donors have relatively low levels of political involvement and they do not tend to engage in direct political activity, except for making contributions. The authors of the major study of PAC contributors have concluded:

If . . . PAC contributors remain simply apolitical financiers of campaigns, the PACs will provide additional channels for special interest articulation, but ironically, they will represent a major potential for the increased importance of *elite* and not *mass* based electoral politics. As long as those who provide their funds remain politically disengaged, PAC leaders will be free to select one set of candidates one year and a different set the next with no institutional accountability or responsibility to those who provide the PAC funds.[81]

THE NEW AMERICAN SCENE

Money is a vastly more important ingredient in our politics than ever before. This is more a result of changes in campaign technology and campaign fund-raising techniques than of changes in the law.

With the development of a cash-based politics, the importance of parties has declined. While parties have vastly increased their fund-raising and have vigorously plunged into the new-style campaigns, the mating of the FECA and new fund-raising technologies has given birth to PACs, which are major institutional competitors for parties.

These developments have also modified long-standing political arrangements. The link between parties and their candidates is weakened. Politics has become more professionalized, bureaucratized, centralized, and nationalized. PACs now share the fund-raising and campaigning roles long reserved for

---

80. Sorauf, "Political Action Committees in American Politics," pp. 95-97.

81. Jones and Miller, "Financing Campaigns," p. 206.

parties. In the competition between the parties, the Republicans are vastly outstripping the Democrats in amassing money, waging campaigns, and adapting to the new style of American politics.

These changes, together with the development of a new contributor base that is largely disengaged from parties and other political institutions, have raised serious issues of accountability. Those who raise and spend campaign funds, and thus disproportionately influence politics in the modern era, are increasingly removed from voters, from traditional grass-roots activists, and, indeed, even from contributors themselves. The financial constituency in American politics is becoming increasingly powerful and independent; the voting constituency is increasingly removed from all the activities of politics—except casting ballots—that influence the outcomes of elections and the shape of national polity.

The new face of American politics turns away from deeply rooted beliefs about the preeminent role of voters and voting districts in controlling elections and government. But the voices of concern about these conditions are not yet numerous enough or loud enough to force reforms that will shift dominance in American politics back to voters.

Political Financing and the Constitution

By RALPH K. WINTER

ABSTRACT: The author examines the various arguments and legislative proposals offered in support of the regulation of campaign financing in light of the need for a democracy to protect free political communication and of current First Amendment doctrine. He concludes that the arguments advanced either lack a sufficient logical or empirical basis or are founded on ideas that are at odds with a system of free expression. Examination of the legislative proposals leads to the conclusion that they either limit political speech, disadvantage challengers seeking to unseat incumbents, or are too remotely related to valid legislative goals.

Ralph K. Winter is a U.S. circuit judge serving on the Court of Appeals for the Second Circuit. Before entering judicial service, he was the William K. Townsend Professor of Law at Yale Law School and wrote several articles opposing the regulation of campaign financing. He also represented numerous litigants in constitutional challenges to campaign finance legislation, including the plaintiffs in Buckley v. Valeo.

IN addressing the relationship of the First Amendment to the use of money or in-kind resources for purposes of political communication, one must keep in mind the nature of law and particularly the nature of constitutional law. A body of law fashioned by courts interpreting the First Amendment should be rooted in the purposes of that provision and should be principled. That is to say, interpretation should be based on values and ideas derived from the amendment and capable of being neutrally applied so that the resulting body of law is coherent in the subfield of political financing as well as in the larger area covered by the amendment. For example, some are prepared in the name of political equality to limit the use of money or valuable resources for political communication. If such regulation is to pass constitutional muster, we must accept as constitutionally valid the logical ramifications flowing from the goal of equality, including an ultimate power in government to regulate all significant sources of political communication.

The First Amendment as presently construed applies to virtually all communicative conduct. It thus protects the arts,[1] including material offensive to many,[2] and commercial speech,[3] although the permissible area of regulation in both cases is somewhat ill defined. I note this at the outset because the core of the First Amendment is the protection of political speech, and the maximum constitutional protection afforded the arts and commercial speech ought to serve as the minimum afforded political speech.

That political speech is entitled to the highest protection afforded by the First Amendment is an easily defended position. Like arts and commercial speech, political communication has informative and educational aspects. In addition, however, political speech effectuates those constitutional procedures providing for democratic rule. Without protection for political speech, the information and choices afforded the electorate would be diminished, and political opposition would become risky if not impossible. Such a consequence would be inconsistent with both the specific electoral procedures the Constitution provides and the general form of government it creates.

Moreover, the regulation of speech, if undertaken, must be by government, hardly a neutral participant in political debate. This must be stressed because one fact is systematically glossed over by those who seek to regulate political finance, namely, that such regulation is enacted by officeholders, who have a powerful incentive to maximize the resources of political communication available to them and to minimize those available to their opponents.

Supreme Court decisions generally accord political speech great protection even when that speech involves the expenditure of very large sums of money. They have thus protected mass publication of the Pentagon papers,[4] limited the application of the law of libel in the case of the mass publication of defamatory advertisements purchased for substan-

---

1. See, for example, *Southeastern Promotions, Ltd* v. *Conrad*, 420 U.S. 546 (1975); *Memoirs* v. *Massachusetts*, 383 U.S. 413 (1966).

2. *Miller* v. *California*, 413 U.S. 15 (1973); *Paris Adult Theater Inc.* v. *Slaton*, 413 U.S. 49 (1973).

3. *Bates* v. *State Bar of Arizona*, 433 U.S. 350 (1977); *Virginia Pharmacy Board* v. *Virginia Consumer Council*, 425 U.S. 748 (1976); *Bigelow* v. *Virginia*, 421 U.S. 809 (1975).

4. *New York Times* v. *United States*, 403 U.S. 713 (1971).

tial sums,[5] and protected the expenditure of money for the purchase of advertisements advocating certain public positions by commercial corporations.[6] Constitutional protection has been extended to more personal acts with political content notwithstanding that many view these acts as inherently offensive. One may thus freely wear clothing bearing the words "fuck the draft"[7] and desecrate the flag as a political statement.[8]

More important, for purposes of the present discussion, the Court has expressly declined to permit regulation of political speech in the name of equality of resources. In *Mills* v. *Alabama*,[9] for example, the Court invalidated a law prohibiting last-minute editorial attacks on candidates by newspapers during election campaigns even though the candidates lacked an effective means of reply. In *Miami Herald Publishing Co.* v. *Tornillo*,[10] moreover, the Court struck down a right-of-reply statute that compelled newspapers to give candidates they had attacked free reply space. Again, this decision rejected as a ground for limiting political speech a self-evident inequality of resources with which to communicate with the public.

Tornillo, however, has not been fully extended to the broadcast media, for the Court upheld the so-called fairness doctrine in the *Red Lion Broadcasting Co.* v. *FCC* decision.[11] That doctrine limits the broadcast media's right to express certain views without according an opportunity for similar expression by those holding other views. *Tornillo* remains the general rule, however, for *Red Lion* was specifically restricted to the case of broadcast frequencies, which are limited in number and are owned by the government. The First Amendment has thus been construed to hold that the public interest in free and unfettered political debate outweighs claims of unfairness or inequality.

Of course, a compelling governmental interest can justify regulation that affects speech. The two leading decisions in this area are *Red Lion* and *United States Civil Service Commission* v. *National Association of Letter Carriers*,[12] upholding the Hatch Act's prohibitions on political activity by certain governmental employees. Other grounds justifying the regulation of political speech relate to the time, place, and manner of such speech.[13] Thus, demonstrations that impede the use of public highways or interfere with the administration of justice may be prohibited.[14] Similarly, the use of "loud and raucous" sound trucks may be prevented.[15] This then, briefly, is the legal context in which the regulation of the use of money must be addressed.

MONEY AND POLITICAL COMMUNICATION

It is sometimes argued that speech and the use of money or in-kind resources to speak are two different things. This is a profoundly flawed contention. It is simply beyond argument that effective communication in modern society pervasively requires large expenditures. If

---

5. *New York Times* v. *Sullivan*, 376 U.S. 254 (1964).

6. *First National Bank of Boston* v. *Bellotti*, 435 U.S. 765 (1978).

7. *Cohen* v. *California*, 403 U.S. 15 (1971).

8. *Spence* v. *Washington*, 418 U.S. 405 (1974) per curiam; *Smith* v. *Goguen*, 415 U.S. 566 (1974); *Street* v. *New York*, 394 U.S. 576 (1969).

9. 384 U.S. 214 (1966).

10. 418 U.S. 241 (1974).

11. 395 U.S. 367 (1969).

12. 413 U.S. 548 (1973).

13. *Police Department of the City of Chicago* v. *Mosley*, 408 U.S. 92, 98-99 (1972).

14. *Cox* v. *Louisiana*, 379 U.S. 536 (1935).

15. *Kovacs* v. *Cooper*, 336 U.S. 77 (1949).

government may regulate access to necessary resources by controlling expenditures of money, then it has a weapon that can be used to regulate all communication. The arts, for example, require theaters, cameras, salaries, printing technology, and so forth. If investment in the arts were forbidden, they would cease to exist in any meaningful form. Similarly, organs of the institutional press require substantial capital investment and incur costly operating expenses. As a result, they are largely controlled by persons of means. Even more modest methods of communication—handbills, bullhorns, stenciled T-shirts, even flags to burn—involve the expenditure of money. If the speech protected by the First Amendment is legally distinct from the use of money or resources to speak, then there simply is no effective First Amendment protection for speech.

As is the case with the arts, money and political communication are inseparable. Only the most serious and compelling of governmental interests can justify regulation, and even then the regulation must be narrowly tailored to suit the particular goal. I therefore turn to the various goals asserted for the regulation of political finance.

Skyrocketing costs

Calls for the regulation of political finance routinely recite statistics showing that the costs of political communication have been rising at a dramatic speed. The fact is undeniable. The significance of the fact, however, is not at all clear, and its repetition in this particular context apparently reflects an assumption that dramatically increasing costs are evidence of a serious illness in the political system. Unpacking the claim, however, demonstrates how unfounded such an assumption is.

First, persons seeking to engage in political communication must purchase resources in a market in which prices are determined by competition. Political speakers are, in fact, a small fraction of those who compete for such resources generally. Commercial advertisers, for example, use most of the same resources to communicate with the public, and the amount spent in a year on such advertising by one or two of the largest advertisers equals or exceeds the total amount spent by all those engaged in political communication. The rise in the costs of political communication is largely caused by factors independent of the political system.

Second, the last 20 years have witnessed a dramatic increase in political activity because of the proliferation of political events such as nominating primaries and caucuses. Complaints about rising costs, therefore, are to some extent complaints about the extent of political activity in this country. The fact that those who complain about costs almost invariably support the proliferation of political events is one of the ironies of the debate over political financing.

Moreover, apart from public financing schemes, the measures proposed as a response to the rising costs of political communication do not aid campaigns in meeting those costs. Rather, the proposals put a cap on expenditures by limiting the amount of resources that may be purchased by a campaign, an action that directly limits the amount of political speech. Upon examination, the concern over skyrocketing costs appears to reflect an underlying disdain for political campaigns generally.[16]

16. *Buckley* v. *Valeo*, 519 F.2d 821, 897 (D.C. Cir. 1975) *per curiam,* describing presidential elections as "quadrennial Romanesque political extravagances."

Reliance upon skyrocketing costs as a justification for the regulation of campaign financing also fails to take into account the self-interest of incumbents. Whereas the various suggestions for limiting expenditures to purchase resources for political communication apply to every means used by challengers to communicate with the public, incumbents have available to them vast resources usable for the same purpose but paid for by the government. At the time that the Federal Election Campaign Act (FECA) was passed in 1974, for example, the cost of franked mail sent by incumbent members of Congress to constituents was increasing at about twice the rate of campaign costs generally and in election years exceeded all sums spent by all challengers on all campaign activities. In addition to franked mail, incumbents have available inexpensive television and radio taping facilities, computer resources to keep track of individual constituents' interests, paid staff, and many local offices, including mobile units. Expenditure limits thus have a differential impact on challengers and incumbents.

Finally, it should be noted that the regulation of campaign finances itself increases the costs of campaigns. By limiting individual campaign contributions to $1000,[17] the FECA imposes upon candidates the heavy costs associated with fund-raising from a multitude of sources, such as direct mail. Indeed, much of the rhetoric bandied about with regard to the costs of campaigns usually concentrates on the gross amount of money raised without any mention of the very high costs of raising it. Moreover, by subjecting candidates to a complex regulatory scheme administered by an administrative agency, campaign finance laws impose upon candidates heavy legal and accounting costs.

Furthering equality in political communication

Proponents of the regulation of private political financing claim that such regulation is needed to equalize the ability to speak on political matters. The apprehension, of course, is that private financing of political speech allows wealthy persons and interests to drown out everyone else. Rarely has so sinister a proposition been so attractively packaged, for if government may silence certain speakers in the name of equality, constitutional protection for political communication would soon cease to exist.

No one denies that some persons and groups have advantages—indeed, enormous advantages—in political communication. However, these inequalities are so ubiquitous throughout our polity that controlling the communication of certain persons, groups, or interests will not bring about equality. It will merely create new inequalities. For example, if candidates for office are severely limited in the amount they may spend in political campaigns, their power to communicate with the public would surely be reduced. However, the power of the institutional press such as the networks, major newspapers, radio stations, and magazines would be relatively increased as candidates sought their favor in order to obtain through news coverage the exposure they no longer could purchase through advertising. At that point, pervasive governmental control of the press would be not only constitutionally valid but seemingly imperative. This, I submit, cannot be the law under the First Amendment as it currently stands.

17. 2 U.S.C. § 441a(a) (1982).

The First Amendment singles out the press as a special beneficiary of its protection.[18] This provision, it should be emphasized, is at odds with equality in political communication. Indeed, the principal reason for singling out the press for protection is its unique power to reach the public. A private press serves as a counterweight to government and other interests and is protected precisely because it is more powerful than other means of political communication. There is thus explicit constitutional recognition that equality is not a goal justifying the regulation of political speech.

In fact, private political financing is a far more egalitarian method of political communication than is a free press. Those who provide political financing are more diverse both in number and in viewpoint than is the institutional press. Critics of private political financing correctly point out that a small fraction of the people account for the great bulk of campaign contributions. That small fraction, however, amounts to millions of people, whereas every media firm is operationally controlled by persons numbering at most in double digits. Whether at the town, city, state, or national level, the decision of what is carried on the media is infinitely more centralized than are the sources of private political financing.

It must also be noted that some political financing is provided by surrogates representing the interests of many others unable to speak on a subject. Consider a developer, for example, who spends money seeking public support for amending ordinances that restrict the development of certain tracts of land. Such a use of money is often condemned as pursuing profits for a small special interest group; however, those potential profits represent the inchoate interests of those consumers who would purchase that land and better their own standard of living but cannot know of this opportunity in advance of development.

Because inequalities in political communication are ubiquitous, equality as a goal of regulation also cannot be limited. Its logic, for example, extends beyond candidates for office to organizations pursuing particular issues. Such groups almost always have wealthy patrons and invariably depend upon money to pursue their goals. There is not a major civil rights group, civil liberties organization, public interest lobbying organization, public interest law firm, environmental group, public policy think tank, or New Right organization that cannot be accurately accused of using money to communicate on matters of public interest in a fashion that gives it more power than roughly 99 percent of the rest of the citizenry.

The logic of equality in political communication thus leads not to a free, robust debate but to a governmentally imposed silence, for anything short of that silence may arguably be described as discrimination. The fact is that any person or group engaging in effective political communication is automatically subject to an accusation of inequality. Indeed, political communication is not effective unless it is unequal and rises above other voices. The goal of equality in political communication thus stands the First Amendment on its head. It hardly makes sense, for example, to protect fringe political speech such as

---

18. The First Amendment provides that "Congress shall make no law respecting an establishment of religion, or prohibiting the free exercise thereof; or abridging the freedom of speech, or of the press; or the right of the people peaceably to assemble, and to petition the Government for a redress of grievances."

flag burning or T-shirts that advocate implausible anatomical contacts with the selective service if we are prepared to suppress mainstream political speech.

Those who would regulate in the name of equality also do not address the fact that such regulation must be by the hand of government and according to the judgment of those in power. Those in power thus must determine whether political communication from one source has been heard too much and whether communication from another has not had adequate exposure. One does not have to be extraordinarily cynical to anticipate the speech that those in power will regard as having had too much exposure.

Profound dangers to First Amendment values thus inhere in the regulation of private political finance. In addition, it should be emphasized that an affirmative case based on those values can be made for such financing. A democratic system of government must allow proponents of change to seek that change through that system. Political communication free of regulation by government is a precondition to the pursuit of change, and free financing of that communication is a catalyst of that change.

Many fail to realize how important private financing is to political change because they assume that status quo issues and candidates get the bulk of the available money. Even if that is generally true—there are, in fact, many notable exceptions—it fails to take into account the fact that political money is of different value to different issue groups and to different candidates. In particular, money has a higher marginal value to groups and candidates seeking change than it does to groups and officeholders with high recognition and acceptance among the public. Indeed, history teaches that groups and candidates seeking change have difficulty raising substantial sums of money in small amounts and are in their infancy heavily dependent upon a few sources that contribute large amounts. Private political financing is thus of critical importance to political change and is at the heart of those values protected by the First Amendment.

The concept that $1 of political financing may be of greater value to a new cause or candidate than to the establishment is rarely recognized outside the realm of political technicians. It is, when considered, virtually a self-evident proposition. Consider an example from the world of commerce. Hypothesize a town with one well-known restaurant. Its previous success affords it an ample budget for advertising, and it is now challenged by a new restaurant with limited means. The success of the new firm will be determined more by whether it can purchase enough advertising to reach a critical mass of the public than by whether it is outspent, even grossly outspent, by its established competitor. Each advertising dollar spent by the older firm has far less potential for affecting opinions than those spent by the newer one. Its advertising at best reinforces opinions among past customers. The latter's advertising, however, reaches large numbers of new customers, and once it reaches a critical mass, the restaurant will be viable until it wins or loses on the merits of its food or service. For the old, advertising borders on the superfluous; for the new, it is critical to survival. Money used in reaching a critical mass with a new message thus produces more value than does money used to repeat the familiar.

In an analogous fashion, new political ideas or new candidates are threatened less by the ample resources available to their adversaries than by the danger that they will not be able to accumulate a minimum level of financing for themselves. This also explains why incumbent officeholders, who always have available only to them more resources in governmentally provided goods and services and who have high name recognition as well, are so willing to limit the use of private financing in political campaigns notwithstanding their advantages in that kind of fund-raising.

The most notable, although hardly the only, example of this use of money as a catalyst for change was Eugene McCarthy's campaign for the Democratic presidential nomination in 1968. Based on his opposition to the war in Vietnam, McCarthy's campaign in New Hampshire, although not victorious, demonstrated President Johnson's vulnerability and revealed an antiwar constituency in Democratic ranks that had not been previously verified. The McCarthy campaign was featured at the time as a children's crusade, staffed by volunteers sloshing through the snow to ring doorbells. In fact, given the size of New Hampshire, it was a heavily financed campaign whose viability was assured by sizable early contributions from wealthy individuals followed by what was by any standard extravagant spending. By the end of the New Hampshire campaign, Senator McCarthy had spent $12—in 1968 dollars—per vote received.[19] His own experience as a political David taking on an incumbent Goliath in a campaign written off by the experts led him in later years to be among the most adamant opponents of the regulation of political financing.[20]

Other examples of the use of pools of private money for underdog candidates and causes abound. Senator McGovern's 1972 campaign for the Democratic presidential nomination also relied heavily upon the early accumulation of large contributions from wealthy patrons. Mayor Bradley's successful 1973 campaign in Los Angeles, as a black running in a largely white municipality, and James Buckley's successful New York campaign in 1970, as a third-party senatorial candidate, also were made viable by early large contributions. The major civil rights and civil liberties organizations were for long periods of time supported by sizable gifts from wealthy individuals that enabled them to achieve the viability necessary for mass fundraising. Even now, the scope of their activity may depend upon large contributions.

It is quite clear that private financing nurtures candidates and causes across the political spectrum and that large donors by no means pursue only the self-interest of the wealthy. Before the FECA limited individual contributions, many identifiably liberal or left-wing political candidates were heavily financed; indeed, many believe that the limit on contributions to candidates has been more harmful to candidates of the Left than any other particular political group.

For First Amendment purposes, it matters not whose ox is gored or saved. The point is that the status quo, however well financed, is threatened by aggregations of private funds and that the regulation of such private financing threatens to cut off movements and candidates pursuing political change.

Corruption

It also was argued by those who supported the FECA that it would reduce

---

19. *Buckley* v. *Valeo*, 424 U.S. 1 (1976) *per curiam*, joint app., 2:25.

20. McCarthy actually joined as a plaintiff challenging the FECA in *Buckley* v. *Valeo*.

corruption. Proponents believed that campaign contributions all too often involved quid pro quos. They believed that officeholders agreed not just to listen to contributors—the inequality problem—and decide issues on the issues' merits, but in fact committed themselves to legislation or dispensed jobs in exchange for campaign money. This problem, which seems so obvious to so many, in fact had little empirical support at the time the FECA was passed. The available evidence was largely limited to the awarding of ambassadorships, a practice not to be praised, but one that also hardly justifies the widespread suppression of political speech. Indeed, it is not clear why full disclosure of contributions is not an adequate deterrent.

*Loss of public
confidence in government*

It is also claimed that regulation of political financing is necessary to remedy a loss of public confidence in government. This is a quintessential bootstrap argument. Having persuaded the public that our government is for sale, advocates of political finance regulation now take the fact of that persuasion as a justification for the measures they support. Public confidence in government is indeed important, but one should not ignore how dangerous this rationale is when used to regulate political communication. Many have argued quite as cogently that confidence in the moral fabric of society is undermined by certain films or plays. Many others have argued for the stringent regulation of government employment on the grounds that the public has lost confidence in government because it believes it to be staffed by subversives. The public-confidence argument is little more than a claim that the First Amendment must give way to public opinion.

Candidates' time

Finally, it has been argued that one effect of campaign finance regulation is to reduce the time candidates have to spend on fund-raising and thus to leave them more time for campaigning and communicating with the public. In fact, such regulation has been almost totally counterproductive so far as this goal is concerned. Except for the presidential general election, where full campaign financing is available, the low limits on individual contributions have forced candidates, including those in the partially financed presidential nominating campaigns, to spend more time than ever trying to raise money.

PARTICULAR APPLICATIONS
OF THE FIRST AMENDMENT

Critics of private political financing have suggested numerous legislative measures to remedy the ills they perceive. Some of the more important of these proposals are now examined in light of the previous discussion.

Independent expenditures

Independent expenditures are expenditures by individuals or groups for the purpose of persuading voters to vote for a particular candidate. Such expenditures are not made in coordination with the candidate's campaign but are made independently in ways believed by those making the expenditures to be most effective. Although critics of private campaign financing appear to equate independent expenditures with contributions to candidates' campaigns, the conventional wisdom among politicians is to the contrary. Whereas they prize contributions, they believe independent expenditures to be more harmful than helpful. Campaign managers strongly prefer to control carefully all expenditures made on behalf of their candidate not only to achieve the most efficient use of money, but also to avoid campaign tactics that have the effect of alienating more voters than they persuade. Campaigns generally base expenditure decisions on private polls and other data that identify groups according to intensity of feeling toward the various candidates. Independent expenditures are made in the absence of such information. The use to which independent expenditures are put, moreover, is usually colored by the ideological outlook of the group making them, increasing the danger that uncommitted voters may be alienated.

Constitutional protection of independent expenditures is essential if we are to effectuate the core purpose of the First Amendment. Such expenditures constitute speech designed to persuade voters to believe and act in a particular way—nothing more, nothing less. They are pure political advocacy, functionally indistinguishable from the editorial endorsement of candidates by organs of the media, the endorsement of a candidate by a political or community leader, or advocacy of policies by issue groups that aid particular candidates.

It has been argued that independent expenditures may be a method of corrupting candidates by creating undesirable obligations. This argument is utterly without merit. An independent expenditure by itself creates no obligation. Whatever obligation may be created arises only after the expenditure has persuaded persons to vote for the candidate. This is a crucial distinction because contributions to a campaign may create obligations by the very act of donation. Independent expenditures, however, create obligations only by persuading voters, much as obligations are created by the endorsement of editorial writers or political and community leaders, or, in fact, any speech that persuades voters.

In light of the fact that the regulation of independent expenditures would have profoundly undesirable implications for the protection of political speech afforded by the First Amendment, the Supreme Court held them to be constitutionally protected in *Buckley v. Valeo*.[21]

Expenditures by candidates

Proposals for the regulation of campaign finances routinely include proposals to cap the amount candidates may spend in political campaigns. Various reasons are offered in support of such limitations—as will be discussed later—but it is well nigh certain that the principal reason for their staying power as an idea is their attractiveness to incumbent members of Congress. Limitations on expenditures by candidates regulate virtually every dime spent by challengers for political purposes, whereas they have no effect whatsoever on the abundant perquisites useful for political purposes that government provides to incumbents. In 1974, the year in which the FECA was passed, over $38 million was spent on the congressional frank, the heaviest use of the frank at that time being near the dates of primary and general elections.[22] In the same

---

21. 424 U.S. 1; see also *FEC v. National Conservative Political Action Committee*, 105 S. Ct. 1459 (1985).

22. *Buckley v. Valeo*, joint app., 2:23.

year, the total spent by challengers in all primary and general election campaigns was barely over $20 million.[23] In addition to the frank, of course, incumbents have other perks useful for political purposes such as a staff, a variety of offices, and access to cheap broadcast facilities. It is true that only the most crass incumbents openly use such perks on the eve of elections, but the fact remains, as every politician knows, that these resources are enormously useful for communicating with voters in order to generate electoral support. Limitations on expenditures, therefore, fall far more heavily upon challengers than upon incumbents even when such limitations are set at a very high level.

Of course, it is not to be expected that such limitations will be set at a high level. As argued earlier, the value of campaign money to a challenger is generally greater than it is to incumbents and, generally, the lower the limitation, the greater the damaging effect on the campaigns of challengers. There is abundant evidence in support of this proposition. When the FECA was being considered by the Congress, John Gardner of Common Cause testified before the Congress that low limits on expenditures would tend to freeze out challengers. He proposed a limit he believed to be adequate. The Congress thereafter reduced the limitation on expenditures significantly below that suggested.

There are other reasons for being concerned about limitations on expenditures. A necessary adjunct to such limitations is centralized control over individuals spending their own money in coordination with a campaign. If an expenditure limitation is to be effective, it is necessary to prevent individuals from offering storefronts, handbills, or other useful campaign materials to campaigns without including their value in the campaign's expenditures. Because counting and reporting them as the candidate's expenditures is administratively impossible, control over individual expenditures amounts to a prohibition. It should be noted that the effect of this control is in addition to the limits on contributions, which would in any event restrict an individual's gift of storefronts and the like to a total value of $1000. The effect of expenditure limits is thus to cause campaigns to be more media-oriented and to preclude grass-roots participation by individuals. Directed by a centralized staff, campaigns become an exercise in technocracy rather than a training ground for democracy.

Weighed against the overwhelming reasons for fearing limitations on campaign expenditures, the purported benefits seem slim indeed. At best, proponents of expenditure limitations fall back on the argument of skyrocketing campaign costs or assert that such limitations are necessary to curb any residual temptation to violate limitations on individual contributions. The former argument amounts to a claim that there is too much political speech in campaigns while the latter seems a paradigmatic example of eliminating mosquitoes at a picnic by shotgun blasts. In *Buckley*, the Supreme Court rejected the proffered benefits of expenditure limitations as wholly inadequate justifications for such an outright limitation on the quantity of speech, a decision eminently consistent with the mainstream of First Amendment law.

Contributions to candidates

The most plausible case under the First Amendment for permitting the regulation of campaign financing arises

23. Ibid., pp. 442, 444.

in the case of limitations on contributions to candidates. Critics of private financing make three basic arguments in favor of the constitutionality of limits on individual contributions. First, they point out that a contribution is at best indirect speech by the donor because the candidate exercises total control over the use of money once the gift is complete. Second, they argue that contributions by individuals give the rich an advantage over the poor in shaping public policy. Third, they note that contributions entail opportunities for corruption since they may create an obligation by the very act of giving. In *Buckley* v. *Valeo* the Supreme Court upheld the FECA's limits on individual contributions on the grounds that preventing corruption or the appearance of corruption was a compelling governmental interest justifying such limits.

Neither the arguments of the critics nor the decision of the Court are without reason. There are, however, cogent arguments supporting a different conclusion that are rarely publicized and deserve consideration. It is true that contributions are indirect speech in the sense that their particular use is determined by the candidate rather than by the donor. However, it is also true that millions contribute to candidates for ideological reasons and that contributions are the only means by which they can participate in furthering the views they espouse. For such contributors, this form of political speech is the only way to make their voice part of an effective organization.

Moreover, contributions, including large contributions, are made across the political spectrum. To be sure, those making them may generally be well-to-do, but it is simply not a fact that their purpose is solely to protect the wealthy. There have been countless instances in which candidates who could be counted on to favor higher and more progressive taxes have been the recipients of sizable amounts of campaign money donated by wealthy individuals. In the case of candidates pursuing political causes outside the mainstream, such contributions are critical. They are needed at an early stage as seed money so the campaigns will be sufficiently viable to appeal to a wider portion of the public for money and support. In the hope of scaring off potential challengers, incumbents can often warehouse large amounts of campaign money. The decisive factor, however, is generally not how much the incumbent has, but whether the challenger believes that enough can be raised at an early stage to make the campaign viable. Large private contributions are often essential to that end.

It should be further noted that a limit on the size of individual contributions makes fund-raising more difficult and more costly and thus limits the total amount that may be spent in campaigns. The effect, therefore, is essentially the same as expenditure limitations that disadvantage challengers. In fact, that disadvantage may be increased by limits on contributions because most challengers will find it more difficult to raise money by direct mail than will most incumbents. Direct mail is not only a costly method of raising funds but is also most successful when used by candidates with name recognition and an established mailing list of supporters.

So far as corruption is concerned, it is difficult to perceive why full disclosure of contributions and their sources to the electorate is not an adequate deterrent in light of the extremely sketchy evidence that campaign money actually results in quid pro quo arrangements. As for the appearance of corruption, disclosure enables the electorate to act upon its perceptions.

Finally, whatever merits the arguments favoring limits on contributions have, they seem rather out of step with the actual provisions of the present law. No reason has ever been offered to explain, much less justify, an identical limitation on contributions for House, Senate, and presidential races. There is also no rationale for not adjusting contribution limits for inflation unless their real purpose is to limit candidate expenditures. Moreover, virtually all of the arguments favoring limitations on contributions would lead not to the present law but to a fairly simple rule limiting how much one person might contribute to candidates for federal office without limiting how much of that sum can be given to one candidate. This would be effective in limiting the influence of any particular individual and yet allow challengers and candidates seeking change to accumulate the necessary seed money.

A note on expenditure limitations connected to public funding

As the law currently stands, Congress may condition the acceptance of public campaign financing upon a candidate's accepting limitations on his or her total expenditures. This may seem an unexceptional restriction, but two matters should be considered. First, a candidate's choice is not between free private financing and public funding, but between the latter and private financing subject to the low limits on individual contributions. As a consequence, the acceptance of a limitation on total expenditures by a campaign is not entirely voluntary, and the offer of such funding in exchange for the waiver of a constitutional right appears to be a purchase by the government of an individual's First Amendment rights. In my view, this state of the law cannot be squared with *Buckley*'s invalidation of expenditure limits.

Second, whatever the voluntariness of the candidate's acceptance of limitations on the campaign's expenditures, one effect is to prevent individuals from using their own funds to participate in the campaign because the limit on expenditures requires centralized control over individual expenditures. Given the fact that national presidential campaigns must concentrate on the media, very little of a national campaign budget is likely to be allocated to grass-roots activities involving such individuals. State parties may legally provide some money for specified grass-roots activities, but they need not do so. Many individuals who want to engage in such activities may well find state and local parties unwilling to support them.

It is the law today, therefore, that an individual may not even provide pencils to campaign volunteers in a presidential election without the campaign's counting and reporting them as expenditures within the limits. Since counting and reporting them as campaign expenditures is an administrative impossibility, the effect is again a flat prohibition. The result is thus that a candidate's waiver of his or her right to spend money has a compulsory effect upon the candidate's supporters. To my knowledge, no one has ever suggested a reason justifying this result, except perhaps the skyrocketing cost of campaigns, since it is clear that any individual funding of grass-roots activities would be subject to the limitation on individual contributions.

A note on political action committees

Much ink is expended these days in deploring the role that corporate and labor political action committees (PACs) play in political campaigns.[24] The plaintiffs in *Buckley* directly raised the specter of the concomitant effect of the limits on individual contributions and the creation of PACs the administrative costs of which might be borne by corporations and unions. They suggested that the effect would be to regulate the content of campaigns by limiting individual contributions often based on ideology while institutionalizing the influence of corporations and unions on a large scale. The Court, urged on by those who now are the most vigorous critics of PACs, rejected this argument and presumably would not be inclined to reconsider it.

One should, however, distinguish between the problems raised by PACs and issues regarding corporate or union expenditures to debate particular policies, as in referenda. PACs raise two distinct problems. First is the fact that PACs are controlled by a particular firm or union, and it alone determines which candidates get the PACs' contributions. The money, however, is raised from employees or members who have no say in its use and who may have contributed out of a desire to please superiors or union officers. The political speech and the views of the actual donors are thus only indirectly related. Second, if there is a corruption problem, it is surely greater in the case of PACs.

24. See Fred Wertheimer, "Campaign Finance Reform: The Unfinished Agenda," this issue of *The Annals* of the American Academy of Political and Social Science; Richard Bolling, "Money in Politics," ibid.

The use of corporate or union money to debate issues through advertising and other means raises none of these problems and thus stands on a different constitutional footing.[25] Indeed, the only argument for permitting regulation of such expenditures is the equality argument.

A note on rich candidates

In *Buckley,* the Supreme Court held that Congress could not limit the amount an individual spent on behalf of his or her campaign, there being no danger of one's corrupting oneself with one's own money. Many now fear that political candidacies are too much the exclusive province of the rich. I would suggest, however, that the result in *Buckley* is constitutionally sound and that the practical effect perceived by critics is hardly inevitable. If, in fact, the rich are now much more able than others to run for elective office, that simply proves that the current limits on contributions prevent challengers who lack private wealth from raising seed money. The remedy is thus to raise the level of contribution limits, not to prevent the rich from using their own money to run for office, a measure that would simply insulate incumbents from a group able to raise sufficient funds to challenge them.

CONCLUSION

Whatever one's view on the merits of regulating political financing, it can hardly be disputed that this regulation raises First Amendment issues of the most sensitive nature. The protection of political communication is the core pur-

25. *First National Bank of Boston* v. *Bellotti,* 435 U.S. 765 (1978).

pose of that constitutional provision, and the use of money is indispensable to effective political communication. Because regulation must be enacted by officeholders, the danger that the regulation will not be neutral is very great. The justifications for such regulation must thus be scrutinized with the greatest care for their neutrality, their cogency, and their implications for political speech. When so scrutinized, the justifications offered for limiting private financing of political communication seem heavily outweighed by their effect on political speech.

Political Finance in the Liberal Republic: Representation, Equality, and Deregulation

By STEPHEN HARDER

ABSTRACT: The intervention by Congress in the private funding of federal election campaigns is fundamentally misconceived. The field should be deregulated. Proponents of intervention believe that the unregulated private financing of election campaigns subverts our representative institutions. This is because, they believe, first, that disparities in campaign spending often decide elections; second, that the pattern of campaign contributions received by a legislator significantly influences that legislator's lawmaking behavior; and, third, that the private financing of political activity injects the economic inequalities of the marketplace into the sphere of political rights. However, a whole view of the complex worlds of elections and legislation suggests that these beliefs, despite their superficial plausibility, are unsupported by reason and experience. In fact, the private market for political finance, left unregulated, should consistently deny to any discrete group of participants the market power necessary to influence elections or legislation significantly. Furthermore, the partial regulation attempted to date has been easily circumvented, and more comprehensive regulation is substantially barred by the constitutional sanctity of political speech and association. Finally, a system of private political finance, free from government intervention, is reconcilable with the legitimate operations of our representative government and with the true meaning of political equality.

Stephen Harder is an associate at the New York law firm of White & Case. In 1979, he received his A.B. degree in East Asian Studies from Princeton University. He spent the next four years in Beijing representing two American corporations. Mr. Harder recently obtained a joint M.B.A.-J.D. degree from Columbia University.

EVERY campaign for election to the Congress, and until 1976 every campaign for election to the presidency, has been entirely financed from private sources. This does not mean that all political activity, or even most of it, has been financed by private individuals. The economic value of the concerted political activities of the commercial media, churches, federal officeholders, state and local governments, myriad lobbying organizations, corporations, unions, schools, and other concentrations of social and economic power is virtually impossible to determine, but that economic value is clearly enormous. Significantly, neither current law nor proposed legislation attempts to monitor or regulate such economic activity.

This traditional reliance on private political finance does not mean that our government should be subject to auction. The direct exchange of money for ballots or bills is certainly illegitimate and must be prevented to preserve the integrity of our representative government. Vote buying and bribery of elected officials were early made criminal.[1] The direct funding of election campaigns by corporations and unions, which benefit from many legal immunities and derive their treasuries from market power rather than the political choices of individuals, has also been proscribed since the first half of this century.[2]

Yet, except for such basic and obviously necessary restrictions, the market for the private financing of political campaigns had remained substantially free of effective government intervention until a decade ago.[3] Now, however, political finance is dominated by an imposing structure of regulation. The Presidential Election Campaign Fund Act and the Presidential Primary Matching Payment Account Act establish a complex though partial system of government financing for presidential election campaigns, while the Federal Election Campaign Act of 1971, as amended, attempts to regulate the still entirely private system of funding congressional elections.[4] This regulatory structure has been further complicated by several Supreme Court decisions, beginning in 1976 with *Buckley* v. *Valeo*,[5] that have radically limited the power of Congress to make coherent law in this field.

Why must the government regulate private political finance at all? The argument for regulation is based on three premises. Unregulated private political finance will, it is claimed, distort the outcomes of elections,[6] subvert the process of legislation,[7] and undermine political equality.[8] If these premises are well

---

1. 18 U.S.C. §§ 201-11.
2. 2 U.S.C. § 441(b).
3. Some nominal restrictions on political contributions were contained in the Federal Corrupt Practices Act of 1925, 43 Stat. 1070 (1925); however, these sanctions were seldom enforced and were easily circumvented. See generally Alexander Heard, *The Costs of Democracy* (Chapel Hill: University of North Carolina Press, 1960), pp. 344-70.
4. The presidential fund act and the primary act are codified, respectively, at 26 U.S.C. §§ 9001-13 and 26 U.S.C. §§ 9031-42. The Federal Election Campaign Act is codified at 2 U.S.C. §§ 431-55. See generally Michael J. Malbin, ed., *Parties, Interest Groups, and Campaign Finance Laws* (Washington, DC: American Enterprise Institute, 1980); idem, ed. *Money and Politics in the United States: Financing Elections in the 1980's* (Washington, DC: American Enterprise Institute, 1984).
5. *Buckley* v. *Valeo*, 424 U.S. 1 (1976).
6. J. Skelly Wright, "Money and the Pollution of Politics: Is the First Amendment an Obstacle to Political Equality?" *Columbia Law Review*, vol. 82 (May 1982).
7. Elizabeth Drew, *Politics and Money: The New Road to Corruption* (New York: Macmillan, 1983).
8. Richard Briffault, "The Federal Election Campaign Act and the 1980 Election," *Columbia Law Review*, vol. 84 (Dec. 1984).

founded, they constitute a serious indictment of the American representative system as it has existed for almost 200 years. They are, however, unsound.

THE CONTEXT OF INFLUENCE

A single vote, for all its surface simplicity, is the sum of a complex political calculus hidden in the mind of the voter. Partisan and ideological identifications, perceptions of current affairs shaped in large part by the commercial media, affiliations with church, employer, and union, and economic and social status all certainly play an important part. Similar factors influence legislators, although their calculations are further complicated by the public nature of their vote. This forces them also to consider the interests and reactions of various affected groups, possible electoral consequences, the demands of party and of other coalitions necessary to government, relations with their colleagues, and, possibly, implications for their sources of campaign funding.

Political scientists have sought to weigh the various elements in these hidden equations of the vote. One prevalent method for doing so is the statistical correlation, in which votes are plotted against party affiliation, economic indicators, or opinion polls. The results are often interesting but frequently misinterpreted, especially in the debate over campaign finance regulation.

First of all, many proponents of the regulation of private political finance forget that statistical correlations require measurable elements. Certain elements in the political equation, such as party, geography, sex, race, and especially money, are easily assigned a numerical value. But quantification of such intangible concepts as ideology or voting record is more suspect. Other important factors in political decisions, such as media influence, political charisma, the wisdom of a particular bill, even the role of history, are fundamentally immune to any kind of numerical analysis.

More important, a correlation is not a cause. Thus, affiliation with the president's party may strongly correlate with a vote for the president's policies, but is this vote caused by shared political vision, by fear of professional reprisal by party leaders, or perhaps by the potential availability of campaign resources distributed by the party to supportive members? The mere existence of a correlation, however strong, does not give a complete or sufficient picture of the motivation of the legislator. Yet if we are to question the legitimacy of the political process, as the argument for the regulation of political finance does, then motivation is crucial.

Unfortunately, the superabundance of easily quantified data on campaign finance has narrowed the attention of many commentators to a very small part of the political world. Anyone convinced that campaign finance now explains much about politics enjoys a statistical field day. Correlations between campaign contributions and voting patterns abound. Not surprisingly, the role political finance plays in the political process, when viewed in this artificially magnified statistical isolation, appears to be significant.

But we should not allow the extent of measurement to become the limit of our understanding. The influence of political finance on the political process must be viewed in light of the multitude of significant yet ultimately immeasurable forces exerted on those who exercise the authority of the vote.

Money and elections

"Big spending media campaigns do not always win," asserts one advocate of regulation, "but they win much more often than they lose, distorting the expressed will of the people by the sheer inequality of the financial resources and the avalanche of campaign messages."[9] If we ignore for the moment the conceptual difficulties raised by the notion of an "expressed will of the people" distinct from an election result, the sense of the criticism becomes clear: campaign spending is alleged to be often a decisive cause of election outcomes.

But candidates do not spend campaign funds in a vacuum. Many important forces shape the ultimate decision of a potential voter before the campaign manager writes the first check. Many of these forces are beyond the immediate influence of the candidate: voters are often strongly predisposed by party, race, gender, religion, or class. The power and opportunity to interpret to the voter such wider phenomena as the economy, foreign affairs, or the record and program of the candidate and the candidate's party are shared by the candidate with government officials, party leaders, corporate media, and the various elite groups that control church, company, union, school, journal, and ideological organization in this country. The political activities of these groups are not limited to the comparatively brief period of heightened political discourse represented by the official election campaign.

Election campaigns cost money, but money is only a secondary resource to a candidate. The real political resources—in other words, the only resources that can conceivably weigh in the balance of the voter's decision—are the candidate's personality, record, and program or those of the candidate's opponent. Money is needed to fund the organization, research, and communication necessary to place these real resources before the voters, but it is no substitute for them.

Of course, an extreme lack of money may leave real political resources so underdeveloped as effectively to preclude victory. But potentially close elections almost always attract abundant funding. For instance, in 1982 the mean expenditure of House incumbents winning reelection with more than 60 percent of the vote was about $200,000. Yet in closer races, where the incumbent won with less than 60 percent of the vote, 31 Republican challengers spent a mean $324,000, and the 22 Democratic challengers who defeated Republican incumbents spent a mean of $292,000,[10]

These reflections suggest an alternative analysis to the one obviously implied by the following simple statistical correlation cited by a proponent of regulation:

Spending data for the House . . . races in 1978 graphically show the extent of inequalities in spending and their correlation with winning and losing . . . the winner outspent the loser in 78.8% [of the 407 contested] races. Where the spending margin was more than two to one, as it was in 159 races, the bigger spender won 93% of the time.[11]

Political reality is more obscured than revealed by such "graphic" statistical correlations. Over 90 percent of House incumbents run for reelection. In 1984, incumbents won 94 percent of their races. As a group they obviously

---

9. Wright, "Money and the Pollution of Politics," pp. 622-25.

10. Malbin, *Money and Politics,* p. 284.

11. Wright, "Money and the Pollution of Politics," p. 622.

enjoy a huge advantage over their challengers in the real resources of politics: name recognition, a positive local image cultivated in part through state-financed ombudsman activities, the chance to build a popular record through bill sponsorship, and so forth. In addition, they benefit from some free access to the media as well as much government-financed travel and communications. The monetary value of these perquisites of office, which is not monitored under any election law, has been placed at close to $1 million per House election.[12] House incumbents easily attract adequate financial backing, while their challengers, often relatively unknown and untested, are usually short of funds. The spending data cited previously by the proponent of regulation, far from proving that money buys elections, merely reflect these facts of political life.

More relevant to a real understanding of the role of money in elections is the very unequal impact that results from the spending of equal amounts of money by incumbent and challenger. "Multiple regression estimates confirm that, with other variables controlled, campaign spending by non-incumbents has a substantial impact on their share of the vote; incumbent campaign expenditures have little effect."[13] These estimates also corroborate the thesis that money has a diminishing marginal utility in election campaigns. The incumbent, whose real political resources have been substantially developed with the aid of much unreported, often government-subsidized spending, gains relatively little from the additional spending of officially reported campaign funds. The challenger gains much.

This whole view of the role of money in elections helps to explain the legendary nervousness of congressional incumbents. They know that if the real resources of politics are squandered, campaign funds, however easily raised, are of little avail. In 1982, for instance, when the mean expenditure by House incumbents in contested elections was $265,000, the 23 incumbents who lost their bids for reelection still outspent their victorious opponents, on average, by $124,000.[14] Perhaps in response to a growing awareness of the limited effect of campaign spending on election results, the total amount of official spending in House election campaigns declined, after a decade of steady growth, from $174 million in 1982 to $162 million in 1984—a decrease in real terms of 11 percent.[15]

Money funds campaigns; it does not buy office.

Money and legislation

Legislators seeking reelection do need campaign funds. Advocates for the regulation of political finance are convinced that the natural concern to raise campaign funds significantly affects the exercise of legislative authority. One supporter of state funding of election campaigns writes:

It is clear that the politicians' anxiety about having access to enough money corrodes and even corrupts the political system.... At the

---

12. Norman J. Ornstein et al., *Vital Statistics on Congress,* 1984-85 ed. (Washington, DC: American Enterprise Institute, 1984), pp. 116-37. See also T. E. Mann, *Unsafe at Any Margin: Interpreting Congressional Elections* (Washington, DC: American Enterprise Institute, 1978).

13. Gary C. Jacobson, *Money in Congressional Elections* (New Haven, CT: Yale University Press, 1980), p. xvi.

14. Malbin, *Politics and Money,* p. 284.

15. "Incumbents Relied More on PAC Gifts in 1984," *Congressional Quarterly Weekly,* 8 June 1985, pp. 1115-17.

least politicians increasingly consider how their votes will affect their own—and their opponents'—ability to raise money. At worst votes are actually traded for money.[16]

The complex reality of the legislative process, however, belies such vague generalizations of endemic corruption.

The legislator stands at the vortex of the representative process. Each year the 435 members of the House cast hundreds of votes for thousands of pages of legislation drafted in thousands of committee meetings. Expertise and time are limited. The interests of nation and district are often obscure; the legislator has no choice but to rely for guidance on party leaders, professional staff, agency reports, sophisticated lobbyists, think tanks, and more knowledgeable colleagues. Even where principle seems clear, a vote may be sacrificed to other ends: votes are traded, governing coalitions enforced, compromises struck, and public reactions weighed. It is a rough-and-tumble world in which the legislator votes.

How important a factor in this complex calculus is the pattern of contributions to a legislator's campaign? The only persuasive analysis of this question must look carefully at the concrete reality facing the typical elected representative.

Absent a system of government financing, the candidate for elective office obtains campaign funds from these sources: individual donations, including sometimes the personal assets of the candidate; the candidate's party; and organized political committees. There are currently some 4000 political action committees in this country.

The mean campaign expenditure of a House candidate in 1982 was $228,060. In the same year, the portfolio of contributions for the average House member consisted of 6 percent from the party, 30 percent from political committees, and 64 percent from individuals and the candidate's personal funds.[17] It is not unusual for the number of contributing political committees to exceed one hundred or for contributing individuals to number in the thousands. Thus the purely economic impact of losing the contribution of any individual or discrete group of individuals would seem minimal.

The campaign portfolio of Congressman Dan Rostenkowski, chairman of the House Ways and Means Committee, provides a concrete example. Congressman Rostenkowski was reelected in 1980 with 84 percent of the vote. He raised a total of $274,580 in campaign funds. About 58 percent, or $159,100, came from 192 different political committees. The average committee contribution was $828, or 0.3 percent of the total funds raised. The individual contributions of only 11 committees exceeded 1 percent of the total; those of only 2 exceeded 2 percent. Only 1 committee gave the maximum contribution allowed by law: the National Automobile Dealers Association gave $10,000, still only 3.6 percent of the total campaign portfolio.

Congressman Tom Foley, House majority whip in the Ninety-seventh Congress, won reelection in 1980 with 52 percent of the vote. Of the $188,192 in campaign funds he raised, 67 percent, or $126,935, came from 192 different political committees. The average committee contribution was $661. Only 14 of the 192 committees contributed an amount in excess of 1 percent of the total; those of only 3 exceeded 2 percent. The largest

16. Drew, *Money and Politics*, p. 146.

17. Ornstein et al., *Vital Statistics*, p. 80.

single contribution, $5000, from the Associated Milk Producers, Inc., accounted for only 2.6 percent of the total campaign portfolio.[18]

When such real instances of campaign contributions are viewed against the background of a complex political reality, the purported rationale for regulating private political finance vanishes like a mirage. Campaign funds themselves are of only limited utility, and even the largest contribution can usually be easily replaced. Further, it is far from certain that a vote against the presumed interests of a contributor will lose the contribution. Even if it does, the inconvenience of replacing most single contributions cannot weigh heavily in the scales of the legislator's mind when balanced against concerns of conscience, credibility, party, ideology, electoral consequences, and collegial relations.

Of certain concern to any legislator is the possibility of driving a well-organized supportive group into active electoral opposition, but that concern is conceptually distinct from a concern for finances. This crucial distinction is often ignored by both politicians and commentators. A relatively large contribution is a very consistent proxy for a large and well-organized group. The contribution can be replaced, but the support of the group cannot. What appears to be preoccupation with campaign funds is often a shorthand expression for a concern for constituency.

Let us, however, assume the implausible, that campaign contributions are the decisive consideration. Let us assume, too, that the legislator is to exercise his or her legislative authority

18. Laurie Duker, ed., *A Common Cause Guide to Money, Power & Politics in the 97th Congress* (Washington, DC: Common Cause, 1981), pp. 140-46, 224-29.

not in a floor vote but in a committee drafting session. The subject may be arcane and beyond the ken of electorate or press. Surely here, the argument for regulation typically runs, a contributor can be quietly repaid by a favor.

But how, exactly? The drafting of technical legislation in a complex society is often a zero-sum game. It is almost impossible to draft a single clause without incidentally disadvantaging one organized interest and benefiting another. Political committees representing opposing interests may well have made contributions to the same legislator. Here is where the analysis of many advocates of regulation becomes disingenuous: while elaborately documenting the winning contributors and their contributions, they conspicuously fail to note the often substantial contributions of the losers. In Rostenkowski's case, contributors American Banking Association and Securities Industry Association are surely in conflict on many details of banking regulation; just as contributors American Family Corporation, an insurance group, and the American Medical Association are certainly at odds on important aspects of health care regulation. Even when the potential losers are diffuse and unorganized, their interests may be represented by such powerful and sophisticated surrogates as Ralph Nader, the American Civil Liberties Union, or the U.S. Treasury.

The inescapable conclusion, that considerations of campaign finances cannot alone exert a significant influence on legislation, is amply documented by empirical research. In sophisticated multiple-regression analyses of House votes, partisan and ideological factors appear much more closely correlated to legislative outcomes than do contribution patterns. On less volatile issues, a mild correlation between campaign contributions and votes has been observed.[19] Yet this correlation is best explained not by pervasive congressional venality, but by the success of sophisticated political committees in identifying for financial backing representatives who are more likely to support their interests.

The notion that any significant number of the 435 members of the House, men and women who have sacrificed much for the opportunity to exercise legislative authority, will consistently mortgage that authority for fractional contributions of campaign funds of limited utility—a notion that underpins the argument for the regulation of political finance—is little short of bizarre. Financial pressure from discrete sources of contributions, in the real world of legislation, is at most a weak force, having apparent effects only when the other stronger forces normally impinging on the legislator are insubstantial or contradictory. Thus one might say that mere money matters most where it matters least: affecting the occasional vote on the marginal issue. On any issue of real importance, even the most self-interested legislator simply cannot afford to be swayed by the proffer of campaign contributions. This more realistic view of political finance offers scant justification for the sweeping regulation currently in force.

AGAINST REGULATION

Justifications for regulation, however questionable, are one thing; the consequences of regulation are another. Regulation of political finance requires governmental controls over the economic relations between individuals, political committees, parties, and candidates. Serious questions must be posed concerning not only the efficacy but also the constitutionality of such controls.

Competition and intervention

The efficacy of economic controls depends on the character of the market to be regulated. Controls are most manageable—and most easily justified—where market actors are few and where product substitution or market entry are naturally restricted. The existing $1 billion private market for state, local, and federal political finance, however, is not susceptible in these ways to government control.

The existing market for political finance is almost a textbook example of a perfectly competitive market. Buyers and sellers are numerous; thousands of candidates and political committees compete for the contributions of tens of thousands of individuals. Substitution is easy; no one has a natural monopoly on political inspiration or government office. Entry and exit are unrestricted; anyone can run for office or form a committee, and no one is forced to contribute. Finally, information is generally sufficient for individual choice; however, stricter disclosure requirements would make the market even more competitive and efficient.[20]

What is traded in this market for political finance? The ultimate sources of political finance are individuals. Many undoubtedly make political contributions for the same reasons they give to charity, college, or church: a sense of shared values or general philanthropy. For others the activities surrounding political fund-raising may satisfy psy-

---

19. Larry J. Sabato, *PAC Power: Inside the World of the Political Action Committees* (New York: W. W. Norton, 1984), pp.122-25.

20. Heinz Kohler, *Intermediate Microeconomics* (Glenview, IL: Scott, Foresman, 1982), p. 42.

chic needs for status and social relations. No doubt a number of larger donors, including political committees and parties—the chosen intermediaries of individuals who would rather pool their resources under the management of political professionals than contribute directly to candidates—contribute with the additional hope of securing access to legislators. A few donors may even desire to render a legislator so dependent on their particular contribution as to obtain an economically coercive influence over the legislator's actions —but, as discussed previously, this is exceedingly difficult if not impossible to accomplish.

There is nothing sinister about this market. It does not allocate political authority. Elections do that. Nor is it even the dominant means of allocating access to legislators. Most access to legislators is monopolized by party leaders, staff, lobbyists, press, and creditable constituent representatives. Contribution patterns are one possible factor considered by the legislators or the staff in allocating the remainder of the available time. The market for political finance is simply where election campaigns are funded by groups and individuals in return for access, status, and inspiration.

The best evidence of a competitive market is the diffusion of market power. In 1982, the single largest supplier of political finance to congressional candidates, outside the national parties, was a political committee promoting the interests of realtors, which contributed a total of $2.1 million. In the entire congressional market of $288 million, this sum constituted less than 0.6 percent of the total.[21] The diffusion of market power in the case of legislators is also exemplified by the examples of the 28 House committee chairmen who faced contested races in 1980. Despite their great influence over the shape of legislation, they raised in 1980 an average total of only $180,000, a figure only 9 percent above the mean for all House incumbents in that year.[22]

When the nature of the market for political finance is fully understood it becomes obvious that any serious limits on the amounts that individuals and groups may contribute directly to candidates will certainly force a large proportion of the blocked resources out of the market for direct campaign contributions and into the nearest substitute, the market for independent expenditures.

The election law defines "independent expenditures" as spending by an individual or group made "without cooperation or consultation with any candidate...[but] expressly advocating the election or defeat of a clearly identified candidate."[23] Independent spending can be thought to exist in two forms. On the one hand, groups whose intended direct financial support for a candidate is blocked may simply organize a shadow campaign, funding commercials and phone banks much as the candidate would. On the other hand, groups who feel strongly about issues that no candidate has addressed may spend money to force these issues into the public debate. The two forms are separable only in theory; in practice any form of independent spending may place the independent spender in the same economic relation to a candidate as that of a more orthodox contributor who makes a direct contribution.

21. Sabato, *PAC Power*, p. 17.

22. Duker, ed., *Common Cause Guide*, pp. 224-28; Ornstein et al., *Vital Statistics*, p. 65.

23. Federal Election Campaign Act, 2 U.S.C. §§ 431.

Many forms of private financing have been prohibited in presidential campaigns since 1976. Independent spending related to presidential candidates has increased markedly, from less than $300,000 in 1976 to $16.7 million in 1984. Limits on contributions to congressional candidates have been in place since 1974. Independent spending in congressional campaigns has increased from $386,000 in 1976 to $5.75 million in 1982.[24] It seems abundantly clear that any attempt to intervene strongly in the market for political finance cannot succeed unless the government can substantially control independent spending—but such control is impossible.

Political finance, political speech

Congress tried to control independent spending, and thus preserve the coherence of its regulatory structure, by forbidding individuals and political committees to make independent expenditures exceeding $1000 during any federal election campaign. The Supreme Court, however, unequivocally struck down all such limitations on independent expenditures—even in the context of elections otherwise completely financed by the government.[25]

Some proponents of regulation, understandably frustrated by this judicial undermining of a coordinated scheme of regulation, have charged that the Court, since *Buckley* v. *Valeo*, has simplistically equated money and speech. Yet this criticism betrays an insufficient understanding of the breadth of protection that must be afforded to politically motivated speech and association in a liberal society. In its campaign finance decisions the Court has often cited Justice Brennan's landmark opinion in *New York Times* v. *Sullivan*. A reiteration of the facts of that case suggests the core constitutional obstacle to comprehensive regulation of political finance.

On 29 March 1960 the Committee to Defend Martin Luther King and the Struggle for Freedom in the South, a political committee based in New York City, sponsored a full-page political advertisement in the *New York Times*. The advertisement cost $4800; today the cost would be $30,000. Entitled "Heed Their Rising Voices," the piece criticized in eloquent, though occasionally inaccurate, terms the record of the elected police commissioner of Montgomery, Alabama. It concluded with an appeal for political finance: "We must extend ourselves above and beyond moral support and render the material help so urgently needed.... We urge you to join hands with our fellow Americans in the South by supporting, with your dollars, this combined appeal." In the context of an election campaign this advertisement would be a classic example of an independent expenditure.

When the police commissioner brought an action for libel, the Supreme Court found the actions of the committee and the newspaper so central to the meaning of free speech and free association as to be effectively immune from libel suits by public officials. Justice Brennan wrote of a "profound national commitment to the principle that debate on public issues should be uninhibited, robust, and wide open."[26]

---

24. "Court Strikes Down Limits on Independent PAC Outlays," *Congressional Quarterly Weekly,* 23 Mar. 1985, pp. 532-33.

25. *Federal Election Commission* v. *National Conservative Political Action Committee,*—U.S. —, 105 S. Ct. 1459 (1985).

26. *New York Times Co.* v. *Sullivan*, 376 U.S. 254 (1964).

It is hard to see how the nature of this "profound national commitment" could depend upon the detailed circumstances of the financing of the advertisement. Could the First Amendment rights of a political committee to raise funds or publish, or the right of the public to be exposed to the committee's political ideas, depend upon whether this advertisement cost $4800 or $30,000? Whether the costs were paid by a single benefactor of the committee or a hundred? Whether the same words appeared as a newspaper editorial or a paid advertisement? Whether the advertisement was run once or a dozen times? Or whether its sponsors resided in Montgomery or in New York City? Of course, the First Amendment value of the speech itself is unaltered by these changing circumstances.

In fact, had the attempted criminal prohibition of independent expenditures over $1000 existed in 1960, the police commissioner could presumably have obtained an injunction to prevent publication on the grounds that the advertisement violated the election laws. In other words, an elected official could have used the election laws to suppress criticism of his conduct in office. The result would have been what Justice Brandeis once termed "silence coerced by law—the argument of force in its worst form."[27]

These considerations, and not some simpleminded equating of money and speech, strongly argue that in our liberal republic the government can never be allowed to make political speech and association criminal simply because of the manner of their financing. A contrary conclusion is an invitation to suppression.

27. *Whitney* v. *California*, 274 U.S. 357 (1927).

REPRESENTATION AND EQUALITY

Clearly, the proponents of regulation of political finance face formidable empirical, practical, and constitutional difficulties. A challenge to them on these grounds, while telling, remains only an argument by negation. The most important reason for upholding a private and unregulated system of political finance is positively grounded in basic principles of American government.

The concept of constituency

Elections make no laws. They are not like a town meeting. In a town meeting, a small group of citizens passes directly upon the rules that bind a small community. In a general election, a multitude invests the few with political authority to legislate for all. But, by its very nature, the general election by secret ballot makes impossible the inference of any but the vaguest mandate for legislative action. The legislator asks, "How is legislative authority to be exercised?" Election returns provide no answer.

It is also useful to remember that Congress is not a court. Elected representatives and their constituents are not judges. In a court, the identities of the disputants and the bounds of the conflict are not in question. The judge or jury are disinterested; they must only compare the characteristics of known parties to the precepts of a known law.

In Congress, legislators are, like those who elected them, interested parties. Not only are the legislators bound by the laws they approve, but the public aspect of their actions subjects them to electoral challenge. Furthermore, these interested legislators must make new law, choose new values to guide a changing nation. In this task the major difficulty is not deciding between parties and interests, but ascertaining what conflicts exist between which groups and determining who actually represents the interests of those groups. If legislators fail to know the nation they would govern, their most agonized and conscientious judgments are wasted.

How, then, to know the nation and thereby to truly represent the people?[28] To attempt to answer this question is to illuminate the vital role that private political finance plays in the process of representation.

The individual citizen, considered in isolation, embodies superficial perceptions, unchallenged understandings, cost-free preferences. With regard to almost any public question, the mere summation of the mass of individual wills would only magnify bias and misconception. Defenders of popular sovereignty have always rejected direct democracy, because the first impulse of the isolated citizen crudely multiplied into a majority too often results in the irrational oppression of numerical minorities whose just entitlements and real value to the community are not immediately apparent. Were we governed by opinion poll, no minority would be safe for long.

The real interests of a people, as of individuals, are revealed by compromise. Policy requires not mere preference, but choice. Furthermore, it is only when individuals form and fund groups for political ends that inchoate preference and unchallenged belief crystalize into articulated interest and coherent policy. The elites who lead political groups, if their political influence is to grow, must further this process of self-definition. They must also balance the energy that derives from intensely held convictions with the numerical support that comes to moderation. Political power flows to elites who both inspire their followers and convince them to compromise with others. In this manner, the true interests of the community are given shape as groups form, divide, and coalesce, rising toward the surface of the nation's conscience. In this way the preferences of the individual are refined and enlarged into the interests of the community.

In a market economy where political association is a constitutional right—in other words, in a liberal republic—this entire activity of self-definition of the popular will inevitably has a monetary component. The means of organization, research, and communication will be purchased for money. Thus economic activity becomes an index of political activity. Political activity will always be most intense among groups with reason to fear the unexamined preferences of the multitude. Thus, in any liberal society, those whose ambitions would benefit if the superficial preferences of many were translated, without intermediation, into political power may resent the activities and disparage the legitimacy of well-organized minorities. If, on the other hand, the economic activity associated with political organization is suppressed, numerical minorities lose the only weapons—organization and communication—they have to fight prejudice and exploitation. No society can allow this to happen and for long remain liberal.

These reflections show that the dichotomy often posed by proponents of regulation—namely, between the financial and geographical constitu-

---

28. See generally Hannah F. Pitkin, *The Concept of Representation* (New York: Praeger, 1971).

encies—is misleading. If "constituency" means those elements in society to whom a legislator should legitimately be responsive, then the idea of geographic constituency is both too vague and too narrow.

It is vague because the interests of those individuals who live within the voting district of a particular representative are impossible to understand fully except in the context of the nation as a whole. Conflicts of economic and moral interests are not regional, but interstitial. The significance—one might even say the meaning—of an unemployed steelworker, a small savings bank, a social security recipient, or a toxic-waste site is only made apparent to the community through networks of communication and organization that ignore district boundaries.

The concept of geographic constituency is too narrow because representatives in Congress are not meant to be ambassadors from hostile peoples, but lawmakers for an indivisible nation.

A legislator, then, is legitimately responsible to many constituencies, not just the majority of one day in one district. Campaign contributions from nationally organized political committees may be one factor in this response. Were locally elected legislators somehow insulated from national groups, the result would not be laws miraculously better suited to each separate district, but laws divorced from both national and local reality. Constituency transcends geography.

Thus elections have always, and beneficially, been determined in large part by forces outside the district. Moreover, private political finance, which funds the organization of political groups, not only has a liberalizing influence on political decision making, but also establishes and reinforces the connections between a representative and his or her constituents. Thus the current attack on free and private political finance proceeds from a deep misconception of the representative process.

Equality and influence

Money, education, institutional power, public office—in fact, all the social goods that incidentally become important resources for political organization—are obviously distributed in an unequal, often pathetically unequal, fashion among individuals in our society. While the prevailing allocation of these social goods in our country may be congruent with neither justice nor the common interest, significant disparities in social attainments will exist in any liberal society, however just or enlightened it is. Does, then, a system of free and private political finance mean that social inequalities are to be bred in the bone of the body politic, corrupting the American ideal of political equality?[29] The simple answer, crucial to the legitimacy of our republic, is no.

First, ultimate political authority in America is distributed by the Constitution in a radically egalitarian manner. Suffrage is universal. Elections are direct. The ballot is secret. Representation is apportioned on the basis of one person, one vote. Whatever the persuasive influences on the legislator are, the authority to legislate is directly founded on popular consent. The authority of the individual voter is not subtle—the

29. See generally Alexander Hamilton, John Jay, and James Madison, *The Federalist* (New York: Modern Library, [1937]), nos. 9, 10, 51, 56, 57; Alexis de Tocqueville, *Democracy in America* (New York: Harper & Row, 1966), pt. 2, chaps. 1-4.

ballot cannot make policy or choose specific candidates—but it is absolute.

Second, the rhetoric of certain proponents of regulation to the contrary, there is simply no economic class war in the field of political finance. Admittedly, only a small minority contributes to political campaigns—in 1980 only 13 percent of voting-age Americans—and contribution patterns correlate broadly with levels of affluence. Yet the actual size of the average contribution tends to be modest. In 1980, the last year for which figures are available, only 15 percent of the total funds raised by congressional candidates came from annual individual contributions of over $250. In the same year, the average contribution to a political committee was $100. If 87 percent of the voting-age population in 1980 made no political contributions at all, it certainly was not due to economic constraints. While in 1980 all congressional candidates were raising a total of $127 million in campaign funds, the national expenditure on chewing gum—presumably consumed by poor and rich alike—was over $1 billion.[30] Clearly, the absence of most Americans from the lists of political contributors represents not a failure of economic power, but of political inspiration.

Third, political influence—the capacity to draft policy for, nominate leaders to, and negotiate on behalf of political groups—is, and always will be, unequally distributed. The control of political groups will always be monopolized by the interested and the organized. All politics is a struggle for power by coalitions of interests and values. True republics are distinguishable from other forms of government not because the underlying political forces are different, but because the struggle for political dominance takes place largely in public.

Here lies the reason why private political finance is necessary to true political equality: the suppression of private political campaigns does not eradicate the unequal distribution of social goods. It does not render innocuous the forces that underlie all politics. It only drives the interplay of interest and inequality from the public forum into the shadows. Are private political campaigns illegal? Then powerful interests will exert their full power to influence the nominating or primary process, outside of and prior to the heightened public scrutiny of elections. Is legislation passed that irrationally discounts the interests of significant minorities? Then the gap between the law of the community and social reality will be filled with cynicism and corruption.

The indispensable role of private political finance, properly understood, is to bring the conflict of powerful social forces into the public forum. Only then can the exercise of the equal right to vote have a meaningful impact on the political process and serve to counterbalance inevitable disparities in social attainment.

CONCLUSION

The discussion that has been presented here outlines the argument against government regulation of political finance. The justifications for regulation betray a superficial understanding of our political process. The market for political finance in the past has displayed a protean capacity to evade par-

---

30. Sabato, *PAC Power*, p. 59; Herbert Alexander, *Financing the 1980 Election* (Lexington, MA: D.C. Heath, 1983), pp. 373, 422; *Washington Post*, 18 Nov. 1982.

tial control, and it is constitutionally invulnerable to total control. The restrictions now in place succeed only in making it more difficult for many candidates to fund their campaigns, while biasing in an unprincipled fashion the structure of voluntary political association. Left unregulated, the market for political finance is of such breadth and competitiveness as to afford almost no chance for illegitimate economic coercion of political authority.

Finally, it can be seen that the advocates of government regulation of political campaigns would, in the name of representative government and political equality, impose a system that furthers neither value. The ideal of public funding of politics is a dream of islands, of an abstract politics conducted in isolation from political forces. The unjustly disadvantaged should be raised up, but this can be accomplished only by enlightening the powerful and the organized and not by tampering with the rules of the political process itself. If America is to continue as a liberal republic—indeed, if our shared ideals of representative government and political equality are to be fully realized—then political finance must remain private and substantially free of government regulation.

Should There Be Public Financing of Congressional Campaigns?

By CHARLES McC. MATHIAS, Jr.

ABSTRACT: In spite of seemingly comprehensive campaign finance reforms enacted by Congress beginning in 1971, the current system of financing congressional campaigns threatens to erode public confidence in the electoral process and in government itself. The sheer volume of money in campaigns has led to the perception that those who pay the campaign bills wield disproportionate influence in the process, or at a minimum enjoy greater access to elected representatives than do individual citizens. Public funding of congressional races is a workable means of lessening candidates' reliance on private contributions. Moreover, it is the only effective means of placing reasonable limits on overall campaign spending.

Charles McC. Mathias, Jr., Republican from Maryland, has been a member of the United States Congress since 1960 and has served in the Senate since 1968. He currently is chairman of the Senate Committee on Rules and Administration, which has oversight of the Federal Election Commission and laws governing campaign finance. He is a graduate of Haverford College (B.A., 1944) and the University of Maryland Law School (LL.B., 1949).

SAMUEL Johnson once remarked that nothing is so conducive to a good conscience as the suspicion that someone may be watching.

This observation reminds us of the purpose and underlying principle of campaign finance reform. In a perfect world, there would be no need to proscribe certain behavior in the setting of political campaigns, since individuals would not seek influence through their contributions, candidates would never be beholden to large donors, and the system itself would remain an open one. In the real world, campaign finance laws are necessary rules of behavior designed to protect the political process and promote certain basic democratic values. These laws and their enforcement help ensure that elections and government itself are free of abuses that would subvert democratic society.

The dynamics of the electoral system have such far-reaching ramifications for how we conduct ourselves as a democratic nation that we cannot view campaign finance in isolation from other facets of the democratic process. Our understanding of the nature of representation and participatory democracy, what we mean by consent of the governed, and our view of the legitimate function of government are integral to any discussion of what we want campaign finance reform to accomplish. The way in which we conduct our elections must then defer to these broader principles and values.

The role of money in elections is a troubling spectacle to this nation in 1986. The first stages of reform have given us a great wealth of information on campaign finances, but the statistics also warn that the problems of big money in the process persist. The potential for abuse lingers on because of unfinished business: the Congress's failure to provide for public financing of congressional campaigns.

The concept of public financing of elections in this country is not new. In 1907, President Theodore Roosevelt supported the concept in his state-of-the-union message. In 1907, the Progressive Republican program was seen as the only way to get corrupt money and excessive money out of elections, and that is truer than ever 79 years later. Campaign finance data of the last 14 years and the current role of money in politics demonstrate conclusively that the American public would be better served by a system of publicly funded congressional elections than by any other single campaign finance reform now under consideration.

MONEY IN CAMPAIGNS

The sheer volume of money in the political process should be sufficient to prove the case for limiting its influence. Campaign finance experts estimate that campaign spending for all elective offices reached $1.2 billion in 1980.[1] The 1982 midterm elections saw campaign spending top $900 million.[2] If the cost of congressional mass mailings in the amount of $100 million is added to the total, we again reach the billion-dollar figure. Another record-setting year was 1984: candidates for the House and Senate spent more than $374 million.[3]

1. U.S., Congress, Senate, Committee on Rules and Administration, *Hearings on Campaign Finance Reform Proposals of 1983,* 98th Cong., 1st sess., 26 and 27 Jan., 17 May, and 29 Sept. 1983, pp. 99, 124.
2. "A $900 Million Election Stirs Reform Cries," *U.S. News & World Report,* 20 Dec. 1982, p. 28.
3. U.S., Federal Election Commission, *FEC Reports on Financial Activity 1983-1984. Final*

The costs of running for federal office have increased dramatically in the past decade or so. The 1984 total compares with approximately $88 million just ten years before.[4] Even discounting for inflation during this period, the overall cost of running for Congress has more than doubled since 1974.

Even more striking than the totals are the growing number of House and Senate candidates who are spending astronomical sums of money. In 1974, 10 candidates for the House spent more than $200,000. By 1978, 128 candidates exceeded that amount, and in 1982, the number climbed to 353.[5] In 1974, no House candidate exceeded $500,000 in expenditures; 7 candidates reached that level in 1978, and 67 did in 1982.[6] Let us go one step further. In 1978, we saw the first $1 million House candidate. There were 2 at that level in 1980 and 5 in 1982.[7]

Looking at Senate races, one finds striking expenditure increases in the elections just completed compared with the same races six years before. In 1978, 21 Senate candidates spent more than $1 million in the general election; in 1984, at least 30 candidates spent that much. In 1978, 6 candidates spent more than $2 million, and in 1984, at least 16 did. Finally, there were 2 candidates who spent more than $4 million in 1978, and 7 candidates exceeded that incredible sum in 1984. The latter year, 1984, also saw one record-breaking $26 million Senate race.[8]

There is another noteworthy development allied with these huge increases in campaign costs. The system seems to be attracting more people with vast personal wealth, who are uniquely able to bear the high cost of seeking public office. In 1982, for instance, half of the candidates for the U.S. Senate reportedly were millionaires.[9]

What do these figures suggest about the current state of campaign finance? The views of candidates and officeholders provide one perspective. Senator Alan Cranston, Democrat from California, testified before the Senate Committee on Rules and Administration in 1981:

To raise my $3 million campaign fund in 1980, I averaged a fundraiser every 2½ days, every 60 hours, for two straight years. The demand of such a strenuous fundraising schedule substantially decreased the amount of time I was able to spend meeting with, talking with, and listening to people who are not prospective contributors, and reduced my ability to do many other things we normally associate with a political campaign in a democratic society.[10]

Report. U.S. Senate and House Candidates (Washington, DC: Federal Election Commission, 1985), p. xii.

4. Common Cause, *Campaign Finance Monitoring Project: 1974 Congressional Campaign Finances,* vol. 1, *Senate Races* (Washington, DC: Common Cause, 1976), p. vi.

5. Norman J. Ornstein et al., *Vital Statistics on Congress,* 1984-85 ed. (Washington, DC: American Enterprise Institute for Public Policy Research, 1984), p. 67.

6. Ibid., p. 68.

7. "House Seat Can Cost $1 Million," *Washington Post,* 25 Oct. 1984.

8. U.S., Federal Election Commission, *FEC Reports on Financial Activity 1977-1978,* interim report no. 5, *U.S. Senate and House Campaigns* (Washington, DC: Federal Election Commission, 1979); idem, *FEC Reports on Financial Activity 1983-1984.*

9. "Elections: It Doesn't Hurt to Be a Millionaire," *U.S. News & World Report,* 15 Nov. 1982, p. 8.

10. U.S., Congress, Senate, Committee on Rules and Administration, *Hearings on the Application and Administration of the Federal Election Campaign Act of 1971, as Amended,* 97th Cong., 1st sess., 20 and 24 Nov. 1981, p. 96.

Senator Thomas Eagleton, Democrat from Missouri, related the following in 1983 testimony:

When I ran for the Senate in the 1968 general election, I spent $200,000. By 1974, it had grown to $513,000. By 1980, it had grown to $1,456,000. By 1986, under existing trends . . . it will be $2 million plus. . . . There is no way I could raise such an amount from small contributors within Missouri.

What has changed . . . is that money, always a necessary tool of waging a campaign, has now become the be-all and end-all of the political campaign. Fundraising has gone from a campaign ingredient to an all-pervasive campaign obsession. Senators start raising their war chest sometimes three or even four years before their reelection date.[11]

Another witness, a political consultant, commented after listening to Senator Eagleton's remarks that the senator's estimate of the cost of his next campaign was probably off by about half—it was more likely to cost $4 million.[12]

Concern with campaign fund-raising is not a partisan affair. Senator Barry Goldwater, Republican from Arizona, has spoken out strongly on the topic:

Unlimited campaign spending eats at the heart of the democratic process. It feeds the growth of special interest groups created solely to channel money into political campaigns. It creates an impression that every candidate is bought and owned by the biggest givers. And it causes elected officials to devote more time to raising money than to their public duties.[13]

Senator Goldwater goes so far as to call the present state of campaign finance a "crisis of liberty."

These concerns cannot be lightly dismissed. When we have reached the point at which an officeholder says, "Yes, I am troubled by what I have to do to raise campaign funds; yes, the process is time consuming and detracts from my ability to perform the duties of an elected representative; and yes, the public perception of the process may undermine confidence in the system," all of us should ask whether more remains to be done.

Fund-raising is as burdensome—in some respects, more so—for a challenger. It is a safe bet that many, many qualified men and women decide not to run for office solely because of the prospect of having to raise the enormous amounts of money the experts say are necessary to run a competitive race. Quite simply, the need to attract great financial resources has become a formidable barrier to those contemplating running for federal office. The price tag of campaigns, and the necessity of raising these huge amounts from private sources, should cause us to have grave doubts about how open the system remains. While the ability to attract vast sums of campaign contributions may be one means of testing a candidate's appeal, it should not be the only one, and certainly it should not be the single most important factor in determining a candidate's qualifications for higher office.

Compounding a challenger's fund-raising problems is the increasingly common practice of incumbents' accumulating substantial campaign war chests far in advance of the next election.[14] In part an understandable response to the

---

11. U.S., Congress, Senate, Committee on Rules and Administration, *Hearings on Campaign Finance Reform Proposals of 1983*, p. 50.
12. Ibid., p. 145.
13. Ibid., p. 400.

14. As of 31 Dec. 1982, nine Senate incumbents up for reelection in 1984 had raised over $100,000, and three of these had raised in excess of $600,000.

prospect of costly campaigns, campaign war chests are also, in the candid assessment of one member of Congress, "one of the opportunities incumbents have to frighten off opponents," with the result, he remarked, of "reduc[ing] the possibility of viable choices, which is what democracy and freedom are all about."[15]

While difficulty in raising money and the deterrent effect of incumbents' war chests keep many prospective challengers out of the race, they do not discourage candidates able to make substantial contributions from their personal funds. As the statistics presented before suggest, the incidence of very wealthy candidates seeking political office is on the upsurge. In 1982, 15 Senate general-election candidates contributed $100,000 or more to their campaigns.[16] Preliminary figures for 1984 show that 12 Senate candidates lent their campaigns $100,000 or more.[17] In what seemed certain to be an all-time record, a losing Senate candidate spent over $6.8 million of his personal funds in 1982.[18] Two years later, however, 1984 proved to be another record-breaking year, when a winning Senate candidate spent $10 million on his own campaign.[19]

15. U.S., Congress, House, Committee on House Administration, Task Force on Elections, *Hearings on Campaign Finance Reform*, 98th Cong., 1st sess., 9, 16, 21, and 23 June, 8 July, 22 and 23 Aug., and 12 Oct. 1983, p. 197.

16. Richard E. Cohen, "Giving till It Hurts: 1982 Campaign Prompts New Look at Financing Races," *National Journal*, 18 Dec. 1982, pp. 2146-47.

17. U.S., Federal Election Commission, "Aggregate Loans from the Candidate as Reported by Major Party General Election Senate Campaigns, 1983-84 Election Cycle" (Data generated from a computerized data base, Federal Election Commission, 1985).

18. Cohen, "Giving till It Hurts," p. 2146.

19. Federal Election Commission, *FEC Reports on Financial Activity 1983-1984*, p. 331.

This trend poses the danger that the voices of the affluent will be heard disproportionately on the campaign trail and in the halls of government. Fairness—not to mention the health of representative government—dictates that the political arena be open to all, irrespective of personal wealth. It is a travesty to perpetuate a system of campaign finance that permits the unlimited expenditure of a candidate's personal funds at the same time that it significantly limits sources of funding for other participants.

The contributor's view

There is yet another perspective from which to view campaign fund-raising—that of the contributor. On the positive side, those who contribute may feel they have a stake in the outcome of an election and so may be motivated to greater participation. Giving may also reinforce a sense of group ties or identity, since through association or pooling of resources individuals have a greater collective impact on the process. As they reflect the attitudes and the intensity of feeling of individuals toward a candidate, contributions may also provide some indication of how broadly based support for a candidate is. Knowledge of who his or her supporters are also probably leads to a greater appreciation by a candidate of what the supporters' needs are and promotes responsiveness in meeting those needs, if there are not other countervailing interests at stake.

We have seen in the evolution of campaign giving under the current law, however, an erosion of the positive character of contributions. Most noticeable is the diminution of the role of the individual small contributor. This reduction in importance occurred simply because the scale of campaign expenditures has come to dwarf the resources available to most individuals. In contrast to the individual giver, the highly organized and well-funded interest group has the means not only to survive but to thrive. It is this picture of campaign giving that should concern us.

Under current law, multicandidate political committees, commonly known as political action committees (PACs), are allowed to contribute up to $5000 to a candidate per election. The development of PACs in response to the law has been one of the most striking side effects of campaign finance reforms. Since 1974, the number of PACs has risen dramatically, from 608 to 4000.[20] Not surprisingly, as campaign spending has risen, so has the amount of PAC money contributed to congressional candidates, from $34 million in 1978 to over $105 million in 1984. The percentage of PAC money as a part of overall campaign receipts also has edged steadily upward.[21]

Perhaps more disturbing is the pattern of PAC giving. There is, for instance, a demonstrable bias in favor of incumbents in PAC contributions. Figures for the 1984 election showed that House incumbents received $81 million in PAC funds compared to $19 million for challengers.[22] In the eyes of some, PAC giving suggests an ominous trend—an ever increasing dependence by officeholders on highly organized special interests for campaign funds. That groups in the private sector have an important stake in the decisions of government and will seek a voice in formulating governmental policy is understandable. The growing presence of PACs, however, has raised fears that these special interests have come to play a disproportionate role—a role that may carry with it the seeds of actual or potential corruption.

In response to concern about PAC giving, some have called for an increase in the limits on individual contributions, an argument strengthened by the fact that no adjustment has been made since the limits were set in 1974. The $1000 limit, however, is even now beyond the reach of the vast majority of individual contributors. Raising limits on individuals might not awaken fears that candidates will once again become beholden to individual large contributors, but it would continue to shift the basis of campaign support toward those with greater financial resources. It would not solve the basic problem of how to keep the system open and fair.

If campaign contributions carry their own political message, as we must acknowledge they do, the missing element in today's campaigns is the unarticulated view of those who are not well organized, who lack the financial resources and perhaps the motivation to be active participants in the process. If they are to be represented in government and their interests taken into account, their presence should be acknowledged at the stage at which the issues are framed and the agendas set for making future public policy—in campaigns for elective office. The current system of campaign finance has made it increasingly difficult to accomplish this goal.

---

20. U.S., Federal Election Commission, "PAC Numbers Show Slight Drop in 1985" (Press release, Federal Election Commission, 1985).

21. U.S., Federal Election Commission, "FEC Final Report for '84 Elections Confirms Majority of PAC Money Went to Incumbents" (Press release, Federal Election Commission, 1985).

22. Ibid.

CONGRESSIONAL POWER TO REGULATE MONEY IN CAMPAIGNS

Congress, in attempting to regulate the role of money in campaigns, faces a difficult question: the degree to which money in politics is entitled to protection as speech under the First Amendment. The Supreme Court in *Buckley* v. *Valeo*[23] reviewed the constitutionality of limits on campaign contributions and expenditures enacted by Congress in the Federal Election Campaign Act of 1971, as amended in 1974. The Court's analysis began, significantly, with its observation that "virtually every means of communicating ideas in today's mass society requires the expenditure of money."[24]

The Court saw contribution limits as only a marginal restriction on the contributor's ability to engage in political communication, characterizing contributions as mere speech by proxy.[25] While the Court found that contribution limits worked a more significant restraint on freedom of political association, it upheld the limits, citing an earlier decision that "even a 'significant interference' with protected rights of political association may be sustained if the State demonstrates a sufficiently important interest and employs means closely drawn to avoid unnecessary abridgment of associational freedoms."[26] The Court found such justification by looking to the act's primary purpose of preventing the fact or appearance of undue influence. "To the extent that large contributions are given to secure political *quid pro quos* from current and potential officeholders, the integrity of our system of representative government is undermined."[27]

On the other hand, the Court found that limits on expenditures by candidates and their supporters imposed direct and substantial restraints on the quantity of political speech. Moreover, since the expenditure limits, unlike limits on contributions, did not serve the purpose of eliminating the reality or appearance of corruption, the Court found no justification for such a restriction.

Following this analysis, the Court struck down a $1000 limit on expenditures by individuals that were totally independent of the candidate's campaign. The Court reasoned that such independent expenditures provided only limited assistance to a candidate and could even prove counterproductive to a candidate's campaign. Thus the Court concluded that independent expenditures did not pose the danger of eliciting improper commitments from a candidate. In reviewing the Federal Election Campaign Act's limit on a candidate's expenditures of his or her own personal funds, the Court noted that a candidate using his or her own funds would be less dependent on contributions from others and consequently more immune to the risks of undue influence.

The Court specifically found that neither equalizing the relative ability of individuals and groups to influence the outcome of elections nor equalizing the relative financial resources of the candidates was a sufficient or even permissible governmental interest to justify the serious First Amendment intrusions represented by expenditure limits. Thus, the Court held, limits on overall campaign expenditures, on independent

23. 424 U.S. 1 (1976).
24. Ibid., p. 19.
25. Ibid., p. 21.
26. Ibid., p. 25.
27. Ibid., p. 26.

expenditures, and on expenditures by a candidate from personal funds were unconstitutional.

The *Buckley* decision fails to recognize that the integrity of the electoral process is threatened if the only effective participants are those with vast financial resources. *Buckley* thus represents a giant step backward in the effort to reform campaign finance. As Judge J. Skelly Wright notes in a persuasive critique of the Court's ruling, congressional regulation of campaign spending can be a powerful tool to enhance, not limit, First Amendment liberties.[28]

Even if Congress continues to be limited by the *Buckley* holding, however, an important means to limit excessive campaign spending still remains. The Court also held that Congress may impose limits on overall spending and on the expenditures of personal funds by a candidate in the context of a publicly financed campaign.

Why public finance?

In view of the serious problems associated with money in campaigns and the legal restraints on congressional power to regulate, a system of public finance is the next essential reform. Partial public funding with realistic expenditure ceilings would enable candidates to run competitive campaigns in which private funding would continue to play an important but not a dominant role. A grant of public funds would free candidates from the incessant demands of fund-raising and offers the hope of shortening the seemingly endless campaign season. A system of public finance that includes a limit on the amount candidates may contribute to their own campaigns would eliminate the unfair advantage enjoyed by those with great personal wealth. And most important, public financing in congressional campaigns would restore a missing equilibrium between the sources of campaign funding and give officeholders a greater measure of freedom to address issues in the broad national interest. Such results would go a long way toward renewing public belief in the integrity of the electoral process.

Some will say that such further reforms will only lead to more creative means of circumventing the limits, that "special interest money has always found its way into the political system . . . [and] always will."[29] All reform, however, is based on the notion that there are values at stake that make it worthwhile and, in some instances, imperative to control the potential for abuse in a system. That reforms at times have failed to achieve their stated goals, or that they have produced unintended and perhaps undesirable consequences, should not lead us to abandon efforts to safeguard the integrity of a process so vital to the preservation of democratic values.

Perhaps as important as stating what public funding would do is stating what it would not do. The most serious concern is that publicly funded congressional campaigns, with limits on spending, would divert money into other channels—specifically, into independent expenditures. The emergence of independent expenditures in the aftermath of *Buckley* reasonably could

28. J. Skelly Wright, "Money and the Pollution of Politics: Is the First Amendment an Obstacle to Political Equality?" *Columbia Law Review,* 82(4) (May 1982).

29. Committee on Rules and Administration, *Campaign Finance Reform Proposals of 1983*, p. 107, n. 5.

lead us to expect a growth, even a surge, in independent spending following enactment of public finance legislation. Witnesses in congressional hearings have been blunt in saying so.

An example cited is the publicly funded 1980 presidential general election, in which individuals' circumscribed ability to contribute to the presidential campaign gave impetus to the creation of political committees operating independently of the major candidates' committees. A similar phenomenon is projected for congressional campaigns, which, we are told, will become battlegrounds for a kind of independent-expenditure guerrilla warfare in which "Terry Dolan . . . and anyone else with the guts, the desire, and the lists . . . [can] become the future political kingmakers."[30]

Regulating independent expenditures

Even if independent expenditures increased dramatically, we do not have to accept as inevitable that they would wreak havoc on the political system. Instead, we should ask what means exist for regulating independent expenditures, if they become a problem.

The Supreme Court, in striking down limits on independent expenditures in *Buckley*, stated, "Independent advocacy . . . does not presently appear to pose dangers of real or apparent corruption comparable to those identified with large campaign contributions."[31] Unfortunately, in a more recent case the Supreme Court again struck down limits on independent expenditures, holding unconstitutional a $1000 limit on independent spending by political committees in support of candidates in presidential general elections who accepted public funding. The Court in a 7-to-2 decision held that the expenditures in question were entitled to full First Amendment protection and, absent a showing of any "tendency . . . to corrupt or to give the appearance of corruption,"[32] the $1000 limit was constitutionally infirm. As Justice White notes in his dissent, the Court's continuing reluctance to defer to Congress in Congress's effort to regulate campaign finance remains a formidable barrier to achieving a system broadly designed, in his words, to "eliminate the danger of corruption, maintain public confidence in the integrity of federal elections, equalize the resources available to the candidates, and hold the overall amount of money devoted to political campaigning down to a reasonable level."[33]

Even though the Supreme Court for the present appears unconvinced that there are compelling reasons for limiting independent spending, Congress can still take steps to curb the abuses associated with such spending. First, Congress should encourage rigorous enforcement of the requirement that there be no coordination with a candidate's campaign.[34] Second, Congress should consider new legislative means of counteracting the harmful effects of independent expenditures in more direct ways.

A question to be considered at the outset is whether the independent expen-

30. Ibid., p. 145.
31. 424 U.S., p. 46.
32. *FEC* v. *National Conservative Political Action Committee*, 105 S.Ct. 1459 (1985).
33. Ibid., p. 1475.
34. On the adequacy of the FEC, see William C. Oldaker, "Of Philosophers, Foxes, and Finances: Can the Federal Election Commission Ever Do an Adequate Job?" this issue of *The Annals* of the American Academy of Political and Social Science.

ditures are in compliance with existing law; that is, are they truly independent? Current law defines an independent expenditure as

an expenditure by a person expressly advocating the election or defeat of a clearly identified candidate which is made without cooperation or consultation with any candidate, or any authorized committee or agent of such candidate, and which is not made in concert with, or at the request or suggestion of, any candidate, or any authorized committee or agent of such candidate.[35]

To the extent that these guidelines are observed, it was the Court's view at least that "independent expenditures may well provide little assistance to the candidate's campaign."[36] It is still far from clear whether independent expenditures may be able to influence, let alone decide, election results. One of the largest independent expenditure committees, the National Conservative Political Action Committee (NCPAC), established its reputation in 1980 when four out of the six liberal Senate incumbents it targeted in its negative campaigning lost their reelection bids. In 1982, however, of nine targeted House and Senate candidates against whom NCPAC spent amounts ranging from $127,000 to $783,000, only one was defeated. NCPAC spent over $600,000 in the U.S. Senate race in Maryland in 1982 in a negative campaign that by most accounts helped the candidate it attacked and hurt his Republican opponent, who lost the election by a wide margin.[37]

That independent expenditures may be unpredictable in their effect and that in some instances they have backfired do not mean that they cannot have harmful consequences for the political process. If these occur, Congress should consider new legislation to address the problem.

Public finance and political parties

The discussion of the consequences of public finance would be incomplete without asking what effect it would have on the political parties. In spite of early predictions, it is obvious that campaign finance regulation has not brought about the demise of the major parties. The Republican Party, in a way now being copied by the Democrats, has adapted remarkably well to both the law and the new technologies of campaigning. Within the constraints of contribution limits, the Republican National Committee, the National Republican Senatorial Committee, and the National Republican Congressional Committee have all been enormously successful fundraisers, able to assist Republican candidates up to the maximum allowable limits under current law. Although parity does not now exist between the two major parties in fund-raising ability, it will no doubt come to pass before the decade is out.

Public funding need not affect the contributions and coordinated spending efforts parties are currently able to make on behalf of candidates. Ways of further expanding the parties' role might well be explored, both in the context of publicly funded congressional races and through other legislative proposals to encourage party-building efforts. As significant as the monetary contributions of parties are, considerable advantages flow from an ongoing organizational structure and a steadily growing body of expertise on

---

35. 2 U.S.C. § 431(17) (1979).
36. 424 U.S., p. 47.
37. *Campaign Practice Reports* (Washington, DC: Congressional Quarterly, 1982), 9(21):1.

effective campaign techniques. Some, in fact, see parties taking over many of the functions of political consultants in providing campaign services to candidates, a development that would further enhance the role of parties as formidable players in campaign finance.

Proposals for publicly funded campaigns also have raised the conflicting concerns that the major parties will face an onslaught of third-party and independent candidacies and that such a system will altogether freeze out candidacies from other than the major parties. Both fears seem exaggerated.

A system of public finance cannot constitutionally exclude independent and third-party candidates. Yet the concern that public finance would artificially bolster independent and third-party candidacies seems unwarranted. Virtually every public finance proposal discussed in Congress has imposed a threshold eligibility requirement. The requirement may consist of a specified amount of money that a candidate must raise in order to qualify for public funds or a certain number or percentage of signatures of qualified voters or of ballots cast in the election.

To the extent that third-party candidates or independents are able to meet reasonable qualifying thresholds, they are entitled to some measure of public funding, a result that should not threaten the stability of the system. While public funding may to some extent stimulate fund-raising efforts or other activity by third-party candidates in order to qualify for public funds, it is difficult to see how a system of matching grants would radically change the amount of funds available to non-major-party candidates in the process.

Incumbents and public finance

Finally, a word should be said about the alleged pro-incumbent bias of public finance. This is a subject on which reasonable men and women have disagreed and probably will continue to do so. The most commonly heard argument is that expenditure limits are likely to hurt challengers more severely, since ordinarily they will need to spend more than an incumbent simply to achieve name recognition. A companion argument suggests that spending limits fail to take into account the considerable benefits accruing to an incumbent by virtue of the perquisites of office.

Does a challenger have to outspend an incumbent in order to win? The figures show that some challengers who outspent incumbents won and that, conversely, some who were outspent by the incumbents won.[38] What may well be as important to a competitive race by a challenger is the certainty that an adequate level of funding will be available, to enable a challenger to develop his or her campaign strategy well in advance.

A lack of funds at a critical stage in a campaign can be devastating, and an abundance of funds so late in the campaign that planning opportunities have been lost can be of little use. The challenger who lacks funds early, for instance, cannot at the last minute produce and run television advertisements that may be crucial. In addition to improving

38. Figures showing relative campaign expenditures by incumbents and challengers in races in which the incumbent was defeated reveal that for the period 1974-82, successful challengers were outspent by incumbents in the aggregate in three out of five of these elections. See Ornstein et al., *Vital Statistics on Congress*, p. 67.

opportunities for campaign management, public funding would introduce the concept of a level playing field in a large number of congressional races in which it would otherwise be absent—hardly a boon to incumbents.

There still may be the fear that public funding fails to take into account the obvious value of incumbency itself. Thus, in reality, challengers will be outspent in every race.

The official duties of members of Congress do encompass activities that can be factors in a member's reelection. Not the least of these is a member's voting record. The use of voting records in past campaigns suggests that this fact is not lost upon challengers or others. An incumbent's record alone may not cancel out the advantages of incumbency, but it should not be ignored when evaluating the fairness of a system of public finance.

The liabilities associated with incumbency do not justify an incumbent's using the resources of his or her office in patently political ways. Reforms undertaken by both houses of Congress in recent years reflect a concern that members of Congress not be perceived as using their position of public trust for political advantage.[39] Ultimately, any system of public finance must take into account concerns about the advantages of incumbency and, if necessary, must include provisions to compensate challengers for such advantages. That such adjustments may be needed should not overshadow the many positive attributes of a system of publicly funded congressional elections.

CONCLUSION

Public funding of congressional races is a workable solution to the problems that are most troubling in the current system of campaign finance. The role money plays in elections has made it increasingly difficult for the democratic process to function properly. If we continue on our present course, eventually we will reach the day when the amassing and spending of campaign money will have fatally undermined public confidence in the process and thwarted the democratic values the system is supposed to serve. The vast sums of money in contemporary campaigns already have had a corrosive effect on participatory democracy. If unchecked, the influence of money will continue to exaggerate and exacerbate an imbalance based on unequal financial resources and will further dispossess those who already have too little say in the decisions of government.

Congress 15 years ago set out to reform the role of money in politics. It is time it finished the job.

---

39. Rule 40, Standing Rules of the Senate, currently prohibits any senator from using the frank for mass mailings in the 60 days preceding an election in which he or she is a candidate (par. 1), precludes use of Senate computer facilities for storing lists that identify individuals by any partisan political designation (par. 5), and prohibits use of Senate radio and television studies in the 60 days preceding an election in which the senator is a candidate (par. 6).

Money in Politics

By RICHARD BOLLING

ABSTRACT: There is one basic problem undermining the ability of Congress to address all other issues effectively. That problem is the corrosive, pervasive, and too often invisible influence of special interest money. Most damaging to Congress is the recent explosion in campaign finance contributions from political action committees. There are other forms of special interest money that are also increasingly corroding the integrity of Congress, such as speaking fees and undisclosed multimillion-dollar lobbying efforts. All of this special interest money is threatening the ability of Congress to govern. We must look for ways to make it easier for congressional candidates to say no to political action committees, say no to the interest groups offering honoraria, and say no to hidden lobbying pressures. The best way we can help Congress to say no is to provide some form of public financing for congressional campaigns.

From 1949 to 1982, Congressman Bolling was the representative for the Fifth District of Missouri in the U.S. House of Representatives, where he served as chairman of the House Rules Committee, the Joint Economic Committee, and the House Select Committee on Committees. He is the author of two books dealing with Congress, Out of Order *and* Power in the House, *and coauthor of* America's Competitive Edge. *He is currently working on a book on improving the effectiveness of federal, state, and local governments in the United States. Congressman Bolling received both his undergraduate and master's degrees from University of the South.*

NOTE: Adapted from a speech delivered by Richard Bolling at Boston College, Chestnut Hill, Massachusetts, in September 1983.

IT is well established, I suppose, that those, like Thoreau or Dante, who spend time in strange or distant or eye-opening places are obliged to report back on what they have seen and learned. This article reports on some of what I have seen during my years in another eye-opening place, the U.S. Congress. While I found it less idyllic than Walden Pond, fortunately I also found it less hellish or populated with sinners than the Inferno.

I am, in fact, an ardent fan of the institution of the U.S. House of Representatives, but these days I am also extremely concerned about the Congress and its ability to govern effectively. My concern does not stem from the magnitude or complexity of the issues that confront Congress. During my 34 years there, my colleagues and I with some success addressed a number of the most difficult and deep-rooted problems this country has known, such as civil rights and poverty, education and health care; and of course, none of these jobs is ever completed. Today's problems may be difficult, but they certainly will and can be faced and dealt with.

Rather, I am concerned because one basic problem is undermining the ability of Congress to address any other issues effectively. That problem is the corrosive, pervasive, and too often invisible influence of special interest money. Most damaging to the Congress is the recent explosion in campaign contributions from political action committees (PACs), which are formed by corporations, unions, trade associations, and ideological groups in order to exercise influence by contributing money to election campaigns. There are other forms of special interest money, however, that are also increasingly corroding the integrity of Congress, such as speaking fees, known as honoraria, and the undisclosed, multimillion-dollar lobbying efforts of various industries and interest groups.

I would like to discuss where the problem of special interest money came from, how severe it is, and what we, collectively, can do about it.

THE SOURCE OF THE PROBLEM

Why has special interest money become such a threat to the Congress? There are two developments that I witnessed during my years in politics that I believe combined to produced the current crisis.

The first was the exponential growth in campaign costs. When I was first elected to Congress in 1948, I could raise only $2500. Money was hard to find, but campaigns were cheap. Some radio was used, and really no television. The average campaign cost for the House was probably less than $10,000. In 1984, in contrast, candidates for the House of Representatives on average spent $205,000. In other words, while the cost of living has increased over fourfold since I first ran for Congress, the cost of staying alive in politics has increased, on the average, by much more than 20 times.

The second development I witnessed that has contributed to the current crisis was that, as congressmen increasingly needed campaign money, interest groups increasingly wanted congressmen. Over the last 15 or so years, as the public demanded government protection and regulation in more areas, such as the environment, consumer products, and job safety, labor and corporate interest groups expanded their efforts to shape the resulting laws. Thus, as the regulatory budget of the federal government increased fivefold since the early 1970s, so did the number of corporate and labor PACs.

Interest groups also began seeking more influence over Congress, perhaps because Congress became the easiest and most productive place to seek it at the federal level. In 1974, Congress passed major amendments to the Federal Election Campaign Act, which had been passed three years earlier. Those amendments established that presidential candidates would have the option of financing their campaigns principally with public funds in the primaries and exclusively with public funds in the general election. Since virtually all the candidates have opted for public financing, the new public financing system has effectively prohibited private contributions in presidential general elections and reduced the role of private money in the presidential nominating process.[1] Unfortunately, however, Congress declined to adopt that reform for itself. With the role of special interest campaign contributions somewhat curtailed in presidential campaigns, and no public financing for congressional races, many special interest groups turned their attention—and much of their money—to Congress.

Over the years, as interest groups developed a greater desire to use their money to influence congressional policymaking, they also became dangerously sophisticated in how to do it. They learned to target their contributions to reach the chairmen and members of congressional committees and subcommittees with jurisdiction over highly prized tax breaks or subsidies or contracts. In the 1984 election, not surprisingly, members of two of the most powerful House committees—the Ways and Means Committee and the Energy and Commerce Committee—received on average more PAC contributions than members of any other House committee. Ironically, the same technologies that made campaigns so expensive—such as polling and direct mail—allowed these groups to target their contributions, their honoraria, and their lobbying efforts to produce the maximum influence.

At this point I would like to make it clear that to corrupt or to influence greatly outcomes in congressional committees or subcommittees usually does not require obtaining the services of many members. Congressional committees are often narrowly divided to begin with, and one or two subservient individuals may make a great difference in the outcome on very important legislation. The system is so fragile and vulnerable that real purity is essential to consistent success for the public interest.

THE EXTENT OF THE PROBLEM

As congressmen needed more campaign funds and as interest groups desired more influence in Congress, the result was an alarming growth in special interest money. It only requires a few figures and examples to see how alarming that growth has been. Consider the most corrosive source of special interest money, PACs. In 1974, there were 608 such committees. Today there are nearly 4000. In 1974 PACs gave $12.5 million to congressional candidates. By the 1984 elections their contributions exceeded $104 million, an eightfold increase in

---

1. Elizabeth Drew shows, however, that large sums of money are being spent that clearly evade the intent, if not the letter, of the law. See Drew, *Politics and Money* (New York: Macmillan, 1983).

just 10 years.[2] Most disturbing, the dependence of congressmen on PAC funds has increased steadily. In 1974 PAC money accounted for only about 14 percent of the funds for an average campaign in the House of Representatives. By 1984, however, House candidates on average were receiving 38 percent of their funding from PACs; 20 of 27 current committee chairs and House leaders got more than half of their campaign funds from these interest groups. In the last two elections, four Senate candidates received over $1 million each from PACs.[3]

Interest groups are pouring increasing sums of money into Congress through other channels as well, such as honoraria. In 1984, for instance, members of Congress received $5.2 million in honoraria.[4] Undoubtedly, some honoraria are modest payments for bona fide speaking engagements. But in other cases, congressmen are receiving $1000 or $2000 for merely having coffee with a handful of an interest group's executives. In many cases, the interest groups that are paying these honoraria are the same groups whose PACs are making substantial contributions. In 1984, members of the two congressional tax-writing committees received over $1 million in honoraria from special interest groups, and members of these two committees received over $16 million from PACs in their most recent election.[5] But unlike campaign contributions, honoraria are going directly into the pockets of members of Congress.

Special interest groups are also buying influence through undisclosed grass-roots lobbying efforts. Certainly there is nothing objectionable about grass-roots lobbying itself, but a number of interest groups are currently spending millions to influence legislation while disclosing few of these expenditures under federal lobbying regulations. For example, in 1983, the banking industry mounted a multimillion-dollar campaign to repeal one of the most needed parts of the 1982 tax act, that concerning withholding on interest and dividends. Banks ran scores of newspaper advertisements and enclosed millions of mini-harangues and preprinted congressional letters in their customers' monthly statements. Within weeks, Congress was inundated with letters urging repeal of withholding. Yet, because few of the trade associations and none of the banks had disclosed their massive expenditures, the withholding provision was all but repealed before Congress knew how much of the uproar had been purchased by the industry.

THE DAMAGE DONE BY SPECIAL INTEREST MONEY

All this special interest money is, in a number of ways, threatening Congress's ability to govern.

First, in many cases, the money is distorting or blocking legislation. In

---

2. *People v. PACs: Common Cause Guide to Winning the War against Political Action Committees* (Washington, DC: Common Cause, 1983).

3. "House Incumbents Get 44¢ of Every Campaign Dollar from PACs in 1984 Election" (Press release, Common Cause, 1985); "1984 Senate Candidates Raised $146 Million, Spent $137 Million and Received $28 Million from PACs" (Press release, Common Cause, 1985).

4. "Senators and Representatives Received $5.2 Million in 1984 Honoraria; Members of Tax Writing Committees Got $1 Million of Total; Tobacco Institute Top Giver at $129,691" (Press release, Common Cause, 1985).

5. "Business PACs Gave $11 Million to Congressional Tax-Writers" (Press release, Common Cause, 1985).

1982, for example, the Federal Trade Commission proposed the used-car rule, which would have required used-car dealers to tell customers about any known defects in the cars they were about to buy. The used-car dealers opposed the rule and, with their PAC money, persuaded Congress to veto it. The 69 senators who voted down the used-car rule received, on the average, twice as much in PAC contributions from the automobile dealers as those who voted against the auto dealers. In the House, the ratio was five to one. A recent study presented to the American Political Science Association concluded that, even accounting for party affiliation and ideology, the more than $1 million contributed by the auto dealers' PAC made a significant—and in some cases decisive—difference in the congressional votes on the rule.

There is an embarrassment of similar cases. Whether it is agricultural subsidies or health care costs or environmental protection or tax loopholes, special interest money is buying too much—and at the public's expense.

The influence of special interest money in these cases is rarely in the form of an explicit quid pro quo. Rather, this money—and especially PAC money—distorts legislation through a more subtle and ongoing process. PACs know that most congressmen run for reelection and will be periodically in need of their money. PACs also know that they will have the power to keep that money flowing to a member of Congress or to cut it off, depending on the congressmen's votes in the years between elections. Because members of Congress know they will need that money, they are hesitant to vote in ways that might offend the PACs, and in many cases, they vote in certain ways specifically to curry their favor.

Second, the torrent of special interest money is drowning out representation. Our representative democracy is founded on the principle that elected officials will freely vote their consciences while earnestly working in their constituents' best interests and actively listening to what those interests are. But a member of Congress may not feel free to vote his or her conscience when that Congress member must depend on special interest groups to provide a third or half of his or her campaign funds. Furthermore, the congressman cannot even know what his constituents' interests are when their letters are being prompted—and in some cases, printed, stamped, and mailed—by some interest group's undisclosed lobbying efforts. The result is that some congressmen are voting for legislation that bears less relation to their constituents' interests than to the special interest money they have been receiving. In other cases, special interest money simply throws Congress into deadlock, and legislation that would have been in almost everybody's interest fails to pass.

Of course, some dispute that all this special interest money erodes representation. They cite James Madison's arguments about pluralism from *The Federalist* and argue that the pressures from the PAC funds of competing groups will cancel each other out. But this argument assumes that there will always be a PAC for each of the countervailing interests. In fact, as Senator Robert Dole of Kansas has observed, "poor people don't make campaign contributions. You might get a different result if there were a Poor-PAC up here."[6] An example is the issue of the used-car rule. The only interest not represented by PAC funds in that fight were the interests of con-

6. Albert Hunt, "Cash Politics," *Wall Street Journal*, 26 July 1982.

sumers and the general public. At a time like this, when the Congress is deciding crucial questions about the course of the economy, about social equity, and about the proper role of government, we cannot afford to have policies that represent only one side—the side with the money and the PACs.

Finally, the explosion in PAC funds and other forms of special interest money is undermining public confidence in the institution of Congress, and for good reason. It may sound idealistic, but I know from experience that Congress must have and must appear to have integrity in order to retain the public's confidence. More and more, the public suspects that at least a portion of the Congress is no longer pure. The cause of this suspicion is that the public sees legislation that, to ever greater extents, looks like special interest wish lists. What the public increasingly discovers is that interest groups are buying the sort of access they as voters could never dream of, and what the public increasingly hears is members of Congress and former members like myself sounding the alarm.

The public justifiably loses faith in the Congress when it hears my former colleague from Missouri, Senator Thomas Eagleton, saying the present campaign-financing system

virtually forces Members of Congress to go hat in hand, begging for money from special interests whose sole purpose for existing is to seek a *quid pro quo.* The scandal is taking place every day and will continue to do so while the present system is in place.[7]

---

7. Statement of Senator Thomas Eagleton, in U.S., Congress, Senate, Committee on Rules and Administration, *Hearings on Campaign Finance Reform Proposals of 1983,* 98th Cong., 1st sess., 1983, p. 52.

The public justifiably loses faith in the Congress when it hears former Congressman James Shannon of Massachusetts saying that

the problem of money in politics hasn't been an obsession of mine, but it's becoming one now.... What's bothering me is when you start seeing guys acting against what you know are their philosophies and constituencies and instincts.... There are some here who say that PACs don't influence public policy. That's baloney.[8]

And the public justifiably loses faith in the Congress when it hears Senator Dole saying that

when these political action committees give money they expect something in return other than good government. It is making it much more difficult to legislate. We may reach a point where if everybody is buying something with PAC money, we cannot get anything done.[9]

In sum, during my service in Congress, I witnessed congressmen's needs for funds and interest groups' desire for influence increase and combine in a way that steadily began to undermine policy, representation, and the institution of Congress. I remember that as we moved through the sixties and through the Johnson administration, there developed an undefinable feeling on Capitol Hill and in Washington—an odor, if you will—that the amount of money flowing in was becoming enormous and that there were some situations developing very rapidly that were just ripe for corruption. During the Nixon administration, as the Watergate scandal broke open, that odor became a stench. By the time I retired, the corruption of special interest money had infected the legis-

---

8. Drew, *Politics and Money,* p. 51.
9. Hunt, "Cash Politics."

lative branch, and, partly as a result, I found myself serving in the most gutless Congress I had ever seen. What I fear today is that special interest money is damaging Congress to the same scandalous degree that it damaged the executive branch during Watergate; the only difference is that the means now being used appear to be sanctioned.

THE FRAMEWORK FOR A SOLUTION

I believe that there is a way out of this problem, and I think an examination of how we have dealt with special interest money in the past gives some guidance for where we should go in the future. Basically, it seems that in the past we have tried, to varying degrees, to reduce the undue influence of special interest money by making it visible, reasonable, and resistible.

The first reaction to special interest money typically has been to make it visible. Thus the key provisions of the first major piece of campaign-finance legislation to pass Congress in recent times, the Federal Election Campaign Act of 1971, required disclosure of contributions to federal campaigns and required PACs to register with the government. Similarly, Congress first attempted to make lobbying more visible by requiring that interest groups report such expenditures, and the Senate initially tried to cope with honoraria by requiring that they be disclosed.

Effective disclosure laws are essential to curbing the excessive influence of special interest money. In the area of campaign finance, for example, disclosure has enabled the press and groups like Common Cause to become effective watchdogs over PAC spending. Of course, the fact that PAC contributions continue to corrupt Congress demonstrates that visibility is not always enough, but in other areas, such as lobbying, effective disclosure is likely all that is necessary or warranted.

The second step toward curbing special interest influence has been to make special interest money reasonable. By this I mean that special interest money must be limited to amounts that are reasonable relative to other sources. That was the step Congress took following Watergate; as it limited the allowable size of contributions from individuals and political parties, it also limited the allowable size of PAC contributions.

That was also the step Congress ultimately took with regard to honoraria. House members limited outside earned income like honoraria to 30 percent of their salaries and—after a tough fight that the late Senator Henry Jackson led in 1983 with courage and wisdom—the Senate ultimately followed suit.

In late December of 1985, however, Congress increased the honoraria limit for Senators—as a regrettable Christmas stocking stuffer. Senators can now receive up to $30,000 in honoraria per year; for House members the limit is $22,000.

Finally, to make special interest money less corrosive, we have tried some measures to make it resistible. That is, Congress tried to wean candidates and elected officials from their dependency on fat-cat donors and interest-group money by providing them with alternative means of support. This was the philosophy behind the provisions in the 1974 laws that established public financing and expenditure limits for presidential campaigns. By providing an alternative source of campaign funds, the laws at least partially freed presidential candidates from the sort of influence-seeking funds that loomed so large in Watergate.

Originally, those laws also specified expenditure limits for congressional candidates. These limits sought to make special interest money more resistible by making campaigns less expensive. Unfortunately, in the 1976 case of *Buckley* v. *Valeo*, the Supreme Court struck down the congressional expenditure limits by ruling that such limits could exist only in conjunction with public financing.[10]

The desire to make special interest money resistible has also been evident in past efforts to control honoraria. Many have argued for adequate congressional salaries in conjunction with limits on honoraria. The reasoning is clear: it is preferable to make Congress beholden to the public than to exclusionary monied interests.

If the solution lies in making special interest money visible, reasonable, and resistible, then there is still much to be done. Lobbying expenditures, for example, are still not visible. The only lobby disclosure law on the books—the 1946 Federal Regulation of Lobbying Act—is weak, loophole ridden, and unenforced. Few corporations or trade associations disclose their grass-roots lobbying expenditures. Moreover, in flagrant disregard of the existing law, many fail to file any disclosure reports whatsoever.

A great deal also needs to be done to keep the flow of special interest money reasonable. In the area of campaign finance, one urgently needed remedy is a limit on the total amount of PAC money that a congressman may accept during a campaign. It is clearly not reasonable to expect that candidates will accept over $1 million from PACs and not be influenced by that money. It is clearly not reasonable to expect that some candidates will accept over half of their campaign money from PACs and still hold the interests of their constituents to be foremost. In the Ninety-eighth Congress, Wisconsin Congressman David Obey and over 150 cosponsors introduced legislation that would limit a candidate's aggregate PAC receipts to $90,000 in House campaigns. In the Ninety-ninth Congress, Senators David Boren and Barry Goldwater and a broad bipartisan coalition have proposed similar PAC limits for both House and Senate candidates. Such legislation deserves active support.

Last, we must continue efforts to make special interest money more resistible. I believe that the overwhelming majority of representatives and senators would more faithfully represent the interests of their constituents if they could afford to do so. Therefore we must look for ways to make it easier for them to say no to PACs, to say no to the interest groups offering honoraria, and to say no to hidden lobbying pressures. The best way we can help members of Congress say no is to provide some form of public financing of congressional campaigns.[11] Although public financing of presidential campaigns has not been trouble free, and even though it also needs improvement, it has been undeniably successful in helping presidential candidates resist special interest money. Watergate demonstrated that, in 1972, the presidency was on the special interest auction block. By contrast, PAC

10. *Buckley* v. *Valeo*, 424 U.S. 1 (1976).

11. See Charles McC. Mathias, Jr., "Should There Be Public Financing of Congressional Campaigns?" this issue of *The Annals* of the American Academy of Political and Social Science.

money now accounts for less than 2 percent of presidential campaign funds. In fact, in the 1984 presidential contest, three candidates declared that they would not accept any PAC funds. We need to provide that kind of flexibility to members of Congress, and public financing is the best way to provide it.

Professor Merton C. Bernstein and I have proposed a variation on the idea of public financing for congressional campaigns. We proposed that public funds be made available that would match PAC contributions and other PAC campaign expenditures dollar for dollar. These funds would be given to the PAC beneficiary's opponent. While at first this sounds expensive, such a program would diminish and perhaps, in time, eliminate the incentive for PACs to make contributions or for candidates to accept them. If a PAC contribution or expenditure buys the favored candidate no advantage because of matching public funds to his or her rival, PAC contributions would soon lose their purpose.

PAC contributions overwhelmingly favor incumbents. In 1984 House elections, for example, of every PAC dollar, $.78 went to incumbents. Therefore present members of Congress might be expected to resist enactment of a campaign financing program that reduces their ability to draw on PAC money. I think that many members of Congress would prefer, however, to reclaim their political fate—and perhaps their souls—from PACs. But even if they remained unmoved by such a morally tempting prospect, we are confident that challengers could adroitly exploit their opponents' continued support of the status quo.

A program of matching public funds to PAC funds could be modeled on the presidential campaign financing laws, under which the Federal Election Commission makes public money available once a candidate receives a sufficient number of individual contributions under a given amount. Each congressional candidate would be required to obtain a minimum number of contributors before qualifying for public funds. There would also be a maximum limit—say $100—on each contribution. Once a PAC made contributions or expenditures on behalf of a candidate above that amount, the candidate's opponent would receive public funds equal to the direct contributions from the PAC and other PAC expenditures, such as the purchase of television time.

In time, I would expect PACs to diminish or disappear—and with them, the need for substantial public outlays. This proposal presents no curb on free speech, and it promises to remove PAC pollution.

It is neither naive nor idealistic to try to control the pernicious influence of money in politics. It is essential to the survival of our democracy. I remember what people said about some of the legislation we successfully ushered through Congress in those 34 years I served. They said there was no way to pass a civil rights act, but we passed not one, but several. They said there was no way to pass a budget act, but we passed it. If they say there is no way to pass lobby disclosure or PAC limits or public financing of congressional campaigns, then, I say, let them be wrong again. I also remember that when I ran for reelection in 1964, I had every party organization and many special interest groups in my district rally against me in the primary. I was able to prevail, however, and part of the reason was that I had a phrase that turned out the volunteers and stirred up the voters. I said that it was going to be "the folks against the factions." Now that may sound naive, but it was true, and it took, and it is why we won.

These reforms to campaign financing are needed. I understand the way special interest money is hobbling the Congress that I served in for many years, and I am worried. I see that the public is not getting the legislation and the representation it deserves, and I am angered. And I hear the public asking if we can make those reforms a reality. I answer not only that we can , but that we must.

Campaign Finance Reform: The Unfinished Agenda

By FRED WERTHEIMER

ABSTRACT: In 1974, following the Watergate scandal, Congress enacted major campaign finance reform legislation. The legislation created a revolutionary new public financing system for our presidential campaigns, but it left congressional campaigns to be financed totally by private money. The presidential public financing system has worked well. Despite some incremental problems, the system has accomplished its basic goal of allowing individuals to run for the presidency without becoming dependent on their financial backers. The system for financing congressional campaigns, on the other hand, is out of control and in need of fundamental reform. The inappropriate role of special interest political action committees (PACs) in influencing congressional elections and congressional decisions is the single biggest problem facing the political process. Congress needs to complete the unfinished campaign finance reform agenda of the 1970s by enacting public financing for congressional campaigns and establishing new restrictions on the total amount that PACs may give to a congressional candidate.

Fred Wertheimer is president of Common Cause, a national citizens' lobbying organization. He joined the organization as a lobbyist in 1971 and became president in 1981. He has been Common Cause's chief lobbyist on campaign finance reform and served as director of its Campaign Finance Monitoring Project. Before joining Common Cause, he served as minority counsel to the House Small Business Committee, as legislative counsel to Congressman Silvio Conte, and as an attorney with the Securities and Exchange Commission. Mr. Wertheimer is a graduate of the University of Michigan and Harvard Law School.

NOTE: The author wishes to acknowledge the important contributions made in the preparation of this article by Common Cause staff members Marcy Frosh, Carole Geithner, Randy Huwa, Ann McBride, and Jane Mentzinger.

OUR democracy is founded on the concept of representation. Citizens elect leaders who are given responsibility to weigh all the competing and conflicting interests that reflect our diversity and to decide what, in their judgment, will best advance the interests of the citizenry.

It is obviously a rough system. It often does not measure up to the ideal we might hope to attain. But we continue to place our trust in this system because we believe our best chance at governing ourselves lies in obtaining the best judgment of elected representatives.

Unfortunately, that is not happening today. We are not obtaining the best judgment of our elected representatives in Congress because they are not free to give it to us. As a result of our present congressional campaign financing system—and the increasing role of political action committee (PAC) campaign contributions—members of Congress are rapidly losing their ability to represent the constituencies that have elected them.

We have long struggled to prevent money from being used to influence government decisions. We have not always succeeded, but we have never lost sight of the goal. Buying influence violates our most fundamental democratic values. We have long recognized that the ability to make large campaign contributions does, in fact, make some more equal than others. In the mid-1960s, for example, Senator Russell Long, Democrat of Louisiana, observed,

One sweet woman was on the opposite side [in an election] and thought they were going to lose and came charging in there with a couple of hundred thousand dollars to pump up their side. . . . Anybody who would suggest that she had no more influence than any other sweet old lady in a calico dress just does not know anything about politics.[1]

Beginning in the early 1970s, Common Cause and other election reform groups pressed for fundamental changes in the campaign finance statutes. The goals were to end secrecy in campaign financing, to limit the influence of large contributions, to enable candidates of modest means to seek office without becoming beholden to campaign donors, and to increase competition in the political process. The reform agenda called for:

—effective campaign contribution and expenditure reporting requirements;

—limits on the size of individual and group campaign contributions;

—a system of public financing of campaigns, including candidate access to federal funds and limits on spending; and

—effective enforcement by an independent agency.

This reform agenda took on a new importance in the wake of Watergate, our nation's greatest political scandal. Watergate revealed that our government was literally up for sale. The money came in the form of funds contributed for the presidential campaign. As the then chairman of American Airlines explained:

The law . . . is based on a system by which candidates for public office must seek funds from persons affected by the actions of such candidates when elected to office. The sys-

1. U.S., Congress, Senate, Committee on Finance, *Hearings on S. 3496, Amendment No. 732, S. 2006, S. 2965, and S. 3014*, 89th Cong., 2d sess., 1966, p. 78.

tem provides no limits on the total amount that may be raised or spent and hence places a premium on pressure to raise greater and greater amounts.[2]

In its final report, the Senate Watergate Committee concluded that, as a result of the systematic solicitation of corporate donors, 12 major corporations gave approximately $749,000 in illegal contributions to the Nixon campaign.[3] Corporate executives testified that they succumbed to such solicitations as a way of gaining access to administration decision makers and also out of fear of experiencing competitive disadvantages if they failed to contribute. Said one Gulf Oil executive, "I considered it considerable pressure when two Cabinet officers and an agent of one of the committees that was handling the election . . . ask[ed] me for funds—that is just a little bit different than somebody collecting for the Boy Scouts."[4]

The Milk Producers Association's pledge of $2 million to President Nixon's reelection campaign was linked in the public's mind to the increase in milk price supports. More than $1.8 million in contributions to the Nixon campaign came from people who received ambassadorial appointments during his administration.[5]

2. D. Michal Freedman, *The Watergate Reforms: Ten Years After* (Washington, DC: Common Cause, 1983), p. 16.
3. U.S., Congress, Senate, Select Committee on Presidential Campaign Activities, *Final Report*, 93rd Cong., 2d sess., 1974, p. 446.
4. Ibid., p. 471.
5. Ibid., pp. 127, 492-93, 579. See Fred Wertheimer and Randy Huwa, "Campaign Finance Reforms: Past Accomplishments, Future Challenges," *New York University Review of Law and Social Change,* 10:44 (1980-81). Unless otherwise noted, figures used in this article are based on analyses prepared by Common Cause of campaign finance disclosure statements filed with the Federal Election Commission.

Reflecting on the meaning of Watergate, John Gardner, founder and former chairman of Common Cause, wrote at the time:

In almost every aspect of Watergate, there was one common element: the flow of secret campaign cash. There are honest donors to political campaigns and honest recipients; but the existence of these does not outweigh the fact that the present system legitimizes the buying and selling of politicians. The old-style, flat-footed cash bribe has been replaced by the campaign gift, its all-purpose, prepackaged modern equivalent.[6]

The result of these revelations, not surprisingly, was an alarming drop in citizens' confidence in their government. Pollster Louis Harris in 1973 told a Senate committee that "public confidence in government generally must be reported as being lower than a constituent democracy can afford."[7]

The nation's greatest political scandal led to one of the nation's most historic and revolutionary reforms, the public financing of our presidential elections. Congress enacted public financing to prevent private campaign contributions from being used as a vehicle for obtaining influence with the president of the United States. Under this system, limits were placed on the size of contributions, overall expenditures were capped, and an alternative source of campaign money was created: public funds generated by the dollar checkoff on the federal income tax.[8]

6. Freedman, *Watergate Reforms*, p. 17.
7. U.S., Congress, Senate, Committee on Government Operations, *Hearings on a Survey of Public Attitudes,* 93rd Cong., 1st sess., 1973, pp. 6-8.
8. FECA Amendments of 1974, Pub. L. No. 93-443, §§ 101-302, 88 Stat. 1263 (1974) (codified as amended in scattered sections of 2, 5, 18, 26, 47 U.S.C.).

Unfortunately, the same progress was not made at the congressional level. Although Congress established limits on contributions by both individuals and PACs and placed limits on overall expenditures,[9] members of Congress were unwilling to take the last crucial step—to establish an alternative public source of campaign funds for their own campaigns. While congressional public financing was passed by the Senate, the House narrowly rejected it, by a vote of 187 to 228, and the provision was dropped in conference. At the same time, in a major step backward and over the objections of reform groups, Congress opened the door for an increased role in special interest giving by repealing a prohibition on the formation of PACs by government contractors.[10] As a result of these actions, campaign contributions remain a powerful vehicle for obtaining access and influence in the United States Congress.

The presidential and congressional campaign-financing systems thus require sharply different types of reform today. Comprehensive legislation must be enacted to remedy the defects in the system for financing congressional campaigns. Limits on overall PAC receipts must be established. A public financing system must be created to provide overall spending limits and adequate alternative funding so that candidates are no longer dependent on special interest group contributions. In contrast, the system of financing presidential campaigns has already been successfully transformed. While significant adjustments are needed in order to deal with new problems that have arisen, such as soft money and independent expenditures, these changes are required to preserve the integrity of an existing system that has accomplished its basic goals.

PRESIDENTIAL
PUBLIC FINANCING

Simply stated, the presidential public financing system is an idea that works; it is the crowning achievement of the amendments adopted in 1974 to the Federal Election Campaign Act. Under the system, candidates who agree to abide by limits on overall campaign spending and the expenditure of personal wealth are able to receive federal tax dollars, funds designated to a separate account by individual taxpayers. Public funds are available to match small private contributions raised by candidates during the nominating process; for the general election, major-party candidates are entitled to full campaign funding with public dollars.

In the three elections for which this new system has been in place—1976, 1980, and 1984—presidential public financing has been successful. Thirty-four of the 35 major party candidates since the law was passed have chosen to participate in this voluntary system. Presidential public financing has checked the increase in presidential campaign expenditures. Presidential contenders no longer must "tin-cup it around the country" in search of campaign funds.[11] In contrast to the presidential contest of 1972, candidates are no longer dependent on a relatively few fat-cat contributors; rather, the funding base for campaigns is broad. PAC contributions play a

---

9. The limits on overall expenditures were struck down by the Supreme Court in the landmark case *Buckley* v. *Valeo,* 424 U.S. 1 (1976).

10. Act of 14 June 1940, chap. 640, § 5 (a), 54 Stat. 772 (repealed 1976).

11. "Fat Cat as Endangered Species," *Washington Post,* 26 June 1980.

minor role in presidential campaigns. PACs gave less than $1.5 million to 1984 presidential candidates, or less than 2 percent of the total funds raised. As the *New York Times* has observed, "Public financing confers on Presidential candidates the freedom not to grovel."[12]

Public financing also confers an added freedom to govern without the strings attached by large donors or public suspicion that such strings exist. The Carter and Reagan presidencies have been relatively free of the hint that government favors have been traded for large campaign contributions. Stories linking the influence of campaign contributions with official actions in the legislative branch are common;[13] for the executive branch, very rare. The Commission on National Elections, headed by Melvin Laird and Robert Strauss, concluded,

Public financing of presidential elections has clearly proved its worth in opening up the process, reducing undue influence of individuals and groups, and virtually ending corruption in presidential election finance.

---

12. "Sneak Attack on Campaign Finance," *New York Times*, 3 June 1985.

13. See, for example, Common Cause, *How Money Talks in Congress: A Common Cause Study of the Impact of Money on Congressional Decision-Making* (Washington, DC: Common Cause, 1979); Wertheimer and Huwa, "Campaign Finance Reforms: Past Accomplishments, Future Challenges," pp. 49, 51, 52, 53; Walter Isaacson, "Running with the PACs" *Time*, 25 Oct. 1982, pp. 20-26; Brooks Jackson and Jeffrey Birnbaum, "Dairy Lobby Obtains U.S. Subsidies with Help from Urban Legislators," *Wall Street Journal*, 18 Nov. 1983; Judith Bender, "The PAC Game on Capitol Hill," *Newsday*, 12 Mar. 1984; Brooks Jackson, "PAC Helps Push Pet Electric Bill," *Wall Street Journal*, 29 Mar. 1984; and Jeffrey Sheler and Robert Black, "Is Congress for Sale?" *U.S. News and World Report*, 28 May 1984, pp. 47-50.

This major reform of the 1970's should be continued.[14]

CONGRESSIONAL CAMPAIGN FINANCING

While the presidential campaign finance system stands as a model for reform, the congressional campaign system is out of control and in need of fundamental repair.

The last decade of congressional campaign financing has been marked by an exponential increase in the number of PACs formed by corporations, labor unions, trade associations, and other groups. In 1974 there were 608 PACs. Today there are more than 4000.

This explosion in PACs can be traced to congressional action—and inaction— in 1974. Ironically, at the very time when members of Congress were acting to clean up presidential elections, they opened the door for PACs to enter the congressional arena in an unprecedented way. The key to the PAC explosion was a provision attached to the 1974 law by labor and business groups, over the opposition of Common Cause and other reform advocates, that authorized government contractors to establish PACs.[15] In addition, by creating public financing for presidential campaigns, but not for congressional races, the 1974 amendments focused the attention and interest of PACs and other private campaign donors on Congress.

The resulting growth in PACs was no accident, and it certainly was not a reform. The growth of PACs, moreover, is certainly no unintended consequence of the 1974 law—the provision was

---

14. *Report of the Commission on National Elections, Executive Summary* (Washington, DC: Georgetown University, Center for Strategic and International Studies, 1985), p. 7.

15. 2 U.S.C. § 441c(b) (1976).

included to protect and enhance the role of PACs in financing campaigns, and it has.

This tremendous increase in the number of PACs has not resulted in balanced representation in Washington. As Senator Gary Hart, Democrat of Colorado, has told the Senate:

> It seems the only group without a well-heeled PAC is the average citizen—the voter who has no special interest beyond low taxes, an efficient government, an honorable Congress, and a humane society. Those are the demands we should be heeding—but those are the demands the PACs have drowned out.[16]

In fact, the increasing number of PACs has largely served to increase the ability of single interests to bring pressure to bear on a congressional candidate or a member of Congress. There are more than 100 insurance company PACs, more than 100 PACs sponsored by electric utilities, and more than 300 sponsored by labor unions. Representative David Obey, Democrat of Wisconsin, has observed that frequently in Washington

> an issue affects an entire industry and all of the companies and labor unions in that industry.... When that occurs, [and] a large number of groups which have made substantial contributions to members are all lobbying on the same side of an issue, the pressure generated from those aggregate contributions is enormous and warps the process. It is as if they had made a single, extremely large contribution.[17]

The increase in the number of PACs, not surprisingly, has also produced a tremendous increase in PAC contributions to congressional candidates. In 1974, PACs gave $12.5 million to congressional candidates. By the 1984 elections, their contributions had exceeded $100 million, an eightfold increase in ten years.

PAC money also represents a far more important part of the average candidate's campaign funds than it did ten or so years ago. In 1974, 15.7 percent of congressional candidates' campaign money came from PACs; by the 1984 election, that proportion had increased to 30 percent.

Yet these numbers only begin to tell the story. The increased dependence on PAC contributions has been greatest for winners, those individuals who serve in Congress and who cast votes that shape our daily lives. In the Ninety-ninth Congress (1985-86), over 150 House members received 50 percent or more of their campaign funds from PACs, including 20 of the 27 committee chairs and party leaders. House winners in the 1984 election received an average of 41 percent of their campaign dollars from PACs. Of all winning House candidates in the 1974 election, only 28 percent received one-third or more of their campaign funds from PACs. By 1984, that figure had grown to 78 percent.

For senators, PAC contributions are also becoming a more important source of campaign dollars. Senators elected in 1976 received a total of $3.1 million from PACs; Senate winners in the 1984 election raised $20 million from PACs. In the 1984 elections, 23 winning Senate candidates raised more than $500,000 each from PACs.

Some have suggested that the growth in PACs is an important new form of citizen involvement in the political process. Yet PAC participation is often

---

16. U.S., Congress, Senate, *Congressional Record*, 99th Cong., 1st sess., 131(165):16683.

17. Statement of Congressman David R. Obey, Democratic Study Group, 26 July 1979, quoted in Fred Wertheimer, "The PAC Phenomenon in American Politics," *Arizona Law Review*, 22:622-23, n. 114 (1980).

likely to be more of an involvement in the corporate process or the union process or the trade association process than it is in the political process. University of Minnesota professor Frank J. Sorauf has noted:

To understand political participation through PACs, we need also to note the nature of the participation. Some of it is not even political activity; buying a ticket in a raffle, the proceeds of which go to a PAC, a party, or a candidate, does not qualify as a political act by most standards. Even the contributory act of writing a check or giving cash to a PAC is a somewhat limited form of participation that requires little time or immediate involvement; in a sense it buys political mercenaries who free the contributor from the need to be personally active in the campaign. It is one of the least active forms of political activity, well suited to the very busy or to those who find politics strange, boring, or distasteful.[18]

In fact, the growth of PACs and the increased importance of PAC money have had a negative effect on two different parts of the political process—congressional elections and congressional decision making. First, PAC money tends to make congressional campaigns less competitive because of the overwhelming advantage enjoyed by incumbents in PAC fund-raising. The ratio of PAC contributions to incumbents over challengers in 1984 House races was 4.6 to 1.0; in the Senate, incumbents in 1984 enjoyed a 3.0 to 1.0 advantage in PAC receipts. On the average, 1984 House incumbents raised $100,000 more from PACs than did challengers. This $100,000 advantage was true even in the most highly competitive House races, those in which the incumbent received 55 percent or less of the vote. In these races, incumbents received an average of over $230,000 from PACs; their challengers received less than $110,000. The advantage enjoyed by incumbents is true for all kinds of PAC giving—for contributions by labor groups, corporate PACs, and trade and membership PACs.

Second, there is a growing awareness that PAC money makes a difference in the legislative process, a difference that is inimical to our democracy. PAC dollars are given by special interest groups to gain special access and special influence in Washington. Most often, PAC contributions are made with a legislative purpose in mind. The late Justin Dart, former chairman of Dart Industries, once noted that dialogue with politicians "is a fine thing, but with a little money they hear you better."[19] Senator Charles Mathias, Republican of Maryland, has stated:

An official may not change his or her vote solely to accommodate the views of such contributors, but often officials, including myself, will agree to meet with an individual who made a large contribution so the official can hear the contributor's concerns and make the contributor aware these concerns have been considered. . . . Since an elected official has only so much time available, the inevitable result of such special treatment for the large contributor is that other citizens are denied the opportunity they otherwise would have to confer with the elected official.[20]

Common Cause and others have produced a number of studies that show a relationship between PAC contributions

18. Frank Sorauf, "PACs in the American Political System" (Background paper, Twentieth Century Fund Task Force on Political Action Committees, 1984), pp. 82-83.

19. "Companies Organize Employees and Holders into a Political Force," *Wall Street Journal*, 15 Aug. 1978.

20. Brief for Appellees, p. 53, *Buckley* v. *Valeo*, 424 U.S. 1 (1976).

and legislative behavior. The examples run the gamut of legislative decisions, including hospital cost containment, the Clean Air Act, domestic content legislation, dairy price programs, gun control, maritime policies, and regulation by the Federal Trade Commission of professional groups or of used-car sales.[21]

PAC gifts do not guarantee votes or support. PACs do not always win. But PAC contributions do provide donors with critical access and influence; they do affect legislative decisions and are increasingly dominating and paralyzing the legislative process.

In the last few years, something very important and fundamental has happened in this country—and that is the development of a growing awareness and recognition of the fact that the PAC system is a rotten system that must be changed. We know that concern is growing when Irving Shapiro, former chairman and chief executive officer of duPont and the former chairman of the Business Roundtable, describes the current system of financing congressional campaigns as "an invidious thing, it's corrupting, it does pollute the system."[22]

We know that concern is reaching new audiences when *Business Week* editorializes that

fears are growing that the proliferation of PACs... is balkanizing the nation's political process as swarms of candidates and well-heeled special interest groups jostle to trade political favors for money.... It would be hard to find a PAC that gives solely to support good government. Most see their contribution as an investment in promoting laws favoring their interests.[23]

And *Chemical Week* warns:

[A] new force has intruded into our system of representative democracy that, if unchecked, could topple it or seriously hurt it. We refer to the phenomenon of Political Action Committees.... The plain truth of the matter, no matter what gloss is put on it, is that PAC money aims at influencing congressional action. The other side of the coin is that new candidates and incumbents alike become beholden to their PAC benefactors. That's the whole point, isn't it?[24]

Criticism of the PAC system is also increasingly heard in the halls of Congress. More and more members from both parties are speaking out about the PAC problem. Consider the following:

[The present campaign-financing system] virtually forces members of Congress to go around hat in hand, begging for money from Washington-based special interest political action committees, whose sole purpose for existing is to seek a quid pro quo.... the scandal is taking place every day and will continue to do so while the present system is in place.[25]

PAC money is destroying the election process. It is breaking down public confidence in

---

21. See, for example, Common Cause, "How Money Talks in Congress"; Wertheimer and Huwa, "Campaign Finance Reforms: Past Accomplishments, Future Challenges," pp. 49, 51, 52, 53; Isaacson, "Running with the PACs," pp. 20-26; Jackson and Birnbaum, "Dairy Lobby Obtains U.S. Subsidies"; Bender, "PAC Game on Capitol Hill"; Jackson, "PAC Helps Push Pet Electric Bill"; and Sheler and Black, "Is Congress for Sale?"

22. Nina Easton, "Swimming against the Tide," *Common Cause Magazine,* 9(5):13 (Sept.-Oct. 1983).

23. "How to Curb PAC Power but Not Free Speech," *Business Week,* 22 Nov. 1982.

24. Patrick P. McCurdy, "Let's Pack in the PACs—All of Them," *Chemical Week,* 15 Aug. 1984, p. 3.

25. Statement of Senator Thomas Eagleton, in U.S., Congress, Senate, Committee on Rules and Administration, *Hearings on Campaign Finance Reform Proposals of 1983,* 98th Cong., 1st sess., 1983, p. 52.

free elections and it is ruining the character and quality of campaigns.[26]

In addition, the growth in the influence of PAC's further fragments our Nation and its elected legislative bodies. It makes it increasingly difficult to reach a national consensus and hold[s] our decisionmaking process hostage to the special interests which PAC's represent.... We cannot expect Members of Congress to act in the national interest when their election campaigns are being financed more and more by special interests.[27]

In addition to the growing role of PAC contributions, the congressional campaign-financing system is also marked by unlimited and skyrocketing spending. In 1974, House and Senate candidates spent $77 million on congressional races. Ten years later, House and Senate candidates spent a record $374 million, almost five times as much.

The cost of winning a seat in Congress is also rising dramatically. In the 1975-76 election cycle, House winners spent $38 million, an average of over $87,000 each. In the 1983-84 election cycle, House winners spent $117 million, an average of $269,956 each. On the Senate side, winners spent $20 million in the 1975-76 cycle, an average of $606,060; in 1984 elections, Senate winners spent $94.8 million, an average of $2.9 million each.

About rising campaign expenditures Senator Goldwater has said,

Unlimited campaign spending eats at the heart of the democratic process. It feeds the growth of special interest groups created solely to channel money into political campaigns.... And it causes elected officials to devote more time to raising money than to their public duties.[28]

And Senator Eagleton has said on the Senate floor:

Throughout the last decade, the money factor has exploded exponentially. Most of us have our "tin cups" for alms-begging; our call lists to fat cats; our endless procession of fundraising receptions; our direct mail pleas; and so forth.

The money race never ends. Senators start the process in the early years of their 6-year terms by "building a war chest" for their reelection. House Members start on the Wednesday after the Tuesday elections to amass the funds for the next go-around.[29]

THE CAMPAIGN FINANCE REFORM AGENDA

A number of changes in federal election law are needed if the campaign finance reform effort begun over a decade ago is to be finished. In some cases, unfinished business needs to be completed. The foremost item of old business, of course, is a fundamental restructuring of the congressional campaign-financing system. In addition, new problems that have emerged in the years since Watergate need to be addressed. Adjustments to the presidential public financing system—a system that is fundamentally sound and that has demonstrated its effectiveness—need to be made. A campaign finance reform agenda today should include congressional campaign finance reform, independent expenditures, and soft money, as well as other issues.

26. Remarks of Senator Barry Goldwater, in U.S., Congress, Senate, *Congressional Record,* 99th Cong., Ist sess., 131(165):16679.

27. Remarks of Senator David Boren, in ibid., no. 164, p. 16605.

28. U.S., Congress, Senate, Committee on Rules and Administration, *Hearings on Campaign Finance Reform Proposals of 1983,* p. 403.

29. U.S., Congress, Senate, *Congressional Record,* 99th Cong., 1st sess., 131(165):16683.

Congressional campaign finance reform

The major unfinished business on the reform agenda is a thorough overhaul of the congressional campaign finance system. Comprehensive legislation is needed that includes the following essential components: limitations on overall PAC receipts, provision of an alternative campaign fund source, and limits on overall campaign spending and on the expenditure of a candidate's personal funds.

Limitations on overall PAC receipts. While current law restricts the amount that an individual PAC may give to a candidate, there is no restriction on the total amount that a candidate may accept from all PACs. Thus in the last two elections we have seen four Senate candidates who have each accepted more than $1 million in PAC funds. An overall limit on aggregate PAC receipts would help shift the focus of congressional fund-raising away from large PAC contributions and back to small contributions from individual donors.

An amendment establishing an overall limit on PAC receipts was adopted by the House in 1979—the Obey-Railsback bill—but was not considered by the Senate. The introduction in 1985 of a PAC-limit amendment by Senators Boren and Goldwater revived congressional consideration of the concept of an aggregate PAC limit.[30]

Alternative campaign funds. Essential to the presidential public financing system are the federal funds made available to presidential candidates. Congressional campaign finance reform legislation similarly needs to provide alternative sources of campaign funds to candidates. This could be done in the form of public funds to match small contributions from individuals, as is done in the presidential nominating process, or grants to candidates, as is done in the presidential general election, or a 100 percent tax credit for small contributions to candidates,[31] or some combination of these systems. The creation of a broad-based alternative financing system will once again make elective office a realistic ambition for individuals without personal fortunes and for those who are unwilling or unable to raise large sums from PACs.

Overall campaign spending and candidates' personal funds. Limits on overall spending and the use of personal funds are a key feature of the presidential public financing system and are needed for congressional campaigns as well. The Supreme Court in its 1976 *Buckley* decision upheld the constitutionality of such limits as part of a system providing public financing for presidential candidates, but the Court struck down the spending limits enacted for congressional races because they were not tied to any public campaign finance system. It is clear from the *Buckley* decision that limits for congressional races along with limits on the use of personal funds can be constitutionally enacted as part of a public finance campaign system.

In crafting reform legislation, it is important to ensure that spending limits are set at levels high enough to allow

---

30. S. 1806, printed in ibid., no. 146, p. 14360; debate on S. 1806 is found in ibid., no 164, p. 16603; see also ibid., no. 165, p. 16678.

31. See, for example, H.R. 2490, printed in U.S., Congress, House, *Congressional Record*, 98th Cong., 1st sess., 129(45):1992; H.R. 4428, in ibid., no. 159, p. 10056; and U.S., Congress, Senate, *Congressional Record*, 99th Cong., 1st sess., 131(143):14065.

challengers to run competitive campaigns. Since any campaign-financing system that includes spending limits must be voluntary under the *Buckley* decision, candidates who felt unable to wage effective congressional campaigns within the spending limits would be free to run their races without public financing. Those who claim that public financing with spending limits favors the reelection of incumbents should not lose sight of the fact that in the first two presidential elections conducted under the presidential public financing system—1976 and 1980—incumbents were defeated, for the first time since 1932. Nor should these critics forget that it is incumbent members of Congress who thus far have failed to rush to enact public financing for congressional races. For the past decade a majority of incumbent members do not appear to have reached the conclusion that public financing and spending limits are an incumbent's advantage.

Enactment of a new campaign-financing system for Congress would free our elected representatives from their dangerous dependence on special interest contributions. A new system is also essential if we are to restore public confidence in the integrity of Congress and its members.

Two additional major changes are needed to protect the integrity of the presidential public financing system and any new system established for congressional campaigns. The changes deal with the issues of independent expenditures and soft money.

Independent expenditures

Under the Court's decision in *Buckley*, contributions made directly to a candidate may constitutionally be limited, but no limits may be imposed on expenditures undertaken independently by a PAC or an individual on behalf of or in opposition to a candidate. Through these so-called independent expenditures, PACs and individuals can evade the intent of limits on direct contributions. They can and do spend substantial sums—far in excess of statutory contribution limits—supporting or attacking candidates.

Independent spenders are unaccountable. They do not have to assume responsibility at election time, nor do they face the political impact of any misrepresentation they may make. A leader in the independent spending movement, Terry Dolan of the National Conservative Political Action Committee, has said, "A group like ours could lie through its teeth and the candidate it helps stays clean."[32]

The persistent use of independent spending in politics alters the political process for the worse.[33] Independent spending can seriously distort the competition between candidates. Candidates are faced with spending not only by their opponents but also by independent groups. Senator Ernest Hollings, Democrat of South Carolina, has noted, "We all have seen how PACs can seriously damage the balance in a campaign through the expenditure of enormous amounts of money. In effect, a candidate budgets to fight one well-financed opponent but then ends up fighting many."[34]

32. Myra MacPherson, "The New Right Brigade," *Washington Post,* 10 Aug. 1980.
33. See, for example, David Broder, "Equal Time for Targets," *Washington Post,* 26 Aug. 1981; "Nick-Pack Strikes Home," *New York Times,* 18 Nov. 1981.
34. U.S., Congress, Senate, *Congressional Record,* 99th Cong., 1st sess., 131(80):8268.

Within the confines of the Supreme Court's decisions in *Buckley* and later cases, there are steps that can and should be taken to curb the impact of independent expenditures. First, the *Buckley* decision specified that independent expenditure activities are exempt from limitation only if they are not coordinated with candidates or the agents of candidates. Additional legislation and regulations should be developed to clarify the standards to be used in assessing the true independence of an expenditure campaign.[35]

Second, and more important, the federal communication statutes should be amended to provide to federal candidates free and equal time to respond to broadcast advertisements purchased by means of independent expenditures. Under a response-time proposal, radio and television stations would be required to provide free and equal time to candidates for federal office in cases where a broadcaster sells time to any person—aside from federal candidates— to broadcast material that either endorses or opposes a candidate. If the broadcast advertisement opposes a candidate, that candidate would be entitled at no cost to an equal amount of broadcast time. If the broadcast advertisement endorses a candidate, other legally qualified candidates for the same office would be entitled at no cost to an equal amount of broadcast time. The response-time concept builds upon existing responsibilities placed on broadcasters— such as the personal-attack rule—and is a constitutional extension of existing communication standards that have been upheld by the courts.

Response time would help to protect the integrity of the present system of contribution limits by assuring that a candidate could respond without major expense to an independent expenditure campaign. Response time would enable candidates to refute misrepresentations made by independent spenders. A response-time proposal would not end independent expenditures, but it would restore some measure of accountability to independent spending activities.[36]

The response-time proposal has been included as a major provision of S. 1310, the Clean Campaign Act of 1985, introduced in the Ninety-ninth Congress by Senators John Danforth, Republican of Missouri, Ernest Hollings, Democrat of South Carolina, and Barry Goldwater, Republican of Arizona.[37] This proposal

---

35. Wertheimer and Huwa, "Campaign Finance Reforms: Past Accomplishments, Future Challenges," p. 64.

36. Fred Wertheimer, "Fixing Election Law," *New York Times,* 3 Sept. 1981. See also Ronald Brownstein, "Soft Money," *National Journal,* 7 Dec. 1985, p. 2828; Center for Responsive Politics, *Money and Politics: Soft Money—A Loophole for the '80s* (Washington, DC: Center for Responsive Politics, 1985); Common Cause, "Comments of Common Cause with Respect to Its Petition for Rulemaking Regarding 'Soft Money,' " (Manuscript, Common Cause, 1985); Elizabeth Drew, *Politics and Money: The New Road to Corruption* (New York: Macmillan, 1983); Thomas Edsall, "Loophole Lets Parties Raise Millions from Firms, Unions," *Washington Post,* 17 Apr. 1984; idem, "'Soft Money' Will Finance Voter Sign Up," ibid., 12 Aug. 1984; Maxwell Glen, "Republicans and Democrats Battling to Raise Big Bucks for Voter Drives," *National Journal,* Sept. 1984, pp. 1618-22; "Soft Money," *Washington Post,* 31 Aug. 1984; "The Soft-Money Loophole," ibid., 1 Nov. 1985; Ed Zuckerman, "Lobbying and Campaign Ethics: The Ethical Implications of 'Soft Money' " (Remarks delivered at George Washington University, Washington, DC, 28 Oct. 1985); idem, "Democrat 'Soft Money' Nets Catch $30 Million," *PACs & Lobbies,* 21 Nov. 1984; idem, " 'Soft Money': A New Life for 'Fat Cats,' " ibid., 16 Jan. 1985; and idem, "More DNC 'Soft Money' Accounts Found," ibid., 6 Feb. 1985.

37. U.S., Congress, Senate, *Congressional*

is also a significant component of the Boren-Goldwater PAC-limitation amendment.[38]

Soft money

In federal elections the amounts that individuals and PACs may contribute are limited; direct contributions from corporations and unions are completely barred; and all contributions in excess of $200 are subject to public-disclosure requirements. In many states, however, parallel regulations do not exist. In the 1980s, so-called soft money has increasingly been funneled to state party organizations. Soft money funds are contributions from sources—corporations or unions—that are not permitted to make any direct contributions in federal elections, and contributions from individuals or groups in amounts above the federal limits.

While soft money is purportedly for use in party-building activities at the state and local levels, there is increasing evidence that these funds are in fact being spent in connection with federal candidates, particularly presidential candidates, in violation of federal law. This is one of the most serious problems in the campaign finance area today. This practice seriously undermines the integrity of the contribution limits and prohibitions contained in the federal law, including the limits on contributions by political parties, the expenditure limits in the presidential public financing system, and disclosure requirements of the federal election law.[39]

In 1984, Common Cause proposed to the Federal Election Commission (FEC) that new regulations be adopted to control the use of the soft-money subterfuge. Under these regulations, national-level political party committees, including party congressional campaign committees, and federal officials would be prohibited from establishing soft-money accounts or from otherwise channeling to state parties for use in federal campaigns contributions that would be illegal under federal law.[40]

A number of additional campaign finance issues have arisen in the 1980s

---

Record, 99th Cong., 1st sess., 131(80):8267; see also Congress, Senate, Committee on Commerce, Science and Transportation, *Hearings on S. 1310, the Clean Campaign Act of 1985,* 99th Cong., 1st sess., 10 Sept. 1985; ibid., 8 Oct. 1985.

38. U.S., Congress, Senate, *Congressional Record,* 99th Cong., 1st sess., 131(146):14361.

39. See, for example, Brownstein, "Soft Money," p. 2828; Center for Responsive Politics, *Money and Politics: Soft Money;* Common Cause, "Comments of Common Cause with Respect to Its Petition"; Drew, *Politics and Money*; Edsall, "Loophole Lets Parties Raise"; idem, " 'Soft Money' Will Finance Voter Sign Up"; Glen, "Republicans and Democrats Battling," pp. 1618-22; "Soft Money," *Washington Post;* "Soft Money Loophole"; Zuckerman, "Lobbying and Campaign Ethics"; idem, "Democrat 'Soft Money' "; idem, " 'Soft Money': A New Life"; and idem, "More DNC 'Soft Money' Accounts Found."

40. In a 5 Nov. 1984 letter to Lee Ann Elliott, chair of the FEC, Common Cause urged the commission to take the following steps regarding soft money practices: (1) to initiate on a priority basis its own broad-ranging factual investigation into soft-money practices, with a view toward prosecuting actual past violations; (2) to initiate a rule-making proceeding to establish the broader administrative tools, such as additional disclosure requirements, needed to facilitate the commission's effective enforcement of the current laws; and (3) to undertake a review of the current laws to determine what additional statutory remedies may be required to assure that soft-money abuses are most effectively curtailed. On 4 Feb. 1985 Common Cause submitted to the FEC "Comments of Common Cause with Respect to Its Petition for Rulemaking Regarding 'Soft Money' " and thereby set out its formal proposal for rule making on soft money.

that require legislative action. Congress should address delegate committee spending, candidate and officeholder PACs, presidential candidate foundations, bundling, the grandfather clause, and the FEC.

Delegate committee spending

While presidential candidates who receive federal matching funds do so in return for a commitment to limit their overall and state-by-state spending, individuals who are seeking selection as delegates to a party's nominating convention are presently not subject to these limitations. Expenditures by the committees of these delegates create the capacity to bypass these spending limits, particularly if the expenditures are made at the direction of, with the encouragement of, or in conjunction with a candidate's campaign.[41] Federal election law needs to be amended to apply the limitations on contributions and expenditures to convention delegates.[42]

Candidate and officeholder PACs

A growing number of presidential candidates and members of Congress are establishing their own PACs. These PACs, like others, may make campaign contributions. In many cases, particularly in the case of presidential hopefuls, these PACs are also used to finance a candidate's political travel and related expenses, expenditures that at this point do not count against the spending ceilings of the presidential public financing system. These PACs also allow larger individual and PAC contributions to be made to the candidate or officeholder involved than could be made to his or her candidate campaign committee. They also place officeholders and office seekers in the position of using PAC money to curry favor. Congress should ban the creation of PACs by members of Congress and by prospective candidates for president or vice-president.[43]

Presidential candidate foundations

An increasing number of public figures, particularly prospective presidential candidates, have set up tax-exempt foundations. Unlike campaign committees, these foundations may accept unlimited amounts of money, including contributions from corporations and unions, and they are not required to report the source of their funds. Donations to these foundations, furthermore, are fully tax deductible.

These foundations, established to do research on issues and to undertake other educational activities, in theory are not linked to any individual. In practice, however, they can pay and have paid for travel by presidential hopefuls and have provided information that forms the basis of campaign position papers—activities that appear

41. Similarly, delegate committees enable individuals and PACs to override the contribution limits to a presidential candidate by making multiple contributions to numerous delegate committees, all of which are intended to benefit directly a single presidential candidate's campaign. Such contributions serve to undermine the effectiveness of the existing contribution limits.

42. Thomas Edsall, "Candidates Find It Easy to Give Spending Curbs the Runaround," *Washington Post,* 3 June 1984; Brooks Jackson, "Loopholes Allow Flood of Campaign Giving by Businesses, Fat Cats," *Wall Street Journal,* 5 July 1984.

43. See Maxwell Glen, "Starting a PAC May Be Candidates' First Step Down Long Road to 1988," *National Journal,* 16 Feb. 1985, pp. 374-77.

to help promote the public officials who created them.[44] At a minimum, tax-exempt foundations that are controlled by or maintained for a political candidate should be required to disclose the source and amount of contributions received.[45]

Bundling

Another development on the campaign-financing landscape that Congress must address is bundling, a practice by which a PAC puts together, or bundles, numerous individual checks made out to a particular candidate's campaign and provides them to the candidate. This practice presently is being used by PACs effectively to evade the contribution limits of the federal election laws. By aggregating these individual contributions a single PAC can provide to a candidate amounts far in excess of the current $5000-per-election limitation. A *Wall Street Journal* story, for example, noted that one insurance company PAC was able to funnel contributions of more than $168,000 to one senator's reelection campaign through bundling.[46]

44. As David Spear, a spokesman for former Senate majority leader Howard Baker, has noted, "If it's not a violation of the law, it's certainly a violation of the spirit of the law . . . candidates ought not to be able to raise campaign funds under the guise of a tax-free foundation." Bryan Abas, "Hart Has a Better Idea," *Westword,* 13-19 Nov. 1985, p. 8.

45. See *Report of the Commission on National Elections, Executive Summary,* p. 8; Paul West, " 'Foundations' Are Promoting Politicians," *Baltimore Sun,* 29 Sept. 1985; and Thomas Edsall, " '88 Candidates' New Tricks Stretch Federal Election Law," *Washington Post,* 20 Oct. 1985.

46. Brooks Jackson, "Insurance Industry Boosts Political Contributions as Congress Takes up Cherished Tax Preferences," *Wall Street Journal,* 10 Oct. 1985. See also idem, "GOP Group Uses Cash Creatively," ibid., 13 Sept. 1984; and

Under current FEC regulations, the bundled contributions are not treated as a contribution by the intermediary PAC unless it actually controls the choice of the recipient. The result is a loophole that is increasingly being exploited by PACs to expand their capacity to exert influence and to undermine the contribution limits.

The bundling loophole should be closed by amending federal election law to provide that bundled contributions would count against the contribution limits of both the individual contributor and the intermediary person or PAC. That is, if a PAC collects or otherwise aggregates contributions that are earmarked or directed to a particular candidate's campaign and assists in transmitting these contributions to that campaign, the contributions will be considered contributions to the candidate by the conduit PAC as well as by the original individual contributor.

Grandfather clause

In 1979 Congress amended federal law to prohibit candidates from converting surplus campaign funds for personal use. Under a grandfather clause included in that amendment, however, any member of Congress who was in office on 8 January 1980 is permitted to keep his or her surplus campaign contributions for personal use after leaving Congress. Members who qualify under this provision may thus take campaign money upon retirement. These surplus campaign funds, in some cases, now range to amounts as high as $600,000. While House and Senate rules prohibit conversion of these funds for personal

Michael Wines, "Bundling: A New U.S. Campaign Custom," *Los Angeles Times,* 3 Oct. 1981.

use while members remain in office, several members who have retired have in fact converted surplus funds for personal use. Other members, still in Congress, seem to regard building up campaign surpluses as a new form of political individual retirement account.[47]

Congress already has recognized the problems inherent in allowing retiring members to convert contributions into personal funds by banning this activity for many members. It should complete the task started in 1979 and remove the grandfather clause, which allows some members to escape the ban.

FEC

While it is important to examine the rules for congressional and presidential campaign financing, a careful assessment must also be made of the FEC, the body responsible for enforcing federal election laws.

The commission has failed the public in several important respects. Most significantly, it is ponderously slow in its enforcement proceedings and is often prone to concentrate on technicalities rather than major issues of rule making. While the FEC's efforts at promoting disclosure of the receipts and expenditures of PACs and candidates have been a major success, lax enforcement by the commission threatens to undermine the effectiveness of the prohibitions, restrictions, and limits of the federal election law.

Both external and internal organizational factors act to undermine the effectiveness of the FEC. Congress created the commission with a partisan split and has never clarified the roles of the staff director and general counsel, the two statutory officers of the commission. Consequently, the FEC has failed to have management and policy direction. Congress also consistently underfunds the agency, making it more difficult for the commission to carry out its various responsibilities.

The performance of the FEC is critical to the effective implementation of federal election laws. Congress needs to consider changes in both the structure and the administration of the commission to ensure the proper implementation of federal election laws.[48]

CONCLUSION

In the spring of 1973, Common Cause chairman John Gardner told the Senate Commerce Committee that "there is nothing in our political system today that creates more mischief, more corruption, and more alienation and distrust on the part of the public than does our system of financing elections."[49] Despite major progress in improving the presidential campaign-financing system,

---

47. At the end of the 1984 election cycle, for instance, members of the House who could convert surplus funds upon retirement had average cash-on-hand figures of $106,935; their colleagues who were not grandfathered averaged $50,421. See Lee Norrgard, "You Can Take It with You," *Common Cause Magazine*, p. 9 (May-June 1985); Maxwell Glen, "Finishing a Campaign in the Black Becoming More Prevalent in the House," *National Journal*, 22 June 1985, pp. 1467-69; Kevin Chaffee, "Money under the Mattress: What Congressmen Don't Spend," *Washington Monthly*, pp. 32-38 (Sept. 1984).

48. See generally Common Cause, *Stalled from the Start* (Washington, DC: Common Cause, 1981); see also William C. Oldaker, "Of Philosophers, Foxes, and Finances: Can the Federal Election Commission Ever Do an Adequate Job?" this issue of *The Annals* of the American Academy of Political and Social Science.

49. Statement of John Gardner, in U.S., Congress, Senate, Commerce Committee, *Hearings on S. 372*, 93rd Cong., 1st sess. 1973, p. 1.

that observation remains true today with regard to the congressional campaign-financing system. As former Watergate special prosecutor and current Common Cause chairman Archibald Cox has observed, inaction has resulted in "a Congress still more deeply trapped in the stranglehold of special interests which threatens to paralyze the process of democratic government."[50] Congress needs to complete the reforms begun in the wake of Watergate by fundamentally transforming its own campaign-financing system and by making other adjustments needed to preserve the integrity of presidential public financing, campaign reporting requirements, and limitations on contributions by individuals and PACs.

A consensus has been reached in this country that PACs are inimical to our system of representative government.[51] The question now remaining is whether that public consensus can be translated into congressional action.

No solution that may be adopted will be final and perfect. We will always need to reevaluate and adjust any campaign finance system. The presidential public financing system demonstrates the need for periodic adjustments. But more important, the experience of presidential public financing shows us that fundamental improvement in our campaign finance laws is indeed attainable.

We can and must have a better system for financing congressional campaigns. Representative government is at stake.

50. Archibald Cox, Address before the Commonwealth Club of California, San Francisco, CA, 7 Jan. 1981.

51. A May 1984 Harris survey, for example, found that "a 70-20 percent majority of all likely voters across the country feels that candidates for federal office should refuse to accept PAC funds." Louis Harris, "PACs: Good or Bad Influence," *Harris Survey,* 31 May 1984.

Democracy or Plutocracy? The Case for a Constitutional Amendment to Overturn *Buckley* v. *Valeo*

By JONATHAN BINGHAM

ABSTRACT: In the early 1970s the U.S. Congress made a serious effort to stop the abuses of campaign financing by setting limits on contributions and also on campaign spending. In the 1976 case of *Buckley* v. *Valeo*, the Supreme Court upheld the regulation of contributions, but invalidated the regulation of campaign spending as a violation of the First Amendment. Since then, lavish campaigns, with their attendant evils, have become an ever more serious problem. Multimillion-dollar campaigns for the Senate, and even for the House of Representatives, have become commonplace. Various statutory solutions to the problem have been proposed, but these will not be adequate unless the Congress—and the states—are permitted to stop the escalation by setting limits. What is needed is a constitutional amendment to reverse the *Buckley* holding, as proposed by several members of Congress. This would not mean a weakening of the Bill of Rights, since the *Buckley* ruling was a distortion of the First Amendment. Within reasonable financial limits there is ample opportunity for that "uninhibited, robust and wide-open" debate of the issues that the Supreme Court correctly wants to protect.

Jonathan Bingham was a Democratic representative from New York from 1965 to 1983, when he retired. Before that, he served as one of Adlai Stevenson's deputies in the United States Mission to the United Nations and as secretary to the governor of the state of New York under Averell Harriman. He is a lawyer and is currently a lecturer in law at the Columbia Law School.

"THE First Amendment is not a vehicle for turning this country into a plutocracy," says Joseph L. Rauh, the distinguished civil rights lawyer, deploring the ruling in *Buckley* v. *Valeo*.[1] It is the thesis of this article that the Supreme Court in *Buckley* was wrong in nullifying certain congressional efforts to limit campaign spending and that the decision must not be allowed to stand. While statutory remedies may mitigate the evil of excessive money in politics and are worth pursuing, they will not stop the feverish escalation of campaign spending. They will also have no effect whatever on the spreading phenomenon of very wealthy people's spending millions of dollars of their own money to get elected to Congress and to state office.

When the Supreme Court held a national income tax unconstitutional, the Sixteenth Amendment reversed that decision. *Buckley* should be treated the same way.

BACKGROUND

The Federal Election Campaign Act of 1971 was the first comprehensive effort by the U.S. Congress to regulate the financing of federal election campaigns. In 1974, following the scandals of the Watergate era, the Congress greatly strengthened the 1971 act. As amended, the new law combined far-reaching requirements for disclosure with restrictions on the amount of contributions, expenditures from a candidate's personal funds, total campaign expenditures, and independent expenditures on behalf of identified candidates.

The report of the House Administration Committee recommending the 1974 legislation to the House explained the underlying philosophy:

The unchecked rise in campaign expenditures, coupled with the absence of limitations on contributions and expenditures, has increased the dependence of candidates on special interest groups and large contributors. Under the present law the impression persists that a candidate can buy an election by simply spending large sums in a campaign....

Such a system is not only unfair to candidates in general, but even more so to the electorate. The electorate is entitled to base its judgment on a straightforward presentation of a candidate's qualifications for public office and his programs for the Nation rather than on a sophisticated advertising program which is encouraged by the infusion of vast amounts of money.

The Committee on House Administration is of the opinion that there is a definite need for effective and comprehensive legislation in this area to restore and strengthen public confidence in the integrity of the political process.[2]

The 1974 act included a provision, added pursuant to an amendment offered by then Senator James Buckley, for expedited review of the law's constitutionality. In January 1976 the Supreme Court invalidated those portions that imposed limits on campaign spending as violative of the First Amendment's guarantee of free speech.

In his powerful dissent, Justice White said, "Without limits on total expenditures, campaign costs will inevitably and

---

1. Personal communication with Joseph L. Rauh, Mar. 1985; *Buckley* v. *Valeo*, 424 U.S. 1 (1976).

2. U.S., Congress, House, Committee on House Administration, *Federal Election Campaign Act, Amendments of 1974: Report to Accompany H. R. 16090*, 93rd Cong., 2d sess., 1974, H. Rept. 93-1239, pp. 3-4.

endlessly escalate."[3] His prediction was promptly borne out. Multimillion-dollar campaigns for the Senate have become the rule, with the 1984 Helms-Hunt race in North Carolina setting astonishing new records. It is no longer unusual for expenditures in contested House campaigns to go over the million-dollar mark; in 1982 one House candidate reportedly spent over $2 million of his own funds.

In 1982 a number of representatives came to the conclusion that the *Buckley* ruling should not be allowed to stand and that a constitutional amendment was imperative. In June Congressman Henry Reuss of Wisconsin introduced a resolution calling for an amendment to give Congress the authority to regulate campaign spending in federal elections. In December, with the cosponsorship of Mr. Reuss and 11 others,[4] I introduced a broader resolution authorizing the states, as well as the Congress, to impose limits on campaign spending. The text of the proposed amendment was:

Section 1. The Congress may enact laws regulating the amounts of contributions and expenditures intended to affect elections to federal office.

Section 2. The several states may enact laws regulating the amounts of contributions and expenditures intended to affect elections to state and local offices.[5]

3. 424 U.S., p. 264.
4. The other representatives were Mrs. Fenwick, Republican of New Jersey; Ms. Mikulski, Democrat of Maryland; and Messrs. Bevill, Democrat of Alabama; Donnelly, Democrat of Massachusetts; D'Amours, Democrat of New Hampshire; Edgar, Democrat of Pennsylvania; LaFalce, Democrat of New York; and Wolpe, Democrat of Michigan.
5. U.S., Congress, House, *Proposing an Amendment to the Constitution of the United States Relative to Contributions and Expenditures Intended to Affect Congressional, Presidential and State Elections,* 97th Cong., 2d sess., 1982, H. J. Res. 628, p. 2.
6. Ibid., 99th Cong., 1st sess., 1985, H. J. Res. 88.

In the Ninety-eighth Congress, the same resolution was reintroduced by Mr. Vento and Mr. Donnelly and by Mr. Brown, Democrat of California, and Mr. Rinaldo, Republican of New Jersey. A similar resolution was introduced in the Senate by Senator Stevens, Republican of Alaska. As of the present writing, the resolution has been reintroduced in the Ninety-ninth Congress by Mr. Vento.[6]

No hearings have been held on these proposals, and they have attracted little attention. Even organizations and commentators deeply concerned with the problem of money in politics and runaway campaign spending have focused exclusively on statutory remedies. Common Cause, in spite of my pleading, has declined to add a proposal for a constitutional amendment to its agenda for campaign reform or even to hear arguments in support of the proposal. A constituency for the idea has yet to be developed.

THE NATURE OF
THE PROBLEM

This article proceeds on the assumption that escalating campaign costs pose a serious threat to the quality of government in this country. There are those who argue the contrary, but their view of the nature of the problem is narrow. They focus on the facts that the amounts of money involved are not large relative to the gross national product and that the number of votes on Capitol Hill that can be shown to have been affected by campaign contributions is not overwhelming.

The curse of money in politics, however, is by no means limited to the influencing of votes. There are at least two other problems that are, if anything, even more serious. One is the eroding of the present nonsystem on the public's confidence in our form of democracy. If public office and votes on issues are perceived to be for sale, the harm is done, whether or not the facts justify that conclusion. In *Buckley* the Supreme Court itself, in sustaining the limitations on the size of political contributions, stressed the importance of avoiding "the appearance of improper influence" as " 'critical . . . if confidence in the system of representative government is not to be eroded to a disastrous extent.' "[7] What the Supreme Court failed to recognize was that "'confidence in the system of representative government' " could likewise be " 'eroded to a disastrous extent' " by the spectacle of lavish spending, whether the source of the funds is the candidate's own wealth or the result of high-pressure fund-raising from contributors with an ax to grind.

The other problem is that excellent people are discouraged from running for office, or, once in, are unwilling to continue wrestling with the unpleasant and degrading task of raising huge sums of money year after year. There is no doubt that every two years valuable members of Congress decide to retire because they are fed up with having constantly to beg. For example, former Congressmen Charles Vanik of Ohio and Richard Ottinger of New York, both outstanding legislators, were clearly influenced by such considerations when they decided to retire, Vanik in 1980 and Ottinger in 1984. Vanik said, among other things, "I feel every contribution carries some sort of lien which is an encumbrance on the legislative process . . . I'm terribly upset by the huge amounts that candidates have to raise."[8] Probably an even greater number of men and women who would make stellar legislators are discouraged from competing because they cannot face the prospect of constant fund-raising or because they see a wealthy person, who can pay for a lavish campaign, already in the race.

In "Politics and Money," Elizabeth Drew has well described the poisonous effect of escalating campaign costs on our political system:

Until the problem of money is dealt with, it is unrealistic to expect the political process to improve in any other respect. It is not relevant whether every candidate who spends more than his opponent wins—though in races that are otherwise close, this tends to be the case. What matters is what the chasing of money does to the candidates, and to the victors' subsequent behavior. The candidates' desperation for money and the interests' desire to affect public policy provide a mutual opportunity. The issue is not how much is spent on elections but the way the money is obtained. The point is what *raising* money, not simply spending it, does to the political process. It is not just that the legislative product is bent or stymied. It is not just that well-armed interests have a head start over the rest of the citizenry—or that often it is not even a contest. . . . It is not even relevant which interest happens to be winning. What is relevant is what the whole thing is doing to the democratic process. What is at stake is the idea of representative government, the soul of this country.[9]

---

7. 424 U.S., p. 27, quoting *CSC* v. *Letter Carriers,* 413 U.S. 548, 565 (1973); see also 424 U.S., p. 30.

8. Quoted by Congressman Henry Reuss, in U.S., Congress, House, *Congressional Record,* daily ed., 97th Cong., 2d sess., 1982, 128(81):H3900.

9. *New Yorker,* 6 Dec. 1982, pp. 55-56.

Focusing on the different phenomenon of wealthy candidates' being able to finance their own, often successful, campaigns, the late columnist Joseph Kraft commented that "affinity between personal riches and public office challenges a fundamental principle of American life."[10]

SHORTCOMINGS OF STATUTORY PROPOSALS

In spite of the wide agreement on the seriousness of the problems, there is no agreement on the solution. Many different proposals have been made by legislators, academicians, commentators, and public interest organizations, notably Common Cause.

One of the most frequently discussed is to follow for congressional elections the pattern adopted for presidential campaigns: a system of public funding, coupled with limits on spending.[11] Starting in 1955, bills along these lines have been introduced on Capitol Hill, but none has been adopted. Understandably, such proposals are not popular with incumbents, most of whom believe that challengers would gain more from public financing than they would.

Even assuming that the political obstacles could be overcome and that some sort of public financing for congressional candidates might be adopted, this financing would suffer from serious weaknesses. No system of public financing could solve the problem of the very wealthy candidate. Since such candidates do not need public funding, they would not subject themselves to the spending limits. The same difficulty would arise when aggressive candidates, believing they could raise more from private sources, rejected the government funds. This result is to be expected if the level of public funding is set too low, that is, at a level that the constant escalation of campaign costs is in the process of outrunning. According to Congressman Bruce Vento, an author of the proposed constitutional amendment to overturn *Buckley*, this has tended to happen in Minnesota, where very low levels of public funding are provided to candidates for state office.

To ameliorate these difficulties, some proponents of public financing suggest that the spending limits that a candidate who takes government funding must accept should be waived for that candidate to the extent an opponent reports expenses in excess of those limits. Unfortunately, in such a case one of the main purposes of public funding would be frustrated and the escalation of campaign spending would continue. The candidate who is not wealthy is left with the fearsome task of quickly having to raise additional hundreds of thousands, or even millions, of dollars.

Another suggested approach would be to require television stations, as a condition of their licenses, to provide free air time to congressional candidates in segments of not less than, for instance, five minutes. A candidate's acceptance of such time would commit the candidate to the acceptance of spending limits. While such a scheme would be impractical for primary contests—which in many areas are the crucial ones—the idea is attractive for

---

10. *Washington Post,* 2 Nov. 1982.

11. In the *Buckley* case the Supreme Court simply assumed that limits on spending were not a violation of free speech when acceptance of such limits was made the condition for receiving public funds. 424 U.S., pp. 85-110. See also Charles McC. Mathias, Jr., "Should There Be Public Financing of Congressional Campaigns?" this issue of *The Annals* of the American Academy of Political and Social Science.

general election campaigns in mixed urban-rural states and districts. It would be unworkable, however, in the big metropolitan areas, where the main stations reach into scores of congressional districts and, in some cases, into several states. Not only would broadcasters resist the idea, but the television-viewing public would be furious at being virtually compelled during pre-election weeks to watch a series of talking-head shows featuring all the area's campaigning senators and representatives and their challengers. The offer of such unpopular television time would hardly tempt serious candidates to accept limits on their spending.

Proponents of free television time, recognizing the limited usefulness of the idea in metropolitan areas, have suggested that candidates could be provided with free mailings instead. While mailings can be pinpointed and are an essential part of urban campaigning, they account for only a fraction of campaign costs, even where television is not widely used; accordingly, the prospect of free mailings would not be likely to win the acceptance of unwelcome campaign limits on total expenses.[12]

Yet another method of persuading candidates to accept spending limits would be to allow 100 percent tax credits for contributions of up to, say, $100 made to authorized campaigns, that is, those campaigns where the candidate has agreed to abide by certain regulations, including limits on total spending.[13] It is difficult to predict how effective such a system would be, and a pilot project to find out would not be feasible, since the tax laws cannot be changed for just one area. For candidates who raise most of their funds from contributors in the $50-to-$100 range, the incentive to accept spending limits would be strong, but for those—and they are many—who rely principally on contributors in the $500-to-$1000 range, the incentive would be much weaker. This problem could be partially solved by allowing tax credits for contributions of up to $100 and tax deductions for contributions in excess of $100 up to the permitted limit. Such proposals, of course, amount to a form of public financing and hence would encounter formidable political obstacles, especially at a time when budgetary restraint and tax simplification are considered of top priority.

Some of the most vocal critics of the present anarchy in campaign financing focus their wrath and legislative efforts on the political action committees (PACs) spawned in great numbers under the Federal Election Campaign Act of 1974. Although many PACs are truly serving the public interest, others have made it easier for special interests, especially professional and trade associations, to funnel funds into the campaign treasuries of legislators or challengers who will predictably vote for those interests. Restrictions, such as limiting the total amount legislative candidates could accept from PACs, would be salutary[14] but no legislation aimed primarily at the PAC phenomenon—not even legislation to eliminate PACs altogether—would

12. A variation of the idea of free television and/or mail, proposed by Common Cause and others, would provide for such privileges as a means of answering attacks made on candidates by allegedly independent organizations or individuals. See Fred Wertheimer, "Campaign Finance Reform: The Unfinished Agenda," this issue of *The Annals* of the American Academy of Political and Social Science.

13. See ibid.
14. The Obey-Railsback Act, which contained such restrictions, actually passed the House in 1979, but got no further. See ibid.

solve the problem so well summarized by Elizabeth Drew. The special interests and favor-seeking individual givers would find other ways of funneling their dollars into politically useful channels, and the harassed members of Congress would have to continue to demean themselves by constant begging.

PAC regulation and all the other forms of statutory regulation suffer from one fundamental weakness: none of them would affect the multimillion-dollar self-financed campaign. Yet it is this type of campaign that does more than any other to confirm the widely held view that high office in the United States can be bought.

Short of a constitutional amendment, there is only one kind of proposal, so far as I know, that would curb the super-rich candidate, as well as setting limits for others. Lloyd N. Cutler, counsel to the president in the Carter White House, has suggested that the political parties undertake the task of campaign finance regulation.[15] Theoretically, the parties could withhold endorsement from candidates who refuse to abide by the party-prescribed limits and other regulations. But the chances of this happening seem just about nil. Conceivably a national party convention might establish such regulations for its presidential primaries, but to date most contenders have accepted the limits imposed under the matching system of public funding; John Connally of Texas was the exception in 1980. For congressional races, however, it is not at all clear what body or bodies could make such rules and enforce them. Claimants to such authority would include the national conventions, national committees, congressional party caucuses, various state committees, and, in some cases, county committees. Perhaps our national parties should be more hierarchically structured, but the fact is that they are not.

On top of all this, the system would work for general election campaigns only if both major parties took parallel action. If by some miracle they did so, the end result might be to encourage third-party and independent candidacies.

Let me make clear that I am not opposed to any of the proposals briefly summarized earlier. To the extent I had the opportunity to vote for any of the statutory proposals during my years in the House, I did so. Nor am I arguing that a constitutional amendment by itself would solve the problem; it would only be the beginning of a very difficult task. What I am saying is that, short of effective action by the parties, any system to reverse the present lethal trends in campaign financing must have as a basic element the restoration to the Congress of the authority to regulate the process.

THE MERITS OF THE *BUCKLEY* RULING

The justices of the Supreme Court were all over the lot in the *Buckley* case, with numerous dissents from the majority opinion. The most significant dissent, in my view, was entered by Justice White, who, alone among the justices, had had extensive experience in federal campaigns. White's position was that the Congress, and not the Court, was the proper body to decide whether the slight interference with First Amendment freedoms in the Federal Election Campaign Act was warranted. Justice White reasoned as follows:

15. See Lloyd N. Cutler, "Can the Parties Regulate Campaign Financing?" this issue of *The Annals* of the American Academy of Political and Social Science.

The judgment of Congress was that reasonably effective campaigns could be conducted within the limits established by the Act. . . . In this posture of the case, there is no sound basis for invalidating the expenditure limitations, so long as the purposes they serve are legitimate and sufficiently substantial, which in my view they are. . . .

. . . expenditure ceilings reinforce the contribution limits and help eradicate the hazard of corruption. . . .

Besides backing up the contribution provisions, . . . expenditure limits have their own potential for preventing the corruption of federal elections themselves.[16]

Justice White further concluded that

limiting the total that can be spent will ease the candidate's understandable obsession with fundraising, and so free him and his staff to communicate in more places and ways unconnected with the fundraising function.

It is also important to restore and maintain public confidence in federal elections. It is critical to obviate and dispel the impression that federal elections are purely and simply a function of money, that federal offices are bought and sold or that political races are reserved for those who have the facility—and the stomach—for doing whatever it takes to bring together those interests, groups, and individuals that can raise or contribute large fortunes in order to prevail at the polls.[17]

Two of the judges of the District of Columbia Circuit Court, which upheld the 1974 act—judges widely respected, especially for their human rights concerns—later wrote law journal articles criticizing in stinging terms the Supreme Court's holding that the spending limits were invalid. For example, the late Judge Harold Leventhal said in the *Columbia Law Review*:

16. 424 U.S., pp. 263-64.
17. Ibid., p. 265.

The central question is: what is the interest underlying regulation of campaign expenses and is it substantial? The critical interest, in my view, is the same as that accepted by the [Supreme] Court in upholding limits on contributions. It is the need to maintain confidence in self-government, and to prevent the erosion of democracy which comes from a popular view of government as responsive only or mainly to special interests.[18]

A court that is concerned with public alienation and distrust of the political process cannot fairly deny to the people the power to tell the legislators to implement this one-word principle: Enough![19]

Here are excerpts from what Judge J. Skelly Wright had to say in the *Yale Law Journal*:

The Court told us, in effect, that money is speech.

. . . [This view] accepts without question elaborate mass media campaigns that have made political communication expensive, but at the same time remote, disembodied, occasionally . . . manipulative. Nothing in the First Amendment . . . commits us to the dogma that money is speech.[20]

. . . far from stifling First Amendment values, [the 1974 act] actually promotes them. . . . In place of unlimited spending, the law encourages all to emphasize less expensive face-to-face communications efforts, exactly the kind of activities that promote real dialogue on the merits and leave much less room for manipulation and avoidance of the issues.[21]

The Supreme Court was apparently blind to these considerations. Its treatment was almost entirely doctrinaire. In

18. Leventhal, "Courts and Political Thickets," *Columbia Law Review*, 77:362 (1977).
19. Ibid., p. 368.
20. Wright, "Politics and the Constitution: Is Money Speech?" *Yale Law Journal*, 85:1005 (1979).
21. Ibid., p. 1019.

holding unconstitutional the limits set by Congress on total expenditures for congressional campaigns and on spending by individual candidates, the Court did not claim that the dollar limits set were unreasonably low. In the view taken by the Court, such limits were beyond the power of the Congress to set, no matter how high.

Only in the case of the $1000 limit set for spending by independent individuals or groups "relative to a clearly identified candidate" did the Court focus on the level set in the law. The Court said that such a limit "would appear to exclude all citizens and groups except candidates, political parties and the institutional press from any significant use of the most effective modes of communication."[22] In a footnote, the Court noted:

The record indicates that, as of January 1, 1975, one full-page advertisement in a daily edition of a certain metropolitan newspaper cost $6,971.04—almost seven times the annual limit on expenditures "relative to" a particular candidate imposed on the vast majority of individual citizens and associations.[23]

The Court devoted far more space to arguing the unconstitutionality of this provision than to any of the other limits, presumably because on this point it had the strongest case. Judge Leventhal, too, thought the $1000 figure for independent spending was unduly restrictive and might properly have been struck down. As one who supported the 1974 act while in the House, I believe, with the benefit of hindsight, that the imposition of this low limit on independent expenditures was a grave mistake.

Let us look for a moment at the question of whether reasonable limits on total spending in campaigns and on spending by wealthy candidates really do interfere with the "unfettered interchange of ideas," "the free discussion of governmental affairs," and the "uninhibited, robust and wide-open" debate on public issues that the Supreme Court has rightly said the First Amendment is designed to protect.[24] In *Buckley* the Supreme Court has answered that question in the affirmative when the limits are imposed by law under Congress's conceded power to regulate federal elections. The Court answered the same question negatively, however, when the limits were imposed as a condition of public financing. In narrow legalistic terms the distinction is perhaps justified, but, in terms of what is desirable or undesirable under our form of government, I submit that the setting of such limits is either desirable or it is not.

Various of the solutions proposed to deal with the campaign-financing problem, statutory and nonstatutory, raise the same question—for example, the proposal to allow tax credits only for contributions to candidates who have accepted spending limits, and the proposal that political parties should impose limits. All such proposals assume that it is good public policy to have such limits in place. They simply seek to avoid the inhibition of the *Buckley* case by arranging for some carrot-type motivation for the observance of limits, instead of the stick-type motivation of compliance with a law.

I am not, of course, suggesting that those who make these proposals are wrong to do so. What I am suggesting is that they should support the idea of

---

22. 424 U.S., pp. 20-21.
23. Ibid., p. 21.
24. *Roth* v. *United States*, 354 U.S. 476, 484 (1957); *Mills* v. *Alabama*, 384 U.S. 214, 218 (1966); *New York Times* v. *Sullivan*, 376 U.S. 254, 270 (1964).

undoing the damage done by *Buckley* by way of a constitutional amendment.

Summing up the reason for such an amendment, Congressman Henry Reuss said, "Freedom of speech is a precious thing. But protecting it does not permit someone to shout 'fire' in a crowded theater. Equally, freedom of speech must not be stressed so as to compel democracy to commit suicide by allowing money to govern elections."[25]

INDEPENDENT EXPENDITURES IN PRESIDENTIAL CAMPAIGNS

Until now the system of public financing for presidential campaigns, coupled with limits on private financing, has worked reasonably well. Accordingly, most of the proposals mentioned previously for the amelioration of the campaign-financing problem have been concerned with campaigns for the Senate and the House.

In 1980 and 1984, however, a veritable explosion occurred in the spending for the presidential candidates by allegedly independent committees—spending that is said not to be authorized by, or coordinated with, the campaign committees. In both years, the Republican candidates benefited far more from this type of spending than the Democratic: in 1980, the respective amounts were $12.2 million and $45,000; in 1984, $15.3 million and $621,000.[26]

This spending violated section 9012(f) of the Presidential Campaign Fund Act, which prohibited independent committees from spending more than $1000 to further a presidential candidate's election if that candidate had elected to take public financing under the terms of the act. In 1983 various Democratic Party entities and the Federal Election Commission, with Common Cause as a supporting amicus curiae, sued to have section 9012(f) declared constitutional, so as to lay the groundwork for enforcement of the act. These efforts failed. Applying the *Buckley* precedent, the three-judge district court that first heard the case denied the relief sought, and this ruling was affirmed in a 7-to-2 decision by the Supreme Court in *FEC v. NCPAC* in March 1985.[27]

The *NCPAC* decision clearly strengthens the case for a constitutional amendment to permit Congress to regulate campaign spending. For none of the statutory or party-action remedies summarized earlier would touch this new eruption of the money-in-politics volcano.

True, even with a constitutional amendment in place, it would still be possible for the National Conservative Political Action Committee or other committees to spend unlimited amounts for media programs on one side of an issue or another, and these would undoubtedly have some impact on presidential—and other—campaigns. However, the straight-out campaigning for an individual or a ticket, which tends to be far more effective than focusing on issues alone, could be brought within reasonable limits.

LOOKING AHEAD

The obstacles in the way of achieving a reversal of *Buckley* by constitutional amendment are, of course, formidable. This is especially true today when the House Judiciary Committee is resolutely

---

25. U.S., Congress, House, *Congressional Record*, 97th Cong., 2d sess., daily ed., 128(81): H3901.

26. *New York Times*, 19 Mar. 1985.

27. *FEC v. NCPAC*, 105 S.Ct. 1459 (1985).

sitting on other amendments affecting the Bill of Rights and is not disposed to report out any such amendments.

In addition to the practical political hurdles to be overcome, there are drafting problems to solve. The simple form so far proposed[28]—and quoted previously—needs refinement.

For example, if an amendment were adopted simply giving to the Congress and the states the authority to "enact laws regulating the amount of contributions and expenditures intended to affect elections,"[29] the First Amendment question would not necessarily be answered. The argument could still be made, and not without reason, that such regulatory laws, like other powers of the Congress and the states, must not offend the First Amendment. I asked an expert in constitutional law how this problem might be dealt with, and he said the only sure way would be to add the words "notwithstanding the First Amendment." But such an addition is not a viable solution. The political obstacles in the way of an amendment overturning *Buckley* in its interpretation of the First Amendment with respect to campaign spending are grievous enough; to ask the Congress —and the state legislatures—to create a major exception to the First Amendment would assure defeat.

The answer has to be to find a form of wording that says, in effect, that the First Amendment can properly be interpreted so as to permit reasonable regulation of campaign spending. In my view, it would be sufficient to insert in the proposed amendment,[30] after "The Congress," the words "having due regard for the need to facilitate full and free discussion and debate." Section 1 of the amendment would then read, "The Congress, having due regard for the need to facilitate full and free discussion and debate, may enact laws regulating the amounts of contributions and expenditures intended to affect elections to federal office." Other ways of dealing with this problem could no doubt be devised.

Another drafting difficulty arises from the modification in the proposed amendment of the words "contributions and expenditures" by "intended to affect elections." This language is appropriate with respect to money raised or spent by candidates and their committees, but it does present a problem in its application to money raised and spent by allegedly independent committees, groups, or individuals. It could hardly be argued that communications referring solely to issues, with no mention of candidates, could, consistent with the First Amendment, be made subject to spending limits, even if they were quite obviously "intended to affect" an election. Accordingly, a proper amendment should include language limiting the regulation of "independent" expenditures to those relative to "clearly identified" candidates, language that would parallel the provisions of the 1971 Federal Election Campaign Act, as amended.[31]

These are essentially technical problems that could be solved with the assistance of experts in constitutional law if the Judiciary Committee of either house should decide to hold hearings on the idea of a constitutional amendment and proceed to draft and report out an appropriate resolution.

Many of those in and out of Congress who are genuinely concerned with politi-

---

28. U.S., Congress, House, *Contributions and Expenditures*, H.J. Res. 628.
29. Ibid.
30. Ibid.
31. 2 U.S.C.A. § 431(17).

cal money brush aside the notion of a constitutional amendment and focus entirely on remedies that seem less drastic. They appear to assume that Congress is more likely to adopt a statutory remedy, such as public financing, than to go for an enabling constitutional amendment that could be tagged as tampering with the Bill of Rights. I disagree with that assumption.

Incumbents generally resist proposals such as public financing because challengers might be the major beneficiaries, but most incumbents tend to favor the idea of spending limits. The Congress is not by its nature averse to being given greater authority; that would be especially true in this case, where until 1976 the Congress always thought it had such authority. I venture to say that if a carefully drawn constitutional amendment were reported out of one of the Judiciary Committees, it might secure the necessary two-thirds majorities in both houses with surprising ease.

The various state legislatures might well react in similar fashion. A power they thought they had would be restored to them.

The big difficulty is to get the process started, whether it be for a constitutional amendment or a statutory remedy or both. Here, the villain, I am afraid, is public apathy. Unfortunately, the voters seem to take excessive campaign spending as a given—a phenomenon they can do nothing about—and there is no substantial constituency for reform. The House Administration Committee, which in the early 1970s was the spark plug for legislation, has recently shown little interest in pressing for any of the legislative proposals that have been put forward.

The 1974 act itself emerged as a reaction to the scandals of the Watergate era, and it may well be that major action, whether statutory or constitutional, will not be a practical possibility until a new set of scandals bursts into the open. Meanwhile, the situation will only get worse.

Can the Parties Regulate Campaign Financing?

By LLOYD N. CUTLER

ABSTRACT: Most campaign finance reform proposals focus on legislative or regulatory cures. Serious thought should be given instead to encouraging the parties to assume control of their candidates' campaign finance practices. Based on the logic of court decisions giving the parties the right to promulgate criteria for voting in their primaries, the parties would appear also to have legal power to impose campaign finance rules, including expenditures ceilings, on candidates who seek to run under the party's banner. A model set of party campaign finance rules is sketched in the article.

Lloyd N. Cutler practices law in Washington. He was counsel for the League of Women Voters in Buckley v. Valeo, *supporting the constitutionality of the statute. He served as counsel to the president in 1979-80. He is a cochairman of the Committee on the Constitutional System, which is preparing a bicentenary analysis of the structure of the American political system and recommendations for improvement. He holds A.B., LL.B, and honorary Ll.D degrees from Yale University. He is a member of the Council of the American Law Institute and a trustee of the Brookings Institution.*

THOSE who favor the regulation of campaign finance propose a variety of governmental cures for the ills they perceive. Some suggest useful legislative or regulatory changes, as Senator Mathias, Congressman Bolling, and Messrs. Barone, Berman, Oldaker, and Wertheimer thoughtfully do in this volume. Others, like Congressman Jonathan Bingham, suggest the additional and more radical step of a constitutional amendment to expand the congressional power to regulate.

Few people, however, have given serious thought to the possibility that the parties themselves, rather than the government, can and should do more to control the campaign-financing practices of their candidates. This article sketches out the legal bases for party control of campaign finance and a set of model rules that would accomplish the job.

In both parties, there are constituencies that favor campaign reforms that would curtail excessive spending and blunt the pressures of interest groups. Within the Democratic Party at least, there appears to be a strong consensus against the excessive cost of campaigning for federal office and against the pressures that single-interest groups can exert because candidates need and seek their contributions. The national Democratic Party platform has regularly endorsed stronger laws and regulations to control campaign financing.[1] In 1984 the candidates for the Democratic presidential nomination vied with one another in proclaiming greater disdain than their rivals for the tainted money of special interest political action committees.

A similar consensus does not appear on the Republican side, but Republican leaders are increasingly speaking out against campaign financing abuses. For example, Senate majority leader Dole has complained that "when these political action committees give money they expect something in return other than good government. It is making it much more difficult to legislate."[2] Senator Goldwater has observed that "unlimited campaign spending eats at the heart of the democratic process."[3] Senator Mathias has long been an advocate of campaign finance reform. Three Republican senators cosponsored the so-called Boren bill in the last session of Congress.

Notwithstanding this sentiment in both parties, it does not seem to have occurred to party officials or candidates that the party itself can control the campaign-financing methods of its candidates. In the general election campaign, of course, such controls could not be exercised by one party alone, because unilateral regulation would give the uncontrolled candidates of rival parties an unfair financial advantage. Rival parties could only afford to control the

1. "Recent reforms in the election process have aided immeasurably in opening the process to more people and have begun to reduce the influence of special interests. The limitations on campaign contributions and the public financing of presidential elections are two reforms which have worked very well. Business political action committees continue to spend excessively, however. Further reform in this area is essential." "The 1980 Democratic National Platform" (Democratic National Committee, 1980), p. 14. "We must work to end political action committee funding of federal political campaigns. To achieve that, we must enact a system of public financing of federal campaigns." "The 1984 Democratic National Platform" (Democratic National Committee, 1984), p. 41.

2. Albert Hunt, "Cash Politics," *Wall Street Journal*, 26 July 1982.

3. U.S., Congress, Senate, Committee on Rules and Administration, *Hearings on Campaign Finance Reform Proposals of 1983*, 98th Cong., 1st sess., 1983, p. 400.

campaign-financing practices of their nominees if this were done by mutual agreement. In primary and caucus campaigns for a party's own nominations, however, no such problem would arise.

The legal power of a party to control the financing tactics of those who seek the right to run under the party's standard can hardly be in doubt. In *Democratic Party of the United States* v. *Wisconsin ex rel. La Follette*,[4] the Supreme Court upheld the national Democratic Party's right to restrict eligibility for seating as delegates in its national presidential nominating convention to those who are chosen through procedures in which only publicly declared Democrats can participate. The Court invalidated a Wisconsin requirement that convention delegates be bound to vote for presidential candidates according to the results of Wisconsin's open presidential preference primary in which crossing over by non-Democrats was frequent. The Court held that Wisconsin's state interest in the conduct of its primary did not outweigh the party's stronger right of free association under the First Amendment.

In *Republican Party of the State of Connecticut* v. *Tashjian*,[5] the United States Court of Appeals for the Second Circuit extended this principle to Republican primaries for federal offices such as senator and member of the House. Significantly, the Connecticut law the Court struck down was the opposite of the Wisconsin law; Connecticut required closed primaries instead of open ones. Connecticut's Democratic-majority legislature had limited primary voting for all parties to declared members of the party. This law conflicted with the state Republican Party's rule that its primary be open to all voters. In the second circuit's view, a state's preference for open or closed primaries did not outweigh the party's First Amendment right to make the opposite choice. On this basis, the Court invalidated the Connecticut statute. The case is now on appeal to the Supreme Court.

On the reasoning of these cases, a political party's First Amendment right of free association ought to include the right to require the candidates for the party's nominations to abide by the party's rules on campaign financing, even if the party rules are more stringent than the laws and regulations of the state or federal government. Of course, party rules would have to meet the constitutional standards of due process, equal protection, antidiscrimination, and free speech.[6] But *Buckley* v. *Valeo*[7] allows wider constitutional scope for financing controls that are imposed as conditions to the grant of a privilege, such as nomination as the party's candidate, than for controls that are imposed unconditionally on all. For example, while *Buckley* forbade unconditional expenditure limits as violating the First Amendment, it permitted reasonable and nondiscriminatory expenditure limits on all presidential candidates who accepted federal campaign funds under the statutory condition that such limits be observed. A party should therefore be able to impose similar limits on anyone who seeks the privilege of running for election as the party's nominee.

In the world of practical politics, even the most enlightened incumbent legis-

---

4. 450 U.S. 107 (1981).
5. 770 F.2d 265 (CA 2, 1985).

6. See *Smith* v. *Allwright,* 321 U.S. 649 (1944).
7. 424 U.S. 1 (1976).

lators have been reluctant to enact laws that cut back an incumbent's natural fund-raising advantage over his or her challengers. That is why it has never been feasible to pass a law for the public financing of congressional campaigns. But incumbent legislators are no longer powerful panjandrums within their own party structures. They might not be able to block the adoption of party rules to control campaign financing that appealed to party officials and to the party convention rank and file. For this reason, it may be useful to speculate on the controls that parties might impose on how campaigns for the party's nominations may be financed.

The party could impose limits on the size of individual contributions and set maximum levels for both contributions and expenditures. It could limit the amounts an individual and his or her family could expend from their own funds. It could bar contributions from particular sources such as single-interest political action committees. It could bar certain types of expenditures, such as those for canned television commercials. It could set up accounting and disclosure procedures and review panels that could decide charges of violation in time to be relevant to the ongoing campaign. As a further control, it could even require that all contributions be made directly to the party treasurer for the benefit of a designated candidate. Within the limits of what can or should be regulated—and these limits are quite severe—there are any number of variations that may be worthy of experiment.

MODEL RULES

Purely for purposes of illustration, a model set of national party campaign financing rules might look as follows:

§ 101 Terms used in §§ 101-7 shall have the meanings set forth in 2 U.S.C. § 431 [the present federal statute], unless otherwise defined.

§ 102 Each candidate for the party's nomination for election to federal office shall file with the Committee all reports of contributions received and expenditures made that are filed with the Federal Election Commission.

§ 103 No candidate for the party's nominations shall make expenditures in excess of:

(A) $————, in the case of a candidate for nomination for election to the office of president;

(B) the greater of $————, or ————¢ multiplied by the voting-age population of the state, in the case of any campaign for nomination for election to the Senate, or to the office of representative from a state entitled to only one representative;

(C) $————, in the case of any campaign for nomination for election to the House of Representatives, delegate from the District of Columbia, or resident commissioner; or

(D) $————, in the case of any campaign for nomination for election to the office of national convention delegate from Guam or the Virgin Islands.

§ 104 (A) No candidate may make expenditures from personal funds, or from the personal funds of his or her immediate family, in connection with his or her campaigns during any calendar year for nomination for election to federal office in excess of, in the aggregate:

(1) $————, in the case of a candidate for the office of president or vice-president;

(2) $————, in the case of a candidate for the office of senator, or

for the office of representative from a state that is entitled to only one representative;

(3) $———, in the case of a candidate for the office of representative, delegate, or resident commissioner, in any other state.

For purposes of this paragraph, any expenditure made in a year other than the calendar year in which the election is held with respect to which such expenditure was made is considered to be made during the calendar year in which such election is held.

(B) No candidate or his or her immediate family may make loans or advances from personal funds in connection with a campaign for nomination for election to federal office unless such loan or advance is evidenced by a written instrument fully disclosing the terms and conditions of such loan or advance.

(C) For purposes of this subsection, any such loan or advance shall be included in computing the total amount of such expenditures only to the extent of the balance of such loan or advance outstanding and unpaid.

§ 105 No candidate may receive contributions from any person, committee, or other affiliated group aggregating more than $——— in any calendar year with respect to nomination for election to federal office.

§ 106 At the beginning of each calendar year, the Committee shall adjust the amounts specified in §——— of this section in the manner specified in 18 U.S.C. § 608(d), indexing to the consumer price index.

§ 107 No candidate may expend funds for the preparation or broadcast of any canned political commercials, herein defined to be any tape prepared before broadcast other than a tape consisting entirely of a live appearance by the candidate or by an identified supporter speaking on the candidate's behalf.

§ 108 Any contribution to a candidate for the nomination of the party for election to federal office shall be made to the treasurer of the party for the account of that candidate. The treasurer shall establish rules permitting candidates to make expenditures from funds held in their accounts, provided that such expenditures are permitted under §§ 101-8 of these rules.

§ 109 (A) There is hereby created the [party's name] Party Campaign Finance Committee ("the Committee"), which shall consist of five members appointed by the ———, with the approval of the ———. The National Committee of the party shall allocate sufficient financial resources and staff to permit the Committee to fulfill its responsibilities under §§ 101-7.

(B) The Committee shall establish rules of procedure for the filing of complaints of alleged violations of these rules, the answers to complaints, the investigation of complaints, and such other matters as it deems desirable.

(C) The Committee shall establish rules setting forth sanctions for violations of §§ 101-8, including the imposition of restrictions on expenditures by a candidate of funds held for his or her account by the treasurer of the party.

(D) The Committee shall, upon the complaint of any candidate, or upon its own motion, investigate any alleged violations of the foregoing rules. If substantial basis exists for believing a violation has occurred, the Committee shall request and receive written testimony and may hear oral testimony. If the Committee determines that a candidate has violated §§ 101-7, it shall impose sanctions as prescribed in the rules of the Committee.

As these model party rules make clear, any regulation of campaign financing is necessarily complex, and this very complexity can be self-defeating. These model rules, however, are simpler than existing laws and regulations by several orders of magnitude. Amendment would be much easier, and administration would be faster and more flexible. For nomination races, party controls could be put into force more rapidly than additional statutes or a constitutional amendment. If party controls were put in place, top-flight people who now decline to run because they cannot afford to, or because they dislike the pressures of frantic fund-raising, might be persuaded to try for the nomination.

After a few years of trial and experimentation by one major party, its example might improve the party's public image and the quality of its nominees to the point where the other party would be impelled to adopt comparable rules. If this happened, one could envision the day when both parties agreed to apply the same rules not only to the nominating campaigns, but to the final election campaigns as well.

Is all this what Zechariah Chafee once called an iridescent dream?[8] If so, the reasons must be that politicians care less than they profess about controlling campaign-financing abuses, and that the public is too indifferent to respond favorably to the first party willing to make the effort.

8. Zechariah Chafee, *Government and Mass Communications* (Hamden, CT: Archon Books, 1965), p. 709.

Living with the FECA: Confessions of a Sometime Campaign Treasurer

By MICHAEL S. BERMAN

ABSTRACT: Presidential campaigns now require the use of substantial legal and accounting resources principally to assure compliance with the Federal Election Campaign Act. The act was designed to reassure the American public that the federal election process was not irreparably corrupted, and, in presidential campaigns, to provide a more level playing field in the accumulation and use of funds. It may be now that the act has become a burden on the process. Contribution limits, certain matching-fund rules, and state expenditure limits in early primary and caucus states have caused candidates to find creative ways to avoid their impact. The rules governing expenditure of funds on grass-roots activity, the heart of American politics, have become far too complicated. All of this means that a person must think twice before taking on the responsibility of being the treasurer of a presidential campaign.

Michael S. Berman is a partner in the law firm of Kirkpatrick & Lockhart, Washington, D.C. He earned his law degree at the University of Minnesota. He served as counsel and deputy chief of staff to vice-president Walter F. Mondale and previously had served as Senator Mondale's administrative assistant and as a Minnesota special assistant attorney general. He was the treasurer of Mondale's presidential campaign and also served as the campaign's national coordinator during the general election.

IT is the height of the campaign season, during the primaries. A suite of offices is appointed with inexpensive metal furniture. Campaign posters, pictures, and charts adorn the whitewashed walls. The office hums days, evenings, and weekends. More than 50 people work there as full-time, salaried staff. Another 150 volunteers provide part-time help. The group has a budget of $3.8 million.

By the looks of it, the office might belong to a Senate campaign in a good-sized state, but it does not. In fact, it is the accounting, legal, and budget office of the 1984 Mondale for President Committee, Inc., later—during the general election—called the Mondale-Ferraro Committee.

During the 1984 presidential primaries, Mondale's accounting staff alone eventually totaled 18. This staff grew to 38 in the general election, including 11 people committed to budget control. During Mondale's two-year campaign, this accounting team filed 39 reports, totaling 17,115 pages, with the Federal Election Commission (FEC). The Mondale campaign had a 4-person legal staff during the primaries, which grew to 13 in the general election. Two lawyers and the controller have remained on the staff into 1986. The legal staff rendered thousands of hours of advice. Most of this massive effort was directed at compliance with the Federal Election Campaign Act of 1971, as amended (FECA), and the FEC's voluminous, complex, and sometimes intrusive regulations that purport to implement that law.

When the FECA was proposed and enacted in 1971, primarily as a disclosure statute, I was enthusiastic. As a Senate staff member, I worked for the FECA's passage in 1971. When contribution and expenditure limits were added in 1974, I was confident we were going in the right direction. I believed the FECA was a necessary and appropriate response to the rampant excesses of the campaign finance system.

For the decade since, I have had extensive hands-on experience with the FECA. In 1972, as manager of a Senate campaign, my responsibilities included raising and spending money and ensuring compliance with the new law. Through the intervening years, as a lawyer and political advisor, I have observed several campaign and committee treasurers, accountants, lawyers, staff, candidates, and public officials trying to work within the FECA. Most recently, I served as treasurer of the Mondale presidential campaign. I have lived with and experienced federal election law in a real and continuing way.

And now, I confess, I am not as sure as I once was that the FECA, as enforced by the FEC, is a workable solution to the admitted problems endemic to campaign finance. I have come to understand why so many who live with the FECA grow weary of the law and frustrated by the often unnecessary burdens it places on the political process. I sometimes wonder whether we have gone too far in pursuit of goals still worth attaining.

The problems with the FECA go beyond the massive and costly staff effort that is required to document compliance and hack through the bureaucratic undergrowth. A law that was designed to reassure the American people that the election process was not irreparably corrupted is now often used by candidates, political parties, and others as a campaign weapon—a device to embarrass a candidate. In these bloody contests between accountants and lawyers for candidates and the

FEC—in which the FEC serves as an often inadequate referee—the FECA's noble goal of purifying the election process becomes lost.[1]

The FECA has produced other untoward consequences. Far from cleansing the election process, it has spawned what I will call creative efforts to comply with—really to evade—its limits. In addition, it has led to rules that are not only sometimes silly and burdensome, but that also inhibit healthy campaign activities.

CONTRIBUTION DISCLOSURE THRESHOLD

The FECA requires disclosure of all contributions over $200.[2] No one seriously quarrels with the idea of disclosure, but I am persuaded that the $200 disclosure threshold is lower than is necessary or useful in presidential campaigns. Those reams of paper that we in the Mondale campaign filed with the FEC would have been substantially reduced had disclosure been pegged at $500 or more. I estimate that the paperwork would have been reduced by about 75 percent.

What does the public get for this work and expense? Very little, I would venture. Few contributions in the $200-$500 range are noteworthy. The statute assumes that contributions below $1000 are unlikely to corrupt a candidate—a conservative assumption in my view. In fact, a good argument can be made that disclosing the smaller amounts makes more difficult the task of gleaning truly useful information from the mountains of paper or untold feet of microfilm at the FEC.

CONTRIBUTION AND EXPENDITURE LIMITS

The FECA limits the amounts and sources of money a candidate may accept. Individual contributions may not exceed $1000 per election;[3] contributions from political action committees (PACs) may not exceed $5000[4]; corporations and labor unions may not contribute at all.[5] In addition, the FECA imposes limits on the amounts presidential candidates who have opted for public financing may spend in the primary and general elections.[6] These restrictions, as intended, effectively limit the amount candidates can raise and spend.

The ability of a candidate to raise funds to support his or her candidacy is one of the crucial tests of the candidacy's viability, but the burden of raising the necessary funds under the current contribution limits has become too great. It is no longer a test of viability; it has become a test of stamina.

The contribution limit of $1000 per person per election was probably too low for presidential races when it was

---

1. On the whole, I think the FEC and its staff have done as good a job as can be expected under the circumstances. They must interpret and enforce a law that is in many ways badly drafted and that contains pointless restrictions. How well can a commission function when Congress has designed it to be weak and declines to give it the resources it should have to do its job quickly and well? See William C. Oldaker, "Of Philosophers, Foxes, and Finances: Can the Federal Election Commission Ever Do an Adequate Job?" this issue of *The Annals* of the American Academy of Political and Social Science.

2. 2 U.S.C. § 434(b)(3)(A); 11 C.F.R. § 104. 3(a)(4)(i).

3. 2 U.S.C. § 441a(a)(1)(A); 11 C.F.R. § 110.1(a)(1).

4. 2 U.S.C. § 441a(a)(2)(A); 11 C.F.R. § 110.2(a)(1).

5. 2 U.S.C. § 441b; 11 C.F.R. part 114.

6. 2 U.S.C. § 441a(b); 11 C.F.R. § 110.8.

enacted some 10 years ago. It is an anachronism today. The $1000 of 1974 was worth $488 in 1984; and while expenditure limits in presidential races have doubled since 1974, the amount that can be donated by an individual has remained the same.

An argument for setting the limit at $1000 was that greater amounts could be corrupting. But can there really be a serious argument that a $2000, $3000, even $5000 contribution from an individual would be corrupting in a presidential campaign that spends $25 million or $30 million? Based on my experience, I very much doubt it. Accordingly, I believe Congress should amend the FECA to raise the contribution limit to $2500 for individuals in presidential campaigns with automatic increases on the same basis as the expenditure limits.

Because of the current $1000 limit, the matching-fund rules and, to a lesser extent, some of the expenditure limits, potential candidates for president increasingly are using vehicles other than regular campaign committees to finance certain activities in the early stages of their consideration of a presidential race. First, it was independent, multicandidate PACs with the putative candidates as chair or principal spokesperson and/or fund-raiser. Now, some potential future candidates have organized think tanks—tax exempt, contribution-deductible foundations.

Why have many potential candidates turned to these creative devices? In all likelihood, these candidates understand that as the costs of running a modern campaign for president escalate, limits on the size of contributions and on the amount they can spend on the formal campaign can become a significant restraint. Logically, they begin to look for legal means to hold off the impact of these limits as long as possible.

A multicandidate PAC can accept contributions of up to $5000 per year from individuals. It provides an opportunity for the potential candidate to travel the country, meeting new contributors as part of the PAC's fund-raising program, and to provide support to various other candidates who may in the future return the favor.

The foundations have a variety of other attractions. For example, contributions to such a foundation are tax deductible to the donors; there are no contribution limits; and corporations and labor organizations can contribute, which is not possible with organizations like PACs. Although the foundation cannot provide direct or indirect assistance to candidates, the foundation approach permits the potential candidate to travel around the country in an effort to educate the public about issues of importance. I ask, Is this different from campaigning?

Again, I raise the question, Does the FECA serve its goals and does the public interest benefit when unrealistically low contribution and expenditure limits cause candidates to wear themselves out with fund-raising and find new vehicles to attract and spend money beyond these limits? Is anybody fooled by these foundations? Is respect for the law and confidence in the integrity of campaigns enhanced or subverted?

PRESIDENTIAL PRIMARY
MATCHING FUNDS

Under the Presidential Primary Matching Payment Account Act, a candidate campaigning for his or her party's nomination for presidential candidate can opt to receive public financing in the form of grants that match funds that the candidate has raised privately.[7] In order to qualify for matching funds, the candidate must first raise $5000 in each of at least 20 states but only the first $250 of each contribution is considered in determining whether the candidate has reached the qualifying threshold.[8] Once the candidate qualifies, the public fund matches private contributions he or she received up to the first $250 of contributions received from any individual.[9] Without the matching funds, most candidates would find it impossible to finance a primary campaign at an adequate level within the existing contribution limits. Thus, the availability of matching funds operates to some extent as an equalizer among candidates.

The amount of each individual's contribution that can be matched with federal funds, $250, has not increased since matching funds first became available in the 1976 campaign. Since then, the total amount of matching funds that a presidential primary campaign can receive—one-half the primary expenditure limit—has doubled just as the expenditure limits have doubled. But, like the individual contribution limits, the $250 match cap, I believe, should be increased. I suggest indexing it in the same manner as the campaign expenditure limits.

The combination of an ever increasing primary campaign expenditure limit with a static $250 matching cap means that, in each successive election, primary candidates will have to devote increasing amounts of their severely taxed time and energy to fund-raising. That result is, I suggest, antithetical to one of the purposes of public financing—to allow candidates to devote more time to the issues and less to fund-raising. Indexing the $250 match cap would neither materially derogate from the Presidential Primary Matching Payment Account Act's goal of emphasizing smaller contributions from more citizens nor irresponsibly increase the drain on the ample tax checkoff fund. In short, it would be money well spent.

Another reform is needed in this area. Currently, contributions cannot be matched unless they are made and received after 1 January of the year before the actual election year and before 31 December of the election year.[10] The period during which contributions received can be matched should be extended at both ends of the allowable period.

Presidential candidates should not be constrained by the campaign finance laws from beginning their campaigns early if they so choose. If a candidate decides that his or her campaign should begin in earnest two or three years before the general election year and is willing to register a committee at that time, why should the campaign finance law make the candidacy more difficult? If part of the rationale for matching funds is to equalize resources among candidates, the least-known candidate has the greatest incentive for an early start. If the early-starting candidate is not prudent in spending the funds raised and matched, that is his or her problem—and perhaps is a reflection on the candidate's qualifications to hold the job being sought.

The end of the period should also be extended. Many candidates finish the

---

7. 26 U.S.C. § 9031 et seq.; 11 C.F.R. parts 9031-39.

8. 26 U.S.C. § 9033(b) and 9034(a); 11 C.F.R. § 9033.2.

9. 26 U.S.C. § 9034(a); 11 C.F.R. § 9034.2.

10. 26 U.S.C. § 9034(a); 11 C.F.R. § 9034.2(a)(4). The starting date of the period is set by statute, the closing date by FEC regulation.

primary season in debt. The period between the national conventions, which mark the end of the primary season, and the general election, effectively the end of the fund-raising year, is the most difficult time for any candidate to raise primary funds. Even the successful nominee is constrained in fund-raising during this period due to the need to focus on the general election. Thus it is extremely difficult to retire primary debts. Candidates who have met the eligibility threshold for matching funds should be allowed—if they are able—to continue to raise contributions that qualify for primary matching funds until all debt, winding-down, and employment responsibilities have been met. At a minimum, the end of the primary matching period should be extended to one full calendar year after the year of the general election.

With these changes, the public financing law would more nearly match campaign reality.

EXPENDITURE LIMIT CATEGORIZATION IN PRESIDENTIAL PRIMARY CAMPAIGNS

A presidential candidate who elects to accept public funds in the primary or general elections, as all candidates did in 1984, is limited in the amount he or she can spend in those elections.[11] The FECA, in fact, creates three purportedly distinct categories of expenditures in the primaries for purposes of determining compliance with the law: electioneering, fund-raising and compliance expenditures.[12]

11. 2 U.S.C. § 441a(b); 11 C.F.R. § 110.8.
12. 2 U.S.C. §§ 431(9)(A), 431(9)(B)(vi), and 431(a)(B)(vii)(II); 11 C.F.R. §§ 100.8(a), 100.8(b)(21), and 100.8(b)(15).

The limit for electioneering expenditures applies to all costs incurred for general political activity. In 1984, this limit was $20.2 million. This category is further broken down by individual state expenditure limits based on population, which are discussed in the next section. The limit for fund-raising expenditures allows candidates to spend an additional amount—20 percent of the electioneering expenditure limit—on bona fide fund-raising costs. In 1984, the fund-raising limit was just under $4.1 million. Finally, the law allows candidates to make additional expenditures solely for the purpose of paying costs incurred in complying with the federal election laws. Ironically, candidates may spend an unlimited amount in this category.

There is, in fact, a fourth fund that a candidate can establish—one to pay penalties assessed by the FEC.[13] There is no limit on the size of this fund and no limit on the amount that an individual can contribute to such a penalty fund.

Experience suggests that the overall expenditure limit for presidential primary election campaigns is adequate. Only two primary campaign committees were able to raise sufficient funds to approach that limit: Reagan-Bush and Mondale for President. I am not aware of any serious complaint that the overall expenditure limit impinged seriously on a primary candidacy.

But I do believe that having a special expenditure limit for primary fund-raising—above and separate from the regular expenditure limit—serves no useful purpose and simply complicates record keeping and accounting. If a candidate does not spend the maximum allowed for fund-raising, the money cannot be

13. 11 C.F.R. § 9034.4(b)(4).

used for any other purpose. If, on the other hand, a candidate exceeds the fund-raising limit, the overage is charged to the electioneering expenditure limit.

This is another feature of the campaign laws that causes candidates to be, as it were, creative. To take advantage of the additional fund-raising expenditure limit, candidates send out large quantities of direct mail intended to win voters' support. By including a pitch for funds, however, the candidate is able to charge the costs of the mailing to fund-raising. The same technique can be used with broadcast and print media.

In an effort to limit abuse of the separate fund-raising limit, the FEC by regulation automatically allocates to the electioneering limit all expenditures in a state that occur within 28 days of the primary election or caucus in that state. Thus, all expenditures during that period, whether for fund-raising or not, qualify as electioneering expenses for that state. While that regulation is intended to curb abuse, it severely cramps legitimate application of the fund-raising limit. The period in question is just when people in the state are most focused on the election; it therefore is likely to be the most fertile time for the solicitation of campaign funds.

There is an easy answer to such regulatory overkill. The current special fund-raising expenditure limit should be eliminated, and the amount currently governed by that limit should be added to the electioneering expenditures. One expenditure limit is enough to contend with.

STATE-BY-STATE LIMITS IN PRESIDENTIAL PRIMARY EXPENDITURES

The Presidential Primary Matching Payment Account Act and the FECA limit the amount that can be spent in each state by a presidential primary candidate who has opted for matching funds.[14] The amount is based on the state's population. Thus, for example, in 1984 the limit in New Hampshire was $404,000, the limit in Pennsylvania was almost $2.9 million, and the limit in California was just over $6 million.

These state-by-state expenditure limits in the nomination period create an accounting nightmare and serve no useful purpose. The limits have no practical effect in 47 or 48 of the 50 states, because the amounts are adequate, but the limits have a palpable impact in a few important states. The states that come earliest in the nomination process—Iowa, New Hampshire, and, to lesser extent, Maine—are relatively small and accordingly have low expenditure limits. These states, however, have political and media importance that far exceeds their size and, thus, their expenditure limits. In my view, if a candidate wants to spend every nickel he or she can raise in a small early state on the theory that a win there will carry him or her much farther than a war of attrition, that should be his or her choice. The FEC should have no interest in the candidate's campaign strategy. The candidate would, of course, remain subject to the overall primary campaign expenditure limit.

The current law causes campaigns to be as creative as possible in spending funds in or around these early target states. Some of the tactics that have been used to avoid exceeding these unrealistically low state limits include:

—housing staff across borders in a state in which expenditure limits are not likely to be a problem;

14. 26 U.S.C. § 9035(a) and 2 U.S.C. § 441a(b)(1)(A); 11 C.F.R. § 110.8(a)(1).

—using the four-day rule to shuttle people in and out of the state who would more efficiently be left in the state full time;[15]

—making large media buys on television stations that are physically located in towns across the border in adjoining states but that have a reasonably sized audience in the target state. Only the viewership in the target state is charged against the expenditure limit of the target state; and

—renting cars in other states and driving them into the target states.

It is easy enough to say that candidates running in these states should eschew such tricks and simply stick within the current limits. The realities of the political process, however, are such that the stakes are simply too high. A law that ignores these practicalities cannot work.

PARTY EXPENDITURES FOR PRESIDENTIAL NOMINEES

Each major political party is permitted to spend a certain amount of money to support its general election presidential nominee. In 1984, the amount was $7.3 million. Under the FECA, the party may not simply transfer these funds to the nominee; the party must pay vendors or make expenditures directly.[16] Notwithstanding this rule, as a matter of practice, the candidate works out with his or her party the items for which the party will pay, such as media, travel, and so forth. The party issues checks to the appropriate vendors based on invoices received in the ordinary course of business.

The current law creates an unnecessary complication—one more thing that must be handled in an awkward fashion. The ban on direct transfer to the candidate was imposed for the purpose of increasing the influence of the parties by giving them supposed financial leverage over their presidential candidates. As a practical matter, however, the parties cannot and do not exercise much leverage over their candidates in the general election. Even if the leverage argument was valid, the party could exercise this leverage by refusing to raise or transfer this money if the candidate was uncooperative. I see no good reason why the party should not be able to give the funds in question directly to the candidate, to be spent and controlled in the same manner and as part of the same process as the expenditure of the federal general election grant.

LIMITS ON GRASS-ROOTS EXPENDITURES

Grass-roots activity is the very heart of American political activity, but the rules that must be used to allocate the costs of grass-roots activity to the presidential campaign are very complex. They make the federal and state regulation on the sale of securities seem like child's play.

There are any number of sillinesses in this area, but my favorite is the following. Let us assume that the presidential candidate has a headquarters in a given state. If the party is selling

---

15. In its regulations, the FEC requires that salary and travel expenses paid to persons working in a state for five consecutive days or more must be allocated to that state. 11 C.F.R. § 106.2(b)(2)(ii) and (iii). To avoid this allocation, staff are instructed to work in a state for no more than four days, then to leave for a day before returning to the state.

16. 2 U.S.C. § 441 a(d); Advisory opinion 1979-9 and 1975-120.

buttons to raise money for party activity, it cannot sell those buttons in the presidential candidate's headquarters, because that headquarters by definition is paid for with federal funds and those funds cannot be used to raise money for the party. However, if the presidential candidate goes through the trouble of paying the overhead of the headquarters through the national party organization with the funds it can spend on its candidate, those buttons can be sold in his or her headquarters.

The provisions pertaining to grass-roots activity were added to the FECA in 1979 as part of a package designed to stimulate grass-roots activity, which had declined in the previous election campaigns as a result of the FECA's provisions.[17] But the statute was drawn, and subsequent rules have been promulgated by the FEC, to prevent the grass-roots provisions from becoming vast loopholes for evading the FECA's contribution and expenditure limits. Some have suggested that the current grass-roots provisions are being exploited as a loophole.[18] I disagree with their thrust. As I see it, these rules curb healthy campaign activity, are difficult to follow, and result in creativity on the part of campaigns seeking to finance grass-roots programs.

Consider what faces a state or local party organization that wants to conduct a voter registration or get-out-the-vote drive on behalf of its presidential nominee without the costs' being borne by the nominee's committee:

1. No general public political advertising may be used, including mail done by a commercial vendor.[19]

2. The portion of the cost of the activities allocated to federal candidates—the presidential nominees—must come from funds that meet the party contribution limit and other requirements of the FECA.[20]

3. The payments for the activities must not be made from contributions designated for a particular candidate.[21]

4. The payments must not be made from funds sent by the national party specifically to pay for these activities.[22]

5. Payments may be made to cover the cost of phone banks as long as the phones are operated by volunteer workers, but these volunteers may be paid a per diem.[23]

If the local party organization spends more than $5000 in a calendar year for these activities, it must register with the FEC and file reports of its expenditures.

To make matters worse, state laws are often different from federal law, and individual volunteers simply cannot be expected to sort it all out. The net result is that people get frustrated, and an awful lot of the kind of spontaneous participation that makes our process special is lost.

USE OF PRIVATE AIRCRAFT

The FEC's regulations controlling the use of private nonscheduled aircraft

---

17. Pub. L. No. 96-187, 93 Stat. 1339 (1980).
18. See Fred Wertheimer, "Campaign Finance Reform: The Unfinished Agenda," this issue of *The Annals* of the American Academy of Political and Social Science; Michael Barone, "Campaign Finance: The System We Have," ibid.
19. 2 U.S.C. § 431(8)(B)(xii)(1); 11 C.F.R. § 100.7(b)(17)(i).
20. 2 U.S.C. § 431(8)(B)(xii)(2); 11 C.F.R. § 100.7(b)(17)(ii).
21. 2 U.S.C. § 431(8)(B)(xii)(3); 11 C.F.R. § 100.7(b)(17)(iii).
22. 11 C.F.R. §100.7(b)(17)(vii).
23. 11 C.F.R. § 100.7(b)(17)(v).

by federal campaigns are something to behold.[24] Let us assume a campaign wants to send a staff person from Washington, D.C., to Denver for a brief meeting and return. The Denver landing is either at Stapleton International, the airport used by the regularly scheduled airlines, or at nearby Front Range Airport, which does not have scheduled service. XYZ Corporation is willing to make a plane available. The regular charter cost would be $28,000. If the flight is to Stapleton, the campaign need only pay XYZ first-class airfare for the staff person. If the flight is to Front Range, the campaign pays the full charter rate because Front Range does not have scheduled service.

If the aircraft is owned by an individual rather than a corporation, the campaign must pay the full $28,000 charter fee regardless of which of the Colorado airports is used as the destination point.[25] That is because the cheaper rate is only available if a corporate-owned aircraft is used.

PRIMARY DEBATES

It would seem logical that a political party would want to sponsor public debates between candidates seeking its nomination. If it were the national party committee, it might want to do it right, with a proper setting, television coverage, and so forth. Those debates cost money, and there is the rub. Under the FECA any money the party spends for this purpose must be treated as a contribution by the party to the individual candidates.[26]

Let us assume that the debate costs $25,000 to mount and only four candidates participate. The allocable contribution per candidate would be $6250, but the most the party can contribute to any individual candidate in the primary is $5000. Yes, the party could get the individual candidates to pick up the extra $1250, but there will always be some candidate who is reticent to debate and is not about to pay for the privilege of being beaten up in public. Perhaps one of the other candidates would like to pick up the cost for the reticent candidates. That will not work because the willing candidate has received matching funds and since a proportionate part of every dollar spent is presumed to be federal matching funds, a contribution from one presidential candidate to another might not be a qualified campaign expense.[27]

The solution is as simple as it is badly needed. Party-sponsored debates simply should be exempt from the FECA's contribution rules.

ROLE OF THE TREASURER

I had never been reticent to encourage people to accept a position as treasurer of a candidate's committee, but now I hesitate. Until recently, treasurers have generally not been charged with violations of the FECA unless they personally committed some unlawful act. Now the FEC seems bent on taking a different and, to my mind, misguided approach. It has adopted a policy that treasurers can be found to have violated the act in their official capacity if the

---

24. 11 C.F.R. §§ 114.9(e) and 9034.7.
25. 11 C.F.R. § 9034.7(b)(7).
26. The FEC debate regulations do not permit parties to stage debates, so the costs incurred by

the parties are not exempt from the definition of contribution. 11 C.F.R. §§ 110.13 and 100.7(b)(21).
27. 11 C.F.R. §§ 9034.4(a) and 9032.9.

campaign committee is found to have violated the law.[28]

In my view, treasurers should only be liable for the specific acts they commit that violate the statute, for example, knowingly accepting corporate contributions, failing to establish and maintain a reasonable accounting operation, or failing to file the requisite reports in a timely fashion.

There is no way that any campaign treasurer can maintain sufficient day-to-day control over the operation of a large campaign so as to assure that no provision of federal law has been violated. For example, during the general election, the Mondale campaign had over 900 people on the payroll and thousands of volunteers in all 50 states and hundreds of congressional districts. So great a number of people over so much territory cannot be supervised for conformity to every provision of federal law.

No matter how hard presidential campaign treasurers try to assure compliance, it is an all but impossible task. Campaign operatives with only one motive, winning, will come up with new and creative ways to meet their objective. Usually they will be legal; sometimes they will not be. If campaign treasurers are made liable for every untoward act of their campaign committee, even if only in their official capacity, the day could soon come when no reasonable person will accept this responsibility.

CONCLUSION

For most people, the 1984 presidential campaign was over on 5 November 1984. That is not true for those of us who agreed to be the treasurer of a presidential campaign. As I write this article, the campaign has been over for more than a year, and I am still at it. I will be at it when this article is published. If I am really lucky, two or three years after the campaign is over I will have answered the last of the FEC's questions and sent the last box of records to storage.

I am often asked by persons thinking about running for president for general advice. Without fail, I highlight the need to obtain the services of a competent lawyer and a competent accountant before taking the first fledgling steps. If that advice is sound, and I think it is, then just maybe our campaign finance laws have gone too far.

28. Agenda document 83-119, adopted, 18 Aug. 1983.

Of Philosophers, Foxes, and Finances: Can the Federal Election Commission Ever Do an Adequate Job?

By WILLIAM C. OLDAKER

ABSTRACT: This article assesses the effectiveness of the Federal Election Commission (FEC) in today's environment by discussing three types of constraints that limit the FEC's authority: contextual, legal, and administrative. The contextual restraint is seen in the unique political position in which the FEC finds itself, regulating its maker and benefactor, the Congress. The legal constraints involve the First Amendment and its interplay with the statutes that the FEC administers. Finally, the article addresses the administrative constraints under which the FEC must labor, and it examines two frequent charges against the commission: the politicalization of its enforcement procedure and the assertion that the FEC pursues petty infractions. The article concludes that the FEC deserves a mixed review, noting that it stumbles in its attempt to keep the foxes out of the chicken coop and the chickens in during congressional elections. The FEC must be made far more independent to be effective.

William C. Oldaker is a partner in Epstein Becker Borsody & Green, P.C., Washington, D.C. He served as assistant general counsel for litigation and enforcement of the Federal Election Commission during 1975-76 and then as the commission's general counsel from 1976 to 1979. Mr. Oldaker now represents a variety of candidates and political action committees with respect to compliance with state and federal election law.

NOTE: Mr. Oldaker would like to acknowledge the assistance of Kathleen J. Taylor, Esq., in the writing of this article.

OVER 2000 years ago in ancient Greece, a first attempt at campaign reform was made. The great philosopher Plato in his classic work *The Republic* proposed a radical restructuring of the Athenian state. And whom did the philosopher suggest should run the Athenian state? None other than philosopher-kings. Plato proposed a reform so that men like him would take command.[1] Thus one of the oldest principles of election law reform was first illustrated: if allowed to design chicken coops, foxes make notoriously poor architects.

Over the past century, the United States has struggled to find some way—consistent with our traditions, our First Amendment freedoms, and our political culture—to regulate the influence of money in politics.[2] As we near the eightieth anniversary of the first federal campaign finance statute,[3] we face the frustrating conclusion that, while much has changed, far too much remains the same.[4] Throughout this period there have been alternating waves of public attention and inattention, swinging from hope and reform at one pole to cynicism and apathy at the other.

On several occasions, Congress has been moved to action; however, almost every such foray into campaign regulation prior to 1974 was totally unsuccessful.[5] Indeed, as Congress considered scrapping the old system of campaign finance regulation during the infamous Watergate period, Senator Daniel Inouye explained what 60-plus years of political self-regulation had thus far produced:

In every election year candidates for Federal office have avoided, circumvented, and occasionally evaded just about every State and national law that regulates the political fund-raising process. The techniques of avoidance may be complex, but they are well-known. Secret conduits, spurious committees, and other forms of deceit and subterfuge come into existence to assure candidates the money needed to reach the voters.[6]

By 1974, a broad consensus had emerged in Congress that one of the principal reasons that pre-Watergate campaign reform had failed was the lack

---

1. Plato, *The Republic,* ed. Raymond Larson, Croft Classics (Arlington Heights, IL: AHM, 1979).

2. For a brief but insightful history of the early period of campaign finance regulation, from 1890 to 1920, see *United States* v. *UAW*, 352 U.S. 567, 570-77 (1957).

3. The statute, 34 Stat. 864 (1907), was the predecessor of the Corrupt Practices Act, 18 U.S.C. § 602 et seq. (1976 and Supp. 1985).

4. Testimony given before a House committee reviewing election finance in 1906 would be almost totally relevant and timely if offered today. Witnesses then feared the influence of the "great corporations" and the probability of "bought" members of Congress. Samuel Gompers said it was "doubtful" that "the contributions and expenditures of vast sums of money . . . can continue to increase without endangering the endurance of our Republic." Compare U.S., Congress, House Committee of Elections, *Hearing on Contributions to Political Committees in Presidential and Other Campaigns,* 59th Cong., 1st sess., 12 Mar. 1906, with U.S., Congress, Senate, *Hearings before the Committee on Rules and Administration,* 96th Cong., 1st sess., 1979. The first set of hearings led to the enactment of the forerunner of the Corrupt Practices Act; the second, to the Federal Election Campaign Act Amendments of 1979, Pub. L. No. 96-187, 93 Stat. 1339 (1980).

5. For an evaluation of the failure of pre-1974 campaign regulation, made by a "candidate, a fundraiser, and . . . a member of an investigative panel looking into campaign finance practices," see Senator Daniel K. Inouye, in U.S., Congress, Senate, *Congressional Record,* 93rd Cong., 2d sess., 9 Apr. 1974, pp. S01351-53.

6. Ibid.

of a single effective enforcement mechanism or agency charged with the task of policing the election law. Until 1974, the Department of Justice and the comptroller general, neither of which had a vested interest in ensuring that campaign finance law was enforced, jointly shared oversight of the Corrupt Practices Act. The inevitable result of this split in authority between two uninterested agencies was that the election laws were simply not being enforced. The ranking Republican on the Senate committee that created the Federal Election Commission (FEC) claimed that enforcement of the Corrupt Practices Act, the campaign finance law existing then, "has not been done for 40 or 50 years or more" and that disclosure reports "have failed to be filed, and nobody is even concerned over doing anything about it."[7] His House counterpart agreed, "Historically, campaign finance reform legislation has been a failure because of the lack of effective enforcement. The Corrupt Practices Act was almost never effective in its 50-year life."[8]

Thus it was not merely a lack of statutory restrictions, but a lack of any effective enforcement mechanism that marked pre-Watergate campaign finance regulations. That was to change with the 1974 act.[9]

FROM WATERGATE TO *BUCKLEY* TO TODAY'S FEC

It was only after tedious and extensive debate, hearings, and compromise between House and Senate bills that Congress created the FEC in 1974.[10] In the end, Congress created a "commission"—it specifically avoided the term "independent agency"—whose structure was, to say the least, unique.[11] The FEC was to have eight members. Two were to be the secretary of the Senate and the clerk of the House as ex officio, nonvoting members; two were to be selected by the president pro tempore of the Senate, two by the Speaker of the House, and two by the president of the United States. The six appointed members were to be evenly divided between the two major political parties.[12]

If the foxes in Congress were giving up their self-supervisory role, they were not going to turn over the keys to the chicken coop to just anyone. As can be seen, Congress essentially tried to retain the right to select six of the FEC's eight members. It also ensured that there was nothing in the bill that gave the FEC any real authority to make substantial changes in campaign finance law. Con-

---

7. Senator Cook, in ibid., 3 Apr. 1974, p. S9553-4.

8. Congressman Bill Frenzel, in U.S., Congress, House, 93rd Cong., 2d sess., 1974, H. Rept. 1239, p. 140.

9. See Federal Election Campaign Act Amendments of 1974, Pub. L. No. 93-443, 88 Stat. 1263 (1974).

10. The House bill, H.R. 16090, as reported by committee, established a "Board of Supervisory Officers" with seven members: the secretary of the Senate, the clerk of the House of Representatives, the comptroller general, and four individuals, two appointed by the president of the Senate and two by the Speaker of the House, evenly split between the parties. See H.R. 16090, 93rd Cong., 2d sess. § 207(a) (1974); U.S., Congress, House, H. Rept. 1239, pp. 27-31. The Senate bill, S. 3044, established a Federal Election Commission with eight members: the comptroller general, who could not vote, and seven appointed by the president. Two of those seven, however, were to be "recommended" to the president by the Speaker of the House and two more by the president pro tempore of the Senate—split between the parties—with the last three chosen by the president on a two-to-one party basis. S. 3044, 93rd Cong., 2d sess. § 207(a) (1974); U.S., Congress, Senate, 93rd Cong., 2d sess., 1974, S. Rept. 689.

11. See Pub. L. No. 93-443, 88 Stat. 1263, 1280-82.

12. Ibid.

gress provided an added safeguard against any attempted changes by the FEC—any rules or regulations the FEC might make could be vetoed by either house of Congress.[13]

The Supreme Court soon ruled unanimously in *Buckley* v. *Valeo*[14] that Congress's method of appointing federal election commissioners was an unconstitutional breach of the separation of powers. This was the first invalidation of a major congressionally created agency since the New Deal. The thrust of the Court's ruling was that Congress could not make appointments to what was, in fact, an agency of the executive branch. This ruling effectively blunted Congress's effort to have at least some foxes guarding the coop.

Congress reacted to *Buckley* with relative speed. Less than four months later, it reconstituted the FEC as a commission with eight members. Congress again provided for two ex officio, nonvoting officers from its ranks, the secretary of the Senate and the clerk of the House. But this time Congress provided that the six other voting commissioners would be chosen by the president, to be confirmed by the Senate. Again, however, Congress decreed that the six voting members be evenly split on party lines.[15]

Of course, Congress did not abdicate its control over the FEC. Congress retained purported power to veto any proposed FEC regulations.[16] Congress also, of course, controls the FEC's budget. Moreover, in 1980, Congress added a requirement that any FEC enforcement action be based on an affirmative vote of four of the commission's members.[17]

For almost a decade since its reconstitution, the FEC has ostensibly operated independently from Congress, as chief enforcer of our federal election laws. Torn desperately between the tasks of keeping the foxes out of the coop and keeping the chickens in, the commission's job is to keep the politicians more than paws' length away from the contributors and to keep the contributors within the fence of the rules wherever possible. Not only is this an exceedingly difficult and thankless task, but, as I will describe in greater detail, it is an almost impossible job, given the constraints on the FEC.

CONSTRAINTS ON THE
FEC's EFFECTIVENESS

The foregoing history of how the FEC originated and evolved into its present structure provides the background for an analysis of the reasons for the FEC's limited effectiveness in the enforcement field. It is useful to view the constraints on the FEC's authority as falling into three categories: contextual, legal, and administrative. Of course, these categories overlap and have a certain interplay,[18] but generally they

13. Ibid., p. 1287.
14. 424 U.S. 1, 118-43 (1976).
15. The formula, found in Pub. L. No. 94-283, 90 Stat. 475 (1976), is essentially now 2 U.S.C. § 437(c).
16. Though called into doubt by the Supreme Court's decision in *Immigration and Naturalization Service* v. *Chadha*, 462 U.S. 919 (1983), the legislative veto language remains at 2 U.S.C. § 438(d)(2).

17. Added by the 1979-80 act amendments, the four-vote rule is now at 2 U.S.C. § 437g(4)(A)(i).
18. For example, the FEC's failure to meet the challenge posed by independent expenditures—discussed in the present article on pp. 138-41—is in part a contextual one, in that, for example, political forces support independent expenditures; a legal one, given, for example, First Amendment limits from *Buckley* and *Federal Election Commission* v. *National Conservative Political Action Committee*, 105 S. Ct. 1459 (1985); and an admin-

provide, I believe, a workable framework in which to consider certain issues.

Contextual constraints

By "contextual constraints" I mean limitations on the FEC's effectiveness that result from its peculiar position vis-à-vis the Congress. Consider the inherent inhibitions on the commission's freedom to act created by the paradox that every enforcement action directed at a member of Congress bites the hand that feeds the commission. On the one hand, the FEC polices the most sensitive of all congressional activities—reelection efforts; but on the other, Congress retains the power to control the FEC's operations, by limiting its budget, amending the Federal Election Campaign Act (FECA), and, at one time, by rejecting regulations proposed by the FEC. Every enforcement action against a member of Congress is an enforcement action against the commission's boss—a limitation that must be painfully omnipresent to all those at the FEC.

A vivid example of this contextual constraint can be found in the aftermath of the 1980 elections. In August of 1981, the FEC cited 359 House and 84 Senate candidates for failing to file financial reports as required under the FECA.[19] Congressional hostility to the FEC—stimulated by this vigorous effort to put teeth in the FECA's reporting provisions—became glaringly apparent when it came time to renew and vote on the FEC's budget. During the agency's budget-review hearings, the FEC's commissioners were grilled at length on the criteria employed in determining whom to investigate and how they conducted an investigation.[20] They were accused by many in Congress of bureaucratic nitpicking.[21] Indeed, the hearings were so intense they were dubbed an "inquisition."[22]

The end result was that the FEC budget for fiscal year 1982 was slashed over 25 percent.[23] There was even talk of abolishing the commission. This led Common Cause, one of FEC's staunchest supporters, to state: "Members of Congress basically do not want to be regulated. They tend to forget the FEC was created BY them, not FOR them."[24]

Thus, in the final analysis, an adversarial relationship will always exist between Congress and the FEC, the agency created by Congress to regulate it.[25] The FEC will be forced to continue to walk a tightrope—vigorously enforcing the laws passed by Congress, while stopping short of incurring congressional wrath to such an extent that Congress decides to put the FEC out of business.[26]

---

istrative one, in that the FEC chooses not to or lacks resources to enforce vigorously laws that are on the books. Still, while they are related, each of these failings is different and demands a different response. Likewise, a change in political climates—contextual—may produce budget cuts at the FEC—administrative—or a change in the act—legal. The opposite can be true as well. Just the same, differentiation between the categories is useful for our purposes here.

19. This requirement is found at 2 U.S.C. § 434.

20. Clay F. Richards and Gregory Gordon, "The FEC and the Battle with Congress," *Los Angeles Daily Journal,* 9 Sept. 1981.

21. For a more detailed discussion of the investigative or enforcement process, see text in the present article under administrative constraints, pp. 141-42.

22. *Los Angeles Daily Journal,* 9 Sept. 1981.

23. Ibid.

24. Ibid.

25. Ibid. It should be noted that Congress has chosen not to be regulated by other federal watchdogs such as the Equal Employment Opportunity Commission or the Department of Labor's Occupational Safety and Health Administration.

26. *Los Angeles Daily Journal,* 9 Sept. 1981.

Legal constraints

Significant legal constraints also impinge dramatically on the FEC's effectiveness in the enforcement field. These constraints principally result from (1) the First Amendment and its interplay in general with the statutes the FEC administers;[27] and (2) independent expenditures, which are a loophole in the campaign finance laws shielded by the First Amendment.

The First Amendment. The First Amendment, of course, protects both freedom of speech and freedom of association. It has been said, and repeated, that the protection the First Amendment affords to these precious freedoms has its most urgent application in the field of political speech and elections.[28] Thus the real constraints the FECA imposes on federal electioneering naturally raise broad and often delicate First Amendment issues.

Indeed, it now appears to be a given that any statute passed by Congress for the purpose of regulating campaign contributions or expenditures will face an immediate, vigorous, and vocal First Amendment challenge.[29] As a result the FEC frequently finds itself enmeshed in the litigation process defending the constitutionality of a provision of the FECA—a tremendous drain on its meager resources[30]—while at the same time it is required to enforce the challenged statute until a final definitive ruling is made by the Supreme Court.

This constraint is illustrated by the brouhaha that accompanied the 1974 FECA amendments. These amendments, among other things, limited political contributions to candidates for federal office; limited expenditures by candidates; limited expenditures by individuals or groups relative to a clearly identified candidate—that is, independent expenditures; and required political committees to keep and disclose detailed records of contributions and expenditures, including names and addresses of contributors.

These amendments were immediately challenged by several groups and individuals as violating the First Amendment's guarantees of freedom of speech and association as well as the Fifth Amendment's due-process clause.[31] In January 1976, the Supreme Court, in

---

27. These statutes include Federal Election Campaign Act, as amended, 2 U.S.C. § 431 et seq.; Presidential Election Campaign Fund Act, as amended, 26 U.S.C. § 9001 et seq.; Government in the Sunshine Act, 5 U.S.C. § 552b.

28. See, for example, *Buckley* v. *Valeo*, 424 U.S. 1, 14-15; *Monitor Patriot Co.* v. *Roy*, 401 U.S. 265, 272(1971).

29. The First Amendment challenge encompasses not only the right of free speech but also the freedom of association. See, for example, *Buckley* v. *Valeo*, 424 U.S. 1; *Federal Election Commission* v. *National Conservative Political Action Committee*, 105 S. Ct. 1459. In recognition of the probable First Amendment implications, the act provides for speedy review of constitutional questions.

30. The FEC's resources are discussed in the present article under administrative constraints, pp. 141-42.

31. The plaintiffs were a candidate for the presidency, a U.S. senator up for reelection, a possible contributor, the Committee for a Constitutional Presidency—McCarthy '76, the Conservative Party of the State of New York, the Mississippi Republican Party, the Libertarian Party, the New York Civil Liberties Union, Inc., the American Conservative Union, the Conservative Victory Fund, and Human Events, Inc. The commission itself was named as one of the defendants in the two suits filed. One of my first tasks in taking over as assistant general counsel for litigation and enforcement for the FEC was to review the FEC's brief and prepare for oral argument before the Supreme Court over the challenge.

Buckley v. *Valeo*,[32] upheld the FECA's contribution provisions, struck down its expenditure provisions as unconstitutional, and declared its disclosure and record-keeping provisions constitutional.

In *Buckley*, the Court broadly articulated the principles by which the consitutionality of campaign finance regulations would be judged:

The Act's contribution and expenditure limitations operate in an area of the most fundamental First Amendment activities. Discussion of public issues and debate on the qualifications of the candidates are integral to the operation of the system of government established by our Constitution. The First Amendment affords the broadest protection to such political expression in order to assure [the] unfettered interchange of ideas for the bringing about of political and social changes desired by the people.[33]

The Court went on to expound on why campaign finance statutes also implicate the First Amendment freedom of association:

The First Amendment protects political association as well as political expression. The constitutional right of association . . . stemmed from the Court's recognition that "[e]ffective advocacy of both public and private points of view, particularly controversial ones, is undeniably enhanced by group association." Subsequent decisions have made clear that the First and Fourteenth Amendments guarantee "freedom to associate with others for the common advancement of political beliefs and ideas," a freedom that encompasses "[t]he right to associate with the political party of one's choice."[34]

Thus the FEC will continue to have to operate subject to the sometimes acute tension between the First Amendment rights of speech and association and the congressional determination to preclude political corruption. If the FEC is too aggressive, it will be charged, sometimes correctly, as treading insensitively on precious First Amendment freedoms.[35] If, on the other hand, the FEC proceeds too cautiously, it will be accused, sometimes correctly, of countenancing corrupt campaign finance practices.[36]

Independent expenditures. The problem of how to regulate independent expenditures has continued to be a thorn in the FEC's side. The FEC correctly views the vehicle of independent

---

32. 424 U.S. 1.
33. Ibid., pp. 14-15.
34. Ibid.

35. Indeed, the commission on several occasions has run into First Amendment difficulties in determining what specifically constitutes a "communication expressly advocating the election or defeat of a candidate" so as to trigger the reporting requirements of the act. 2 U.S.C. § 431(b)(4)(c). The courts have consistently held that in order for the act to withstand a First Amendment challenge on overbreadth grounds, the act's provisions must be narrowly construed. A statute is void on its face under the overbreadth doctrine if it can be applied in order to punish people for constitutionally protected speech. In *Federal Election Commission* v. *AFSCME*, 471 F. Supp. 315 (D.D.C. 1979), the district court held that a poster depicting President Ford embracing former President Nixon while wearing a button stating "pardon me" was an expression on a public issue, rather than a statement of advocacy for or against the reelection of Ford. Therefore it constituted protected speech immune from regulation by the act. Likewise, in *Federal Election Commission* v. *Central Long Island Tax Reform Immediately Committee,* 616 F.2d 45 (2d Cir. 1980), the appellate court held that the distribution of a member of Congress' voting record on certain economic and tax issues did not fall within the act's requirement of express advocacy of the defeat of the member of Congress and, therefore, could not be regulated by the FEC.

36. See, for example, the discussion of the FEC's reluctance to enforce section 9012(f), in the present article on pp. 139-40.

expenditures as a way around the contribution limits upheld in *Buckley*.[37] Individuals and groups, through this loophole, can spend millions of dollars on promoting or opposing a candidate without any limit and without adhering to the FECA's detailed reporting requirements.[38]

In an attempt to close part of the gap in the election laws after *Buckley*, Congress in 1976 passed the amendments to the Presidential Election Campaign Fund Act. These amendments provided, as had been the case under the old laws, that where a candidate in the presidential general election had opted for public financing no political committee could expend more than $1000 in his or her support. The provision—section 9012(f)—did not limit independent expenditures by individuals or groups other than political committees. Congress thus sought to overcome the constitutional infirmities in the previous broad limit on independent expenditures by restricting those expenditures only where the candidate to be supported had chosen public funding. This approach was stimulated by the fact that in *Buckley* the Supreme Court had sustained a candidate expenditure limit when it was tied to the candidate's acceptance of public funding.

Notwithstanding the plain language of the statute, the FEC appeared reluctant to enforce section 9012(f) when, in 1980, several so-called independent expenditure committees announced their intention to raise and spend millions of dollars to support the candidacy of Ronald Reagan, who had opted for public financing in the general election. The FEC, in fact, took no action whatsoever until Common Cause sued the committees in federal court in the District of Columbia. The FEC, its hand forced, then filed its own suit against the committees in the same court, alleging that the committees were violating section 9012(f). The FEC did not challenge the actual independence of the committees, which Common Cause had done. A three-judge district court dismissed both the Common Cause and the FEC lawsuits, holding that the statute violated the First Amendment. That decision was affirmed by an equally divided Supreme Court—Justice O'Connor recused herself—an affirmance that lacked precedential effect outside the District of Columbia.[39]

In the meantime, Common Cause had filed an administrative complaint with the FEC that alleged that the pro-Reagan committees were not, in fact,

---

37. Congress recognized the potential for abuse posed by independent expenditures in debating the 1974 amendments to the FECA and expressly included limits on such expenditures, noting that controls were essential in order to preclude rendering the direct-contributions limits meaningless. "Admittedly, expenditures made directly by an individual to urge support of a candidate pose First Amendment issues more vividly than do financial contributions to a campaign fund. Nevertheless, to prohibit a $60,000 direct contribution to be used for a TV spot commercial but then to permit the would-be contributor to purchase the time himself, and place a commercial endorsing the candidate, would exalt constitutional form over substance. Your Committee does not believe the First Amendment requires such a wooden construction." U.S., Congress, Senate, 93rd Cong., 2d sess., S. Rept. 689, pp. 18-19.

38. The loophole of independent expenditures has led to "the infusion of massive PAC [political action committee] expenditures into the political process." See *Federal Election Commission* v. *National Conservative Political Action Committee*, 105 S. Ct., p. 1479.

39. See *Common Cause* v. *Schmitt*, 512 F. Supp. 489 (D.D.C. 1980), *aff'd by an equally divided court*, 455 U.S. 129 (1982).

independent of the official Reagan campaign and, accordingly, that their expenditures on his behalf constituted illegal contributions to him. That complaint languished at the FEC for more than three years before it was finally dismissed. In recommending dismissal to the commission, the FEC's general counsel did not conclude that he was confident that there had been no improper collusion between the pro-Reagan committees and the official Reagan campaign. Rather, his recommendation was based in part on his view that the commission lacked sufficient resources to pursue the investigation further than it had.

When the 1984 campaign season rolled around, the FEC again seemed reluctant to enforce section 9012(f), as it was free to do outside the District of Columbia. This time the Democratic Party forced the FEC's hand by bringing a lawsuit against two pro-Reagan so-called independent expenditure committees in federal court in Philadelphia. As in 1980, the FEC took up the fight and brought its own lawsuit in the same court, and, again, a three-judge court invalidated the statute as an unconstitutional infringement of First Amendment rights.

When the Presidential Election Campaign Fund Act's limits on expenditures reached the Supreme Court again in *Federal Election Commission v. National Conservative Political Action Committee (NCPAC)*,[40] they were predictably struck down. Holding that preventing corruption or the appearance of corruption is the only compelling government interest in restricting campaign finances, the Court maintained, notwithstanding Congress's apparent judgment to the contrary, that "the hallmark of corruption"—that is, "the financial *quid pro quo*: dollars for political favors"—was not present as an issue in independent expenditures. While conceding that it was possible that a candidate might take notice of individuals responsible for expenditures by political action committees and reward them with official favors, the lack of prearrangement and coordination with the candidate, according to the Court's majority, militates against such a possibility.[41]

The dissent in *NCPAC* refuted the majority's somewhat naive assertion that independent expenditures did not pose a substantial danger that the candidate for political office would be excessively influenced by the individual or group providing the financial support. Noting that "aggregations of wealth" exercise considerable power over candidates, forcing them to please the "spenders" rather than the voters, the dissent quoted Senator Eagleton concerning congressional campaigning:

> The current system of financing congressional elections ... virtually forces Members of Congress to go around hat in hand, begging for money from Washington-based special interest groups, political action committees whose sole purpose for existing is to seek a quid pro quo. . . . We see the degrading spectacle of elected representatives completing detailed questionnaires on their positions on special interest issues, knowing that the monetary reward of PAC support depends on the correct answers.[42]

That does not complete the story of the FEC's struggles with the problems posed by independent expenditures. In addition to the Common Cause admin-

---

40. 105 S. Ct. 1459 (1980).
41. Ibid., p. 1469.
42. Ibid., p. 1479 and n. 12.

istrative complaint mentioned earlier, the FEC has received a number of complaints alleging that certain purportedly independent expenditures were in fact made collusively.[43] The FEC has dismissed or failed to rule on each such complaint. Perhaps each of its decisions was warranted on the facts presented, but the result has been a perception that the FEC is either hostile to such complaints or simply lacks the resources or know-how needed to investigate them effectively, or both.

Another serious shortcoming is the FEC's failure to develop an adequate common law of or working criteria for judging the so-called independence of an expenditure. None has emerged from the FEC's actions on the complaints brought to it, and the FEC has inexplicably never taken any action on a petition for rule making on the subject that it received five years ago in 1981.

Thus the FEC, while having the power and ability to enforce limitations on direct campaign contributions, is hamstrung by First Amendment considerations and other problems in plugging a real leak—independent expenditures—in the dike erected by Congress to hold back political corruption. Unless and until the leak is plugged, the FEC cannot truly be said to constitute an effective weapon against undue influence in the political arena.

Administrative constraints

The FEC's staff and its overall budget are quite simply inadequate to accomplish its delegated responsibilities. The FEC has two basic functions: its record keeping and disclosing of campaign finance reports, for which it receives high marks,[44] and its auditing of the plethora of campaign expenditures and enforcing election laws. It is this latter enforcement duty that attracts the most criticism, with the FEC being charged with nitpicking and pursuing what many in Congress regard as petty infractions.[45] Contributing to this problem is the FEC's lack of power to initiate enforcement actions or campaign audits; rather, it is permitted to react only when complaints are lodged with it.[46] Moreover, an affirmative vote by four of the commissioners, who are split evenly on party lines, is required to initiate an enforcement action. These statutory constraints on the FEC's enforcement power clearly reflect Congress's fundamental desire to hamstring the FEC.

Congress provided the FEC with certain powers unique to an independent agency,[47] but the FEC still faces monumental administrative limitations in its enforcement ability. Confronted with voluminous possible violations of the statutes it is charged with enforcing, the FEC must, of necessity, exercise discretion in determining against whom it will proceed. Complicating this task is the fact that only 10-20 percent of the

---

43. Specifically, the complaints alleged that the candidates to be benefited by the expenditure had been consulted concerning the best means of utilizing the expenditure in order to further the candidates' interest.

44. *Los Angeles Daily Journal,* 9 Sept. 1981.
45. Ibid.
46. See 2 U.S.C. § 437g(a).
47. Specifically, the FEC, unlike other federal agencies, has the authority to bring suit without Justice Department approval. See 2 U.S.C. § 437d(6). It also can negotiate conciliation agreements requiring an admission from the purported offender. 2 U.S.C. § 437g(a)(4)(A)(i). Because it holds no enforcement hearings prior to bringing suit, it has been labeled "investigator, prosecutor, judge and jury." Senator Ted Stevens, quoted in *Los Angeles Daily Journal,* 9 Sept. 1981.

commission's meager budget is allocated to the enforcement function.[48]

The commission has also been given the responsibility to issue advisory opinions and regulations. While the issuing of regulations is similar to the regulatory function of other administrative agencies, the issuing of advisory opinions is quite unique. The advisory opinion, according to its critics, allows the commission to make law in a very piecemeal fashion without the benefit of adequate comment or criticism that would provide insight into the full implications of its proposal actions.

Each of these problem areas—politicization of enforcement and the piecemeal process of lawmaking through the vehicle of advisory opinions—will be explored more fully.

Politicalization of enforcement. In addition to limited resources and an almost Herculean enforcement problem, the FEC in its administration of its statutes is also bedeviled by two charges. First, it is asserted that political influence affects the FEC's final determinations of which enforcement actions to pursue. Second, the FEC is accused of having its priorities askew; that is, it is accused of pursuing what many in and out of Congress believe are petty infractions and, conversely, of failing to address major issues affecting campaign finance. Indeed the problem can be summed up succinctly: "you can't take the politics out of politics."[49]

Because of its limited resources, where the FEC chooses to focus its attention is inevitably second-guessed and criticized. Many view its enforcement actions as being dictated by the political party in power at the time, despite the three-three split by party in the body of commissioners. Indeed, this charge has been leveled by the Republicans during the Carter administration and by the Democrats during the Reagan administration.

This politicization of the FEC's enforcement actions was highlighted in the Supreme Court's decision in *Federal Election Commission* v. *National Conservative Political Action Committee.*[50] This case involved a suit by the Democratic Party against several political action committees that had announced that they intended to spend substantial sums of money to reelect President Reagan in 1984. The Democrats sought injunctive relief against the political action committees under the provisions of the Presidential Election Campaign Fund Act that limited independent commitee expenditures for candidates to $1000. The FEC intervened in the case, attempting to dismiss the complaint for lack of standing. Seeking the same relief, it then brought a separate action against the same political action committees.

While ultimately holding that the expenditure limitation was unconstitutional, the Court addressed the FEC's enforcement powers. The Court found that the FEC, under both the Presidential Election Campaign Fund Act and the FECA, had exclusive jurisdiction with respect to civil enforcement of those statutes. Moreover, the Court held that it was within the exclusive jurisdiction of the FEC "to determine how and when to enforce the Act."[51]

48. See, for example, Federal Election Commission, *Annual Report* (Washington, DC: Federal Election Commission, 1984), p. 60.
49. *Los Angeles Daily Journal,* 10 Sept. 1981.

50. See *Federal Election Commission* v. *National Conservative Political Action Committee,* 105 S. Ct. 1459.
51. Ibid., p. 1463.

While imbuing the FEC with vast power by ordaining that it alone could enforce the two statutes, the Court, *in dicta,* noted the political realities within which the FEC was operating:

In the present case, for example, there is no indication that the FEC would have filed a complaint against the PACs for a declaratory judgment if the Democrats had not done so first. The FEC might have chosen to focus its resources elsewhere or to pursue an enforcement action at a later date. The Democrats forced its hand; the subject of the litigation was so central to the FEC's function that it had no choice but to intervene once the action had been commenced.[52]

Nor is this politicalization confined merely to a political party. The FEC has also been charged with taking enforcement actions based on petty infractions that help friendly incumbent members of Congress at the expense of their challengers. For example, in 1979, Senator Jacob Javits, a supporter of the FEC, faced a challenge for the Republican senatorial nomination from Alfonse D'Amato. D'Amato spent $400 printing 900 campaign brochures in order to win the nomination; the brochures did not contain the required disclaimer.[53] The FEC had previously failed to take action on similar disclaimer complaints. When a campaign staffer for Javits complained to the FEC, the agency proceeded to enforce the statute against the D'Amato campaign strictly. The end result was that D'Amato signed a conciliation agreement and paid a $250 fine.[54]

Another significant example of the quagmire the FEC is caught in because of political infighting is detailed in *Federal Election Commission* v. *Machinists Non-Partisan Political League (MNPL),*[55] which involved a challenge to an investigatory subpoena of the FEC. In October 1979, the Carter-Mondale presidential campaign filed a complaint with the FEC alleging that various draft-Kennedy groups, formed under the auspices of the MNPL,[56] were violating certain provisions of the FECA.

In response to the complaint, the FEC issued a broadly sweeping subpoena seeking to obtain all communications between the MNPL and the draft-Kennedy groups and all documents relating to the decision by the MNPL and its committees to support or oppose any candidate seeking election to the presidency in 1980. The FEC also sought a list of all employees, officers, and volunteers.

The appellate court, in reviewing the challenge to the subpoena, noted that heightened judicial scrutiny was required because the subject matter of the subpoenaed materials represented "the very heart of the organism which the first amendment was intended to nurture and protect: political expression and association concerning federal elections and officeholding."[57] The court then went on to address the grave political implications that could result if the subpoena were granted:

---

52. Ibid.
53. Clay F. Richards and Gregory Gordon, "FEC under Attack: Nitpickers Persist," *Los Angeles Daily Journal,* 10 Sept. 1981.
54. Ibid.
55. See *Federal Election Commission* v. *Machinists Non-Partisan Political League,* 655 F.2d 380 (D.D.C. 1981), *cert. denied,* 454 U.S. 897 (1981).
56. Interestingly enough, the MNPL had supported Jimmy Carter for president in 1976, but it subsequently became disenchanted with his politics.
57. See *Federal Election Commission* v. *Machinists Non-Partisan Political League,* 655 F.2d, p. 388.

Then this federal agency, whose members are nominated by the President, demands *all* materials concerning communications among various groups whose alleged purpose was to defeat the President by encouraging a popular figure from within his party to run against him. As a final measure, the FEC demands a listing of every official, employee, staff member and volunteer of the group, along with their respective telephone numbers, without any limitation on when or to what extent those listed participated in any MNPL activities. The government thus becomes privy to knowledge concerning which of its citizens is a "volunteer" for a group trying to defeat the President at the polls. This information is of a fundamentally different constitutional character . . . since release of such information to the government carries with it a real potential for chilling the free exercise of political speech and association guarded by the first amendment.[58]

The court found that the commission lacked subject-matter jurisdiction over draft-group contributors and that the subpoena therefore was not valid.

Because of the administrative constraints it faces, as well as the charges, whether founded or unfounded, that the enforcement actions it takes are based on political considerations, the FEC needs to exercise more discretion in selecting which actions it chooses to pursue. Also, its general counsel's office needs to be given more independence to act without having to cater to the commissioners, including the ability to audit randomly. An ideal model is the general-counsel function at the National Labor Relations Board. Unfortunately, Congress is likely to be very wary of increasing its watchdog's enforcement powers.

Law by piecemeal—the advisory opinion. The advisory-opinion section of the FECA[59] allows the recipient or other individual similarly situated to rely on the advisory opinion as an absolute defense to prosecution. Thus, without the benefit of receiving adequate comment or even fully becoming aware of the implication of the opinion being issued, the FEC is making law, albeit piecemeal.

The best example of the flaw in the advisory-opinion process is the SunPAC advisory opinion, AO-1975-23. This advisory opinion is responsible for what can be described as a major and significant change in the financing of American elections. In this landmark opinion, the commission recognized that corporations and trade associations could establish political action committees, which could solicit their employees. This issue had never been considered, let alone addressed, under prior legislation. After publication of the request for an advisory opinion and a brief period for comment by interested persons, the commission adopted the SunPAC opinion by a four-to-two vote. Two commissioners vigorously objected to the opinion, noting that the opinion appeared to give corporations greater leeway than unions regarding solicitation for their political funds.

After the issuance of this opinion, the proverbial genie was out of the bottle, and an enormous growth in corporate and trade association political action committees occurred. Indeed, during the subsequent congressional debate over the 1976 amendments most of the debate centered on how to ensure a balance between labor and corporate

58. Ibid.

59. 2 U.S.C. § 437f.

interests, rather than on undoing what the advisory opinion had wrought.

Clearly, more thought should have been given by the commission to the far-ranging implications of the SunPAC advisory opinion. Instead, only a cursory period for comment was provided.[60] The FECA should be amended to require publication of advisory requests in the *Federal Register,* as well as a mandatory 30-day period of comment and response by the FEC to said comment, similar to the requirement for informal rule making under the Administrative Procedure Act.[61]

IN THE FINAL ANALYSIS, HOW GOOD IS THE FEC?

The FEC, in the final analysis, deserves a mixed review. It competently administers the public financing provisions and seems to function best during a presidential election, perhaps because its administrative staff and budget receive increases or are reallocated to cope with the demands. It is also excellent in providing disclosure of campaign financing, one of its principal missions.

During House and Senate elections, however, the FEC stumbles repeatedly in its attempt to keep the foxes out of the chicken coop and the chickens in. Some members of Congress plainly resent the agency created to regulate the financial aspect of the electoral process. Moreover, because of the problem of regulating independent expenditures, coupled with the proliferation of political action committees, it may be an impossible task to police congressional elections adequately, and it is surely an impossible task to police congressional elections by an inadequately funded agency.

The answer, however, is not to abolish the FEC, as some of its critics advocate. Rather, the FEC needs to have more independence from the stranglehold that Congress has on its internal processes. A far more independent general counsel, with greater powers, is needed. Finally, some method must be devised to get a handle on independent expenditures without infringing on important First Amendment guarantees. The Danforth bill,[62] proposing free air time for responding to political advertisements that are funded by independent expenditures, is a step in the right direction. Reforms in the FEC, along the lines I have mentioned, will go a long way in keeping the foxes out of the chicken coop—a goal this nation has been pursuing for over a century and should continue to pursue.

---

60. Subsequent to the SunPAC opinion, the commission changed its method of making public a request for an advisory opinion, as required by the act. 2 U.S.C. § 437(c). Instead of publishing said requests in the *Federal Register,* it now only publishes notice of receipt of said requests in its monthly newsletter. Neither the act nor the commission's regulations require actual publication of advisory opinion requests.

61. See 5 U.S.C. § 553(b).

62. U.S., Congress, Senate, Clean Campaign Act, H.R. 2534, 99th Cong., 1st sess., 17 June 1985.

Putting on the Candidates: The Use of Television in Presidential Elections

By NEWTON N. MINOW and LEE M. MITCHELL

ABSTRACT: The next presidential election campaign on television is likely to feature many spot commercials for the candidates, short news clips of candidates in on-site appearances staged for television, unanswered addresses to the nation or news conferences by the incumbent, relatively limited opportunities for the principal candidates to address the electorate, and, until the last moment, uncertainty about whether the candidates will appear face-to-face in debates. This use of television in presidential campaigns may have negative effects, including unfairly favoring wealthy interests and incumbents, encouraging political factionalism, and placing pressures on broadcasters that threaten First Amendment principles. The public would be better served by permitting broadcasters to present the two leading candidates without having to provide equal time to all other candidates; by giving the principal candidates television time during the campaign to address the electorate; by the adoption of party rules requiring that candidates participate in televised presidential debates; and by encouraging the use of new communications technologies to provide additional political information to the voters.

Newton N. Minow, an attorney, is a partner in the firm of Sidley & Austin, Chicago. He is a former chairman of the Federal Communications Commission and was cochairman of the Steering Committee for the League of Women Voters Presidential Debates Project in 1976 and 1980.

Lee M. Mitchell is president of The Field Corporation, a private holding company in Chicago, and counsel to the firm of Sidley & Austin. Mitchell has directed or participated in studies of the use of television by candidates and by the legislative and executive branches of government for research and policy organizations.

PRESIDENTIAL elections can be unpredictable, but presidential electioneering on television has fallen into a familiar pattern. Without changes in the use of television in presidential elections, its ability to inform and to involve the public in the most important of our elections will continue to be trivialized by a barrage of candidates' commercials, candidate-engineered news clips, special interest broadcasts, and quibbling over televised debate conditions.

CANDIDATES AS ADVERTISERS

If the pattern of past elections is followed, paid political advertising will be a prominent part of the next presidential election. The candidates will purchase as much television time as they can and will use it to present slickly produced advertisements for their candidacies. While there will be some program-length presentations, most of the air time purchased will be spots of 30 seconds or 60 seconds in length. As the campaign nears its conclusion, these television commercials will grow in number and will be broadcast with such increasing frequency that in areas where there also are congressional and state election contests, television viewers will be buried in a blizzard of candidates' commercials.

In the 1984 presidential election, President Reagan produced as many as 50 separate television commercials for the general election alone and his opponent, Walter Mondale, produced at least 20 commercials.[1] The Reagan commercials were created and produced by a staff whose earlier credits included commercials for Prego spaghetti sauce, Meow Mix cat food, and Gallo wine.[2] The Mondale staff had similar expertise. Not surprisingly, during the primary battles that preceded the general election, the already thin line between candidate advertising and consumer product advertising disappeared entirely when Walter Mondale adopted a slogan—Where's the Beef?—from a fast-food commercial as a campaign slogan. More of the same can be expected in future elections.

Candidate spots are the staple of election campaigning on television in part because television, and particularly network television, is a medium of scarcity. There are only 24 hours of television time in every broadcast day, only 3 hours in evening prime time, and only three major networks that regularly attract audiences in the tens of millions. Consequently, the limited amount of television time is in great demand; network executives want to use it to broadcast entertainment, sports, and news programs that will attract the largest possible audiences for advertisers, and advertisers are willing to pay a great deal for it to reach those audiences. Candidates who want television time, particularly on the networks and in prime time, are best able to get it, and to afford it, in 30- or 60-second pieces.

In 1971, Congress enacted the Campaign Communications Reform Act, which added section 312(a) to the Communications Act of 1934. That section provides that the Federal Communications Commission (FCC) may revoke the license of any broadcast station that fails "to allow reasonable access to or to permit purchase of reason-

1. *Public Opinion,* p. 55 (Dec.-Jan. 1985).

2. *Washington Post,* national weekly ed., 5 Nov. 1984, p. 6.

able amounts of time" by a legally qualified candidate for a federal elective office.[3] As interpreted by the FCC, the provision requires that each broadcast station give or sell qualifying candidates a "reasonable" amount of broadcast time—both spot and program time— once the campaign has begun.[4] What is reasonable in any particular case and the time when a campaign has begun are determined in the first instance by the broadcast station; the FCC will interfere only if the station is demonstrated to have made these determinations unreasonably.[5]

In theory, the reasonable-access provision should permit any candidate who wishes to do so to obtain program-length time in place of or as a supplement to spot advertising time and should make it unnecessary for candidates to reduce their positions on issues to 30-second segments. In practice, however, impediments to longer presentations and more meaningful content remain. Although program-length time must be made available under the law, broadcasters may charge for it; because of its scarcity, program time is expensive, with network time priced at $300,000 or more for one half hour.[6] Moreover, candidates and stations often do not agree on what is reasonable, and an FCC hearing to decide the issue and related appeals can take longer than the campaign.[7]

In some cases, even when program-length broadcast time is available and affordable, a candidate will still prefer spot commercials. The spots use the most effective advertising techniques and can be produced in quantity, focused to deliver different messages to different audiences, and changed quickly in response to new public preference poll results. Since spots have become an accepted part of a political campaign, the public expects nothing better.

Candidates as news

When the candidates are not on television in their own commercials, they will be—or will be trying very hard to be—on the local or network news. It has been many years since the campaign trail was used primarily to come face-to-face with voters. The modern campaign trail leads by careful design to the maximum possible exposure on television news. The candidates determine where they will go and what they will do based upon what they think will be most attractive to a television editor and most likely to be broadcast as a clip on the evening news. A candidate may dash from state to state not to meet the voters in those states, but to create a news event within the largest television markets, usually a news event with an identifiable local backdrop.[8] If a television viewer

---

3. 47 U.S.C. § 312(a)(7).

4. *The Law of Political Broadcasting and Cablecasting: A Political Primer,* 1984 ed. (Washington, DC: Federal Communications Commission, 1984); Irving Gastfreund and Erwin Krasnow, eds., *Political Broadcasting Handbook,* 2d ed. (Washington, DC: National Association of Broadcasters, 1984).

5. *Political Broadcast Catechism,* 10th ed. (Washington, DC: National Association of Broadcasters, 1984), pp. 62, 88; "Commission Policy in Enforcing Section 312(a)(7) of the Communications Act," 43 Radio Reg. 2d 1029 (1978).

6. Broadcasters are required to sell time to federal candidates at the "lowest unit rate" available to commercial advertisers. 47 U.S.C. § 315(b).

7. See, for example, *CBS, Inc. v. FCC,* 49 Radio Reg 2d 1191 (U.S. Sup. Ct. 1981).

8. Ronald Brownstein, "Public Seeing Campaign through Eye of TV Cameras," *National Journal,* 22 Sept. 1984, pp. 1752-57.

somehow missed the candidates' 30-second commercials, he or she is unlikely to miss a similar, and probably even briefer, glimpse of the candidates night after night on television news.

If in the next presidential election one of the candidates is an incumbent president, the campaign also is likely to be marked by the president's appearance on television to report to the people on a pending national issue. The appearance will probably be on all of the major television and cable television news networks simultaneously. Our presidents have learned to take advantage of the power of their office to call television cameras to a news conference or to request, and usually receive, valuable network television time to address the public.[9] In his first term, President Reagan made more than 15 televised speeches to the nation, virtually all of which were broadcast live by the American Broadcasting Company (ABC), Columbia Broadcasting System (CBS), National Broadcasting Company (NBC), Public Broadcasting Service (PBS), and Cable News Network (CNN).[10] As a Library of Congress study reported, this use of television "has been integral to the mass communications strategy of every president in recent times."[11]

The impact of equal time

Local stations and the television networks add their own election programming to the television exposure initiated by the candidates. Often, this programming attempts to deal with election issues or the candidates' personalities and character in more depth, and certainly in a more balanced way, than the candidates' spots or their engineered news appearances. It is likely to be outweighed, however, particularly in frequency, by the array of spots and news clips generated by the candidates.

One reason more broadcaster-produced election programming does not appear is section 315 of the communications act. This provision requires that when a station allows one candidate for an office to use its facilities—by giving or selling the candidate time—it must provide "equal opportunities" to all other qualified candidates for that office.[12] This requirement, known as the equal-time law, arose from the efforts of Congress to regulate broadcasting in the 1920s and 1930s and reflects an early concern about the potential of broadcasting to influence elections. By requiring broadcasters to treat all candidates the same, however, the law has had the effect of limiting programming about the principal candidates.

For example, if the voice or face of the Republican candidate for the presidency is used more than incidentally in a broadcast about presidential election issues or candidates, the broadcaster will be required by section 315 to provide equal time not only to the Democratic candidate, but also to every other candidate for that office, which can and usually does include a number of fringe or special interest candidates. The scarcity and value of broadcast time make it impracticable to provide equal time to all of these candidates. Not surprisingly, broadcasters tend to avoid or at least minimize this type of programming to

---

9. Newton N. Minow, John Bartlow Martin, and Lee M. Mitchell, *Presidential Television* (New York: Basic Books, 1973).

10. Denis Steven Rutkus, "President Reagan, the Opposition and Access to Network Airtime" (Report, Congressional Research Service, Library of Congress, 1984), app. A.

11. Ibid., p. 7.

12. 47 U.S.C. § 315.

avoid the impact of equal time. The public consequently loses a potentially valuable source of information about the principal candidates.

Section 315 has the same effect upon the sale or donation of time to the candidates beyond the limited reasonable time required by section 312. If 30 minutes is given to the Democratic and Republican candidates for the presidency, the same amount of time must be given to every other candidate for the office, including Vegetarian, Socialist, and Libertarian candidates and many others. This obviously is a disincentive to put candidates on the air any more than is absolutely required by the reasonable-access provision.

Presidential debates

The television centerpiece of the next presidential election could be a series of debates between the principal candidates broadcast live by the networks. Presidential television debates originated in the 1960 contest between John Kennedy and Richard Nixon when Congress suspended the equal-time law to relieve broadcasters of the need to give corresponding time to other candidates. The 1960 experience made it apparent that televised debates had the ability to focus the campaign, enhance voter interest, convey information about the candidates' positions, and provide some new insight into their character and personalities. Consequently, it was widely predicted that debates would become a fixed part of the process of electing a president. The predictions, however, ignored the fact that before there could be debates each of the two principal candidates would have to conclude that he or she had more to gain than to lose by participating, and in the 1964, 1968, and 1972 elections at least one of the candidates concluded otherwise. Congress's unwillingness to suspend section 315 in those years—encouraged by the political allies of the candidates who did not wish to debate—offered the candidates a convenient excuse.

In 1976, the FCC reinterpreted the equal-time provision to exclude candidate appearances on debates arranged by an independent sponsor. At the same time, political circumstances led candidates Jimmy Carter, a relative unknown at the time, and Gerald Ford, an appointed rather than elected incumbent, to agree to a series of televised debates. Once again, the debates captured the voters' attention and provided to a national audience of millions a great deal of information about the policies and character of the candidates. The Carter-Ford debates increased the public's expectation that debates would take place regularly, and they did occur in the next two presidential elections.[13] The debates have only been an ad hoc part of the electoral process, however, since they have depended upon the willingness and ability of a private organization, the League of Women Voters, to organize them and have been consistently jeopardized by the jockeying of the candidates for political advantage.

Candidates, their staffs, and their parties generally view debates much as they do television commercials or news shows—as techniques to be used or not used depending upon their assessment of the impact the use will have on their candidacies. If there is a handbook for

13. Lee M. Mitchell, *With the Nation Watching: Report of the Twentieth Century Fund Task Force on Televised Presidential Debates* (New York: Lexington Books, 1979); Joel Swerdlow, *Beyond Debate: A Paper on Televised Presidential Debates* (New York: Twentieth Century Fund, 1983).

candidates and campaign managers, it without doubt includes the admonition that if the candidate is well ahead of his or her opponent in the polls, the candidate—particularly if an incumbent—should stay out of sight and out of debates; if behind or unusually telegenic, the candidate must seek debates.

The public has been accepting of the use of television as part of the gamesmanship of elections in the past because this is how it has always been and because any preference for the use of television to benefit public understanding rather than candidate strategy has no organized constituency. Although the recent experience with debates will make it harder for future candidates to avoid them without the substantial risk of losing important votes, debates remain anything but a sure thing in 1988.

Television broadcasting is a unique communications medium. It can bring together audiences far greater than could assemble in any, or even all, of our public stadiums and auditoriums. It can and does reach into more homes than any of our newspapers and magazines. In some respects, television has become the national culture, cutting through age, economic, and geographic barriers to bring simultaneously to all of us experiences such as the first walk on the moon, the struggle for civil rights at Southern lunch counters, the agony of the Vietnam conflict, a government out of control in the Watergate hearings, the *Tonight Show* with Johnny Carson, and *Good Morning America* with David Hartman. It also has become the place where most people look for the information upon which they may base their political viewpoints and voting choices.[14]

FAULTS IN THE PRESENT SYSTEM

If a system were designed to use television to encourage voter participation and to provide the public with useful information about political issues and candidates, it would not be a system in which the most prevalent form of communication is the 30-second political commercial, followed closely by the 15-second news clip of candidates in made-for-television events. Nor would it be a system in which the talent of television professionals is used relatively infrequently to provide analysis and in-depth reporting of election issues. It also would not be a system in which televised presidential debates must depend upon the outcome of the quadrennial debate about debates among candidates, their advisors, and competing debate sponsors.

The way in which television has been used in presidential elections has a number of serious shortcomings.

First, the cost of television advertising can unfairly disadvantage some political interests and promote factionalization instead of consensus. Concern about the influence of money on candidates, growing use of television advertising, and a corresponding increase in the cost of campaigning led Congress to adopt a system of public financing for presidential elections in 1974.[15] Under this system, presidential candidates in the general election who agree to forgo private fund-raising and to limit their total campaign spending receive federal funds for their campaign. As a result, the two principal presidential candidates generally will have equal funding for their purchases of television time. How-

---

14. *Communications Daily,* 1 May 1984; *Editor & Publisher,* 13 Apr. 1985, p. 9; *Broadcasting,* 15 Apr. 1985, p. 140; ibid., 13 May 1985, p. 58.

15. 26 U.S.C. § 9001 et seq.

ever, the law does not limit expenditures by independent organizations or individuals to support or oppose a candidate.[16]

As long as costly commercial spots are perceived as a principal political battleground, presidential candidates with wealthy followers organized as independent groups will have an advantage. The candidates may have equal amounts of money to spend because they have accepted equal limits on their official campaign spending in return for financing by the government, but their supporters do not operate on the same level playing field. The 1974 effort to limit campaign spending simply shifted the spending battle from the candidates to the independent political action committees and organizations.

Similarly, a campaign that must be fought with paid commercials subjects candidates and the political process to dangerous pressures from single-issue factions able to raise and spend large sums of money to influence an election. Candidates must either try to appease these interest groups or accept the risk that the groups' paid television presentations will distort the election outcome. In such circumstances, elections no longer have the beneficial effect of forging coalitions and consensus; rather, they encourage single-issue factionalization.

Second, the present system puts so much pressure on our private system of broadcasting that it threatens First Amendment principles. As news coverage has become a principal part of the television campaign, the content of the news has come under increasing scrutiny by interests seeking to prove the existence of a media bias toward or against a candidate or political viewpoint.[17] Allegations that network anchorpersons demonstrate a bias in their description of campaign events or that the minutes and seconds devoted to one candidate are greater than those devoted to another place broadcasters under pressure to report on elections antiseptically or to minimize coverage.

The goal of fair and balanced news coverage of elections is quite appropriate. When, however, the importance of news coverage in a campaign is perceived to be so great that it warrants microscopic examination of the content of each news program for some sign of imbalance or bias, too much pressure is being placed on an activity not designed for the purpose. The key to a campaign should not be how the campaign or the candidates are perceived by a news organization or anchorperson, but rather how the candidates themselves and their positions are perceived directly by the public.

The situation becomes even worse when the search for news bias is taken up directly or indirectly by the government. When a member of Congress threatens congressional hearings into such allegations, or when the FCC considers such charges at the behest of proponents of a particular political viewpoint, there results a growing possibility that the content of the news will be influenced by this pressure. If so, the basic First Amendment value of a free and unfettered press has been compromised. An electoral system that puts this pressure on news reports during an election and risks this result clearly is not making the proper use of television.

16. 26 U.S.C. § 9012(f)(i); see *FEC* v. *National Conservative Political Action Committee,* 105 S. Ct. 1459 (1985).

17. See, for example, Michael J. Robinson, "The Media in Campaign '84," *Public Opinion* (Dec.-Jan. 1985); ibid. (Feb.-Mar. 1985).

Third, the present system unfairly favors incumbents over challengers. The ability of an incumbent president to command simultaneous network television before and during a campaign, with little equivalent opportunity for his or her opponent, gives the incumbent a powerful electoral weapon. Likewise, in the chase for news-clip exposure, the incumbent generally has the edge because whatever he or she does is more likely to be considered news. When debates are not assured, a well-known incumbent can prevent a lesser-known challenger from obtaining additional exposure by avoiding joint appearances.

The television advantage of incumbency can be and sometimes has been outweighed by other characteristics of a particular election. For example, Ronald Reagan's own media prominence—as a former actor and media commentator—and the state of the economy combined to overcome President Carter's incumbency advantage in 1980. When other things are generally equal, however, the television advantage could change the election result.

Fourth, the present system of heavy reliance on spots and brief news clips falls far short of providing the wealth of information of which television is capable. Although research has indicated that political commercials can increase viewers' knowledge about candidates, communicate a principal campaign point, and mobilize voter support, it is also true that they can and often do oversimplify difficult issues and reduce them to quick slogans, or so slickly package a candidate that weaknesses in the candidates' positions or character are obscured. Poor choices in selecting among presidential candidates will have much more severe consequences than poor choices in selecting among cat food brands.

REFORMS

These problems with the way television has been used in presidential campaigns have no single or quick solution. Putting television to better use will require that a number of steps be taken.

Equal time

The equal-time requirement should be changed. Television simply cannot be used to inform voters adequately about the principal candidates for the presidency if all of the candidates must have equal time. The continued assurance of equality in the access accorded the principal candidates protects them and the public from the possibility that television station owners could use their stations to favor one candidate over the other. It should be enough for the fringe and special interest candidates, however, to have a right to television time only if they have demonstrated the existence of some basic level of interest in their candidacy among the electorate.

Our political system is a two-party system. The candidates of the two parties should be treated equally by those who control the airwaves. Other candidates who have achieved a following by their actions between elections or by their campaigning in prior elections or who represent parties that have appealed to some substantial number of voters through past efforts are dealt with fairly if they have some, but not necessarily equal, access. A position or a candidate capable of attracting voters can do so given this chance. Thus Congress should amend the equal-time law to create a system of differential equality in which the two principal candidates are treated equally, any other significant candidates receive some but not equal time, and fringe or special interest candidates receive less time and then only if they meet certain standards of minimum support.

The federal law that provides government funds to presidential candidates is an example of how differential equality can be achieved between major-party and minor-party candidates. The law defines a major party as one whose candidate for president in the preceding election received at least 25 percent of the popular vote; a minor party is one whose candidate received more than 5 percent but less than 25 percent of the popular vote; and a new party is one whose candidate received less than 5 percent of the vote.

Each major-party presidential candidate is eligible to receive the same specified amount of federal funding. In general, a minor-party candidate is eligible to receive a portion of this amount based upon the ratio of the minor party's vote in the last presidential election to the votes for the major parties. New-party candidates can become entitled to a similar payment based upon their performance in the current election.[18] Similar benchmarks could be used to provide absolute equality in television time between major candidates and a lesser but adequate amount of television exposure for other candidates.

Freed of the artificial strictures of equal time, broadcasters would, it is hoped, increase their efforts to present in-depth coverage of presidential candidates and campaigns. They also would be able to provide the principal candidates with additional air time to present their candidacies themselves.

Program-length time

Program-length time should be provided for the principal presidential candidates on all television networks simultaneously. This allocation should be stipulated by law. The principal candidates would receive 30-minute segments of time to make their case to the voters at least twice during the campaign. This television time could be used by the candidates as they wished, with the sole restriction that they appear live. The candidates could make a traditional speech, introduce their supporters, advisors, or proposed appointees, create their own panel show, or choose some other format. The candidates' segments presumably would appear back-to-back in order to permit the public to make ready comparisons.

Other countries often follow procedures that assure the candidates for their highest office of specific opportunities to use television to address the voters during election campaigns. In Britain, for example, the parties are given free broadcast time during campaigns; the amount of time depends upon the number of parliamentary seats won in the prior election and the number of candidates put forward in the current election. In the United States, where virtually every home has a television set and usually more than one, where television is the principal and most credible source of news, and where citizens come together by the millions for television events, our presidential candidates should have available to them specific television time to appeal to the voters.

18. Presidential Election Campaign Fund Act, 26 U.S.C. §§ 9002-4; 11 C.F.R. §§ 9002-4.

The existing system of government funding for presidential campaigns could serve as a means of providing television time for the candidates. The time could be purchased from the networks with a portion of the federal funds that are already being allocated to the candidates. A substantial portion of those funds is now being spent on television advertising, at least some of which might then be found unnecessary.

Candidate debates

Televised debates between the principal candidates for the presidency should be made a part of every presidential election. The principal reason that televised presidential debates have not become an assured part of our electoral system is that candidates continue to view them not as an obligation to the electorate but as a campaign stratagem. Perhaps the best way to solve this problem is for the two principal political parties to adopt the position that henceforth debates will be a fixed part of the campaign and that whomever they nominate will be expected to participate. The parties could then turn to an independent sponsor, such as the League of Women Voters, to organize and conduct the debates. The presence of an independent sponsor should make it easier to resolve the many practical issues that must be decided—such as debate scheduling and formats—in producing debates that are as useful as possible to the electorate.

In late 1985, the chairmen of the Democratic and Republican parties indicated their intention to have the two parties sponsor presidential debates in 1988. This was an encouraging first step toward adopting debates by party rule and requiring every nominee to participate. Not only would such action by the parties contribute to a more informed electorate, but it also would be good for the parties themselves. By giving candidates and elected officials direct access to the electorate, television reduced the party role and weakened the party system. As party influence has waned, the parties have had increasing difficulty in enforcing party discipline and, consequently, in enforcing the compromises of which consensus is made. This, in turn, has reduced the effectiveness of the legislative process and in effect has abrogated much of the legislature's powers, transferring them to the executive branch. Although the parties' playing some role in televised presidential debates will not be a miracle cure for these problems, it will help move the parties toward a more contemporary role in a television age.

New technology

We need to encourage experimentation with the use of new communications technologies to inform the electorate. Network television produces the largest audiences of any communications medium. Since one principal goal of political campaigning is to reach the greatest number of prospective voters, network television is the preferred medium and the medium most important to any effort to inform the public. Increasingly, however, technological and regulatory changes have led to the availability of other communications methods that, if properly used, can supplement the role of broadcast television and bring additional information to the electorate.

Cable television is now well established in many communities and, in fact, serves more than half of the television households in the country. CNN has a potential audience of more than 32 million cable subscribers and qualifies as one of the television networks.

Because cable television is able to provide numerous video channels through a single wire, it is free of the limitations of the broadcast spectrum. With a large number of channels, television is no longer a medium of scarcity where political information must compete with entertainment, sports, and advertising for a limited amount of time; rather it becomes a medium able to devote substantial portions of time to particular topics or to narrow viewer interests. One example of this change is the cable service Cable Satellite Public Affairs Network (C-SPAN). C-SPAN makes the entire proceedings of the U.S. House of Representatives and related information about government available to more than 21 million cable subscribers.

The new wealth in television channels that cable brings makes it possible to devote an entire cable channel to the electoral process, much as C-SPAN devotes an entire channel to the legislative process. For example, the political parties might develop their own cable channel to transmit programming about their candidates and positions, or an organization such as the League of Women Voters might do the same. Although such a channel would not command the same audience as the broadcast networks, it would make election information available to any cable subscriber who wished to learn more than what was available from other sources. Polls indicate that cable subscribers are more likely to vote, to work in a campaign, and to be political fund-raisers than nonsubscribers.[19]

19. *Communications Daily*, 31 Jan. 1984.

Cable also makes available numerous local channels in each community served by a cable system. Many of these channels are rarely used and could be converted during elections into local election channels. Local or regional channels—comprising interconnected local channels—would provide candidates with an opportunity to present programming about their views on issues of local or regional concern. Although a political communications system that encouraged different messages to different local or regional constituencies would be potentially divisive, cable could be properly used to supplement the type of national television campaign discussed earlier.

Other communications technologies offer similar opportunities. New low-power television stations, often located in rural communities that before had no local station, can provide another outlet for the presentation of candidate positions on issues of local or regional concern. Videotext systems, which offer users a connection to vast computer data bases, can give citizens who wish to seek it out a complete text of the party platforms, candidate position papers, past voting records, and an almost infinite array of other campaign information. Technology now also allows candidates to hold video meetings in numerous communities simultaneously by projecting their appearance—and even questions from each audience—into meeting halls or theaters by satellite relay facilities.[20]

20. According to Walter Mondale's campaign manager, whose candidate used satellite hookups to appear at meetings with campaign supporters: "If the name of the game is to be seen by as many people as possible, you can be seen by a helluva lot more people with a satellite at 28,000 miles than you can from a bus at 60 miles per hour. It's going

Between elections

Between presidential elections, television time should be made available for a series of national debates. Political information may saturate the airwaves during campaign periods, but it quickly disappears as soon as the post-election analysis broadcast ends. Political issues, of course, remain and, in fact, often become the issues that determine decisions of national concern. The important role of television in creating an informed electorate should not end when the campaign ends.

Between elections, the newly elected president dominates, or has the ability to dominate, the presentation of national issues. The importance and single-person focus of the presidential office, and the president's access to television time through news conference appearances and nationally televised addresses to the nation, create a communications capability well beyond that of any opposition leader. Members of the opposition party or members of Congress who oppose presidential positions can be found on television, but never with the regularity or simultaneous network exposure available to the president. As a result, the president and executive branch of the government can dominate the national agenda and national decision making to an extent never contemplated by our Constitution.

The potential political and governmental imbalance created by the president's unique access to television could be corrected somewhat by a series of live, televised debates—*The National Debates*—between representatives of the two major parties quarterly in non-election years. The parties presumably would choose their most effective leaders to participate, and provision might be made for the use of video material or for other formats that would enhance viewer interest. If properly planned and promoted, *The National Debates* could become the focal point for discussion of major national policies by some of the country's most eloquent and persuasive speakers. As such, it is likely that the events would be broadcast willingly by the television networks and reach a large audience.

A series of major political broadcasts between elections would pick up where an improved system of electoral broadcasting leaves off. The public would have access to the principal arguments of the principal national political figures, would be better informed about national issues, and would be better able to understand the issues and participate actively in the next presidential campaign.

The Republic no doubt will survive if spot advertising and news clips remain the principal use of television in elections, if major candidates appear rarely in other formats because fringe candidates must get equal time, if televised face-to-face debates between the candidates depend upon the campaign strategies of the candidates rather than the public interest, and if the president dominates televised political discussion between elections. But we will be wasting the valuable resource of television by not making full use of its enormous ability to provide information about election issues and involve the public in the electoral process.

It is not hard to do better.

---

to be the wave of the future in presidential politics." *Washington Journalism Review*, p. 50 (June 1985).

Campaign Finance: The System We Have

By MICHAEL BARONE

ABSTRACT: The United States has developed a hybrid system of campaign finance regulation, with rules custom-crafted for different political situations and with unanticipated loopholes that need plugging. The largest loophole is soft money. The public financing systems enacted for presidential contests and for New Jersey's and Michigan's gubernatorial elections cannot easily be adapted to cover the various kinds of congressional elections. Although our current system is complex and has some obvious defects, it is generally defensible.

Michael Barone was graduated from Harvard College in 1966 and Yale Law School in 1969. He was an editor of the Harvard Crimson *and the* Yale Law Journal. *He served as law clerk to Judge Wade McCree of the U.S. Court of Appeals for the Sixth Circuit and worked as a pollster and political consultant for Peter D. Hart Research Associates. Since 1982, he has been a member of the editorial-page staff of the* Washington Post, *writing editorials and columns. He has been coauthor of editions of* The Almanac of American Politics *since 1972.*

THE system of campaign finance law that has evolved in the United States over the last dozen or so years is different from what anyone anticipated or intended in two important respects. First, it is a system the rules of which have been custom-crafted for particular kinds of political races in particular jurisdictions. The tendency to custom-craft is even more pronounced in the proposals for change that have some serious chance of passage. The second way in which the system has changed in ways no one anticipated is that the biggest loopholes that have appeared—most notably the use of soft money—raise issues that everyone thought were long ago settled and allow abuses no one thought were any longer possible.

Let us look first at the way the system has become custom-crafted. Consider public financing of elections. Two forms of public financing are used in presidential elections—matching funds in the primaries, public funding in the general. A different form of public financing exists in the race for governor of New Jersey. There is another, similar system for the gubernatorial race in Michigan. I am told that the Los Angeles city council has enacted a public financing system for itself.

What there conspicuously is not is a public finance system for all congressional elections. Many backers of the 1971 federal legislation hoped that presidential public financing would lead, in time, to public financing of congressional races. Instead, the system became carefully adjusted to the requirements of presidential races. For the most part it works well. It weeds out nuisance candidates and provides tolerable levels of financing for serious candidates, it relieves general election candidates from spending half their time raising money; it allows incumbent administrations to avoid the spectacle of shaking down those dependent on government favor for campaign dollars. But there is no way to adapt this system easily to the very different politics of congressional races.

Nor are the admirable New Jersey and Michigan systems going to be a model for national change. In New Jersey, where the governor is the only elected official and appoints the attorney general and all county prosecutors, the nomination used to be the gift of sometimes not-so-honest county party bosses. The low visibility level of local politics in a state in which most of the media comes from New York City and Philadelphia meant that these candidates did not always get all the scrutiny they deserved from voters. New Jersey's rather generous public financing—though eroded somewhat by inflation—has given the state competent and honest competitors in both parties and has made state politics more visible. In Michigan, public financing has also made for serious competition and has freed the Republicans and Democrats from their historical overreliance on business and labor, respectively.

These systems, however, were each carefully created for particular political contests. How is a public financing system set up that will work fairly and usefully in 50 states and 435 congressional districts? The answer may turn out to be that it cannot be. Consider some of the practical problems. The cost of campaigning varies widely by state and district, not only because of their size, but because of television time-buying requirements. New Jersey, for example, is the second most expensive television state, after California, though it is number nine in population. The focus of competition varies also. In many congressional and some Senate races—which ones depends more on the incumbent's strength than on the state's political leanings—the real contest is in one party's primary. Other seats in Congress—a majority in any given election year—are not contested seriously. How does a public financing system handle such divergent cases? With difficulty—or not at all, since legislators fearing one problem or another gang up and kill any measure.

Some of the current proposals would provide more piecemeal reform. Senators Mathias and Simon push for public financing of Senate races, leaving the House entirely alone and not touching Senate primaries either. The Democratic Study Group endorses a $100 tax credit for congressional campaigns, but only for contributions to House candidates in the taxpayer's home state. Senator Boren would limit the total amount of money any candidate could accept from political action committees, but he would not otherwise limit contributions. And so on.

There is something to be said for custom-crafted campaign finance law. It is harder, I suppose, than a comprehensive system for the public to understand, harder even for professional politicians to keep track of. But already there is a gaggle of professional campaign finance experts that candidates can hire; the free market will provide. What the public expects is a process that is fair, that requires basic disclosure of finances, that enables candidates to raise money honestly and spend enough to get their messages across. In a nation with such widely divergent political traditions and continuingly divergent political practices, custom crafting may make more sense than trying to get everyone into the same procrustean bed.

One consequence of custom crafting, though, is that campaign finance regulation is, like New York City, never really finished; someone is always tearing something else down in one place and putting a couple of buildings up in another. But that, I think, is true whether we have custom crafting or not, as is apparent with respect to the problem of loopholes. To change the metaphor, writing campaign finance law is Sisyphus's work. Every so often that stone will have to be rolled up the hill again. The difference is that, unlike Sisyphus, campaign finance reformers can improve things for a considerable period of time; if they do their work well enough, the stone will stay at the top of the hill for a decade or two.

Consider the problem of soft money, which I think is the chief fault of our system today. Soft money is defined as contributions made to state or local political parties that are legal under state law, but would not be legal under federal law, and that can be used for federal campaign purposes. They include money over federal contribution limits and contributions by corporations and labor unions, and they need only be disclosed as required by state law.

Soft money was explicitly legalized in 1979; Congress wanted to encourage state party-building activities, and soft money has probably done that. But in practice the law is used to evade the fundamentals of federal campaign finance law. Both national parties have now set up soft money accounts, for which they solicit and receive large contributions from individuals—on the order of $100,000—corporations, and unions. Funds are then disbursed to state parties in accordance with formulas that reflect the state parties' eligibility under state law to receive each particular form of contribution; state parties tend to spend money on projects that directly aid the presidential campaign or, occasionally, a senatorial campaign. But—here is the nice part—there is no requirement of disclosure by the national parties of who gives money to the fund. A trip to a state capital—for instance, Harrisburg, Pennsylvania or Springfield, Illinois—allows one to discover that perhaps $1000 or so was donated by a person in California. But hidden will remain what the proprietors of the national party's soft-money fund know: that the donor in California gave them a check for $100,000. In other words, those who receive the benefit of the money know where it came from, but the public is effectively barred from finding out. A person cannot give $1000 directly to a presidential candidate without getting his or her name in the papers, but a person can give $100,000 to a soft-money fund and never have that contribution disclosed save in the most fragmentary way.

Obviously this is a loophole that cries out for plugging. Very likely this Congress or the next will act. It should be noted, however, that the problem rose out of the natural operation of the system. There is a lot of money out there waiting to flow into campaigns, and when there is a single hole in the dike it is not long before the money starts gushing through. With all that hydraulic pressure, there is a great premium on finding a loophole, on testing it out for an election cycle or so to make sure there is no problem, and then on using it in a major way. That is what is happening now with soft money.

Ironically, the system of campaign finance law—any system of campaign finance law that seeks to limit contributions—creates such a pressure. It cannot be avoided; it is inherent in the process, so long as people want candidates to be elected badly enough to spend money on their campaigns. Even a total public financing system does not eliminate the problem, since *Buckley* v. *Valeo* allows independent campaign spending as protected First Amendment activity; there was some pretty extensive—and in some cases dubiously independent—spending in the last presidential campaign. It has taken some time for the soft-money loophole to get really large; it will take somewhat more to get it filled. It will not be the last loophole in our custom-crafted campaign-finance system.

There may come a day when our campaign finance system seems so encrusted with exceptions, special cases, partial loopholes, and local options that it will seem as mindless and indefensible as the diverse laws and taxes in ancien régime France. But I think it is possible to defend, with some vigor, the already quite diverse system we have today. If it tends to help some House incumbents avoid serious competition, it for the most part allows serious candidates to raise enough money to be competitive; if it allows now some evasion of disclosure requirements, it places limits on the influence of those rich enough to contribute huge sums of money to candidates. No system is going to erode completely the advantage enjoyed by those with great wealth or political adeptness. Our current system tends to scale down their edge and yet allows pretty vigorous competition. I can think of lots of ways I would change the system if I could sit down and rewrite all the laws and regulations myself, and I can think of some egregious problems with it—soft money is number one—that need fixing immediately. But for all that, over the last dozen or so years we have evolved, almost willy-nilly, a system that works tolerably well and, with some patching, that can work tolerably well for some time to come.

Book Department

	PAGE
INTERNATIONAL RELATIONS AND POLITICS	163
AFRICA, ASIA, AND LATIN AMERICA	168
EUROPE	172
UNITED STATES	172
SOCIOLOGY	177
ECONOMICS	185

INTERNATIONAL RELATIONS AND POLITICS

CLARKSON, STEPHEN. *Canada and the Reagan Challenge.* Pp. xv, 383. Toronto: James Lorimer, 1982. No price.

Clarkson champions the nationalist approach to stable integration in Canada, contending that such stability peaks at the national rather than provincial or continental level of analysis. Nor is this contention limited to one dimension; economic, cultural, and political integration all must be national in scale. Ergo, Ottawa, like so many Third World regimes, must boldly Canadianize its cultural media, economic resources, and political authority—even if that means redefining its special relationship to America. Hence, despite strong macro forces contrarily favoring provincial and continental integration, strategic micro decisions from Ottawa should pursue the nationalist alternative.

One of Clarkson's apparent strengths lies in stressing multiple dimensions of integration—for example, a Canada-centric economy synergistically requires a Canada-centric culture. This proves more radical, hence more conflictual, with Washington now, but more successful than one-dimensional approaches and less conflictual over time. Alas, while Canada's resources can sustain a national economy and its constitution can sustain a national polity, what sustains a truly national culture? Indeed, within-group—interprovince—variance exceeds between-group—international—variance on this dimension: culturally, Canada is nearly America's fifty-first state. Canada may thus become historic Poland's obverse: the state without a nation.

Another apparent asset is Clarkson's heroic stress on David-like decisions over nine major issues, from acid rain to capital flow, to counter Goliath-like forces favoring subnational or supranational integration—in other words, Balkanization or Americanization. Reinforcing such decisions are Canada's various alternative alliance partners and America's various alternative access points besides Reagan's White House. But can David really counter those global crises in arms, resources, capital, and other arenas that scare provincial premiers and America's president alike into power grabs that frustrate Canadianization? Tragically, the very global crises prompting Ottawa's problem may preclude its capacity to solve it.

Clarkson's third phantom asset is his

book's timing. It coincides with America-firster Ronald Reagan's election and Ottawa's National Energy Program, which respectively dramatize Canadianization's urgency and feasibility. Surely, middle-level powers like Canada should use timing to compensate for scarce capabilities when encountering superpowers. Yet the very events used—elections, programs—the dramatizing effects of which spark Canadianizers, appear mercurial whereas Canadianization is glacial—2000 is Clarkson's earliest target date for its achievement. Sadly, more than a fortuitous cosmic soup of mutually reinforcing but fleeting events is needed not just to spark, but to sustain, the momentum toward Canada's nationhood.

Clarkson's true import is partly his *realpolitik* rationale for nationhood. America needs a strong Canada, even if that Canada is independent rather than weak and dependent. Canada is both a geostrategic buffer between East and West and a diplomatic broker between North and South. Thus, like India in 1947, Canada's movement today is urged more by its external position than by its internal potential for national integration. Accordingly, America should not only tolerate but strengthen Canadianization—which is not, after all, Finlandization. Indeed, in international as in national society it is strengthened middle powers like Canada that promote stability and hence American interests.

Clarkson's other genuine import is to illumine not just Canada's problem of national integration but America's problem of national—as against fragmented—foreign policy despite broadly consensual landslide elections like 1980. Even allowing for his possible bias as a University of Toronto political economist, Clarkson fully documents the United States' poor integration in hemispheric foreign policy. Americans have overlearned James Madison's thesis linking responsible government with fragmented authority, at the cost of fragmented policies and resulting ill will abroad. Unlike Britain, the United States just cannot reconcile a pluralist society with a unitary polity. For a superpower, such irreconcilability is dangerous.

On balance, Clarkson's ambitious study—based on interviews with 200 American and Canadian officials—is better at prognosis than diagnosis of developments in Canada. Such prognosis affords a needed early-warning system given Canada's tranquility, similarity, and hence invisibility to Americans. But Clarkson's prognosis of nationalism is for the near term and not the long term if technological advances accelerate physical mobility and so erode territorial identity, which is the taproot of total national communities. Indeed, today's total community may, in the long term, be supplanted by partial, overlapping communities at differing levels of analysis. But until then, read Clarkson—if only because Canada is literally all that stands between today's superpowers.

CRAIG McCAUGHRIN
Washington and Lee University
Lexington
Virginia

KEGLEY, CHARLES W., Jr. and EUGENE R. WITTKOPF, eds. *The Nuclear Reader: Strategy, Weapons, War.* Pp. xx, 332. New York: St. Martin's, 1985. Paperbound, $10.95.

HUDSON, GEORGE E. and JOSEPH KRUZEL, eds. *American Defense Annual 1985-1986.* Pp. xix, 277. Lexington, MA: Lexington Books; Columbus: Ohio State University, Mershon Center, 1985. Paperbound, $13.95.

International defense issues revolve around both nuclear and conventional weapons, with the latter now encroaching on the gray area in between. Affecting these issues are complex political developments and technological change, which breed public debate from clouded premises. It is improbable that a single voice can cover all significant dimensions of the field. Thus a realistic alternative is to study particular aspects or use sector specialists. American security direction, tied to the international, requires a compass of analysts delimiting possibilities and showing merits or defects in selected courses.

The two cited volumes are leaders of their kind in our period. The first, edited by Kegley and Wittkopf and including their own contributions, through the views of experts discusses war, strategy, and weapons from nuclear global and domestic perspectives. Many articles are republished, being chosen for their relevance. The second volume, shaped by Hudson and Kruzel, with articles by them as well as other leading specialists, is the first of an annual critical review of the Mershon Center at Ohio State University of major U.S. defense policies and issues. Both books group stimulating experts to give focused treatments of global and national security themes.

Starting with the *Reader* and its generalized outlook, we see weapons appraisals by the Harvard Nuclear Study Group of the East-West nuclear balance and scenarios for nuclear war. These last have a plausible spectrum of possibilities, requiring unremitting care in action by the two cautious superpowers. Daily the United States dwells on the opportunistic Soviet record, while the USSR deeply mistrusts America as highly erratic, hence dangerous.

The objectives and means of nuclear war receive searching scrutiny. Reprinted is the Catholic bishops' statement against nuclear war and the subjecting of those near significant military targets to "indirect" attack. Albert Wohlstetter strongly criticizes this position and alleges that the bishops explicitly abandon a nuclear threat while implicitly relying on it. Kattenburg defends mutual assured destruction as moral, deeming as valid the no-missile defense strategy with its current prospect of population and industrial destruction rather than Wohlstetter's advocacy of attacking nuclear and military resources. Others call a nuclear freeze irrelevant, a nuclear build-down practical and desirable, and new conventional weapons capable, possibly, of leaping the nuclear firebreak. In nuclear war, as exchanges become uncontrollable, governments could not be protected, while the well-known effects of electromagnetic pulses from explosions would paralyze economic life. So devastating are the weapons, Desmond Ball convincingly states, that after 50-100 warheads targeted key U.S. facilities, dual American civil-military command controls would give incoherent direction to strategic forces.

The Annual's articles, looking at present American defense, complement the *Reader*. A security debate between the opposite poles of Van Cleave and Ravenal has the former asserting that all U.S. commitments—left undefined—must be pursued, while the latter takes a neo-isolationist position. Again, extremes seem to be no answer. Demands on U.S. power and resources, say others, challenge a laggard North Atlantic Treaty Organization and Japan to ease America's financial burden in order to permit strategic shifts. This familiar argument has equity and common interests to support it.

The Pentagon's handling of programs and forces suffers from differing service objectives and unclear lines of responsibility. The role of the Joint Chiefs of Staff's chairman is ambiguous, and our top military suffers from confused cross-service aims. Philip Odeen is not the first to attribute Congress's "micromanagement"—of foreign policy as well as domestic—to its outsized staff increases. In a readable essay, however, he combines proposals for general reform. He would base defense planning and resource allotments, including costs and delivery schedules, on vital interests and objectives. Otherwise, forces will continue unbalanced and unsuited for joint operations. Importantly, "we need a rigorous process of weapons program infanticide." The chairman of the Joint Chiefs of Staff would be the prime military adviser, control an improved Joint Staff, and ensure policy-responsive crisis planning. Theater commanders, too—in peace and crisis—would control their joint staffs and the readiness funds of their service components to ensure effective planning. Major defense missions would be the planning and resources priority of the defense policy under secretary. Congress would cooperate with a two-year budget cycle, combining a single program-budget review and decision process.

The two books outline the superpower recriminations over violated treaty limits. However, the presented evidence of Soviet evasion and stretching in missile defense is plausible. The United States has no operational ballistic missile defense (BMD), but the USSR has such advanced programs as the massive potential battle radar station at Krasnoyarsk and over 10,000 surface-to-air-missile launchers. Accumulating evidence of a systematic Soviet BMD program could even presage an eventual breakout from the first Strategic Arms Limitation Talks (SALT I) treaty.

U.S. defensive gaps were a backdrop to President Reagan's Strategic Defense Initiative (SDI). His sweeping research call was for a national shield against nuclear attack, which opponents have termed scientific and financial fantasy. Program defenders rise to claim that missile accuracy and mobility have made mutual assured destruction and its absence of BMD highly suspect. A confused public admits deterrence to be effective hitherto, but regards it as unattractive in principle. Even if the United States, at some stage in the president's ongoing proposal, scraps the Anti-Ballistic Missile Treaty, Albert Carnesale in the *Annual* warns that it could not match in any near future the Soviet deployable, varied missile defense. For SALT I to endure, he proposes countering the Soviet BMD-oriented programs with a vigorous drive for penetration aids.

Certainly SDI has Soviet attention, for the president has persisted with the program and its salient ingredient of nonnuclear defensive weaponry. As writers indicate in both volumes, Moscow fears that breakthroughs could devalue their offensive nuclear missiles and that they could not match our nonnuclear technology. Some, seeing that the militarization of space is under way with the Soviets having the first steps, think SDI can energize diplomacy with Moscow, but others would not curtail the initial program in any early negotiation. It seems from press reports that Premier Gorbachev, reading the signs, has gone from intransigence to apparent acceptance of limited American research but not testing.

As an SDI way station, qualified writers in both books assert that a limited, credible BMD of critical military targets such as silos for intercontinental ballistic missiles, bomber bases, and command and control facilities would be technically feasible by the 1990s. This BMD would be at affordable cost and would be consistent with a deterrent strategy, for it would increase the survival of retaliatory forces. This believable and important contribution of both volumes, combined with their amplitude and informed reasoning on other themes, makes them essential reading for the national security professional and the tyro as well.

ROY M. MELBOURNE
Chapel Hill
North Carolina

SAMPSON, GEOFFREY. *An End to Allegiance: Individual Freedom and the New Politics.* Pp. 253. New York: Universe Books, 1984. $17.50.

Gertrude Stein's observation that "a rose is a rose is a rose" could be applied to ideologies as "a liberal is a liberal is a liberal." But is that liberal actually a socialist, a liberal democrat, or a capitalist? Since the labels "communist" and "fascist" are tainted by association, even extremists of the Left and Right might ask to be called liberals.

Noticeably dissatisfied with British socialism—for example, the National Health Service "depersonalizes the patient," and harassment by the Inland Revenue "can drive taxpayers to breakdown"—Geoffrey Sampson advocates libertarianism. His ideology, to the right of center on the spectrum, attacks collectivist planning, as N. K. O'Sullivan refers to a major tenet of conservatism. It is similar to French doctrines of laissez-faire, as supported by the Physiocrats, and poujadism, and sought during the Fourth Republic and used more broadly by Mark Hagopian.

Quoting Gordon Tullock on bureaucrats—they "are as self-seeking as businessmen"—Sampson asks us to protect our opportunities for choice so that we can "experiment with different conceptions of the good life." He is comfortable with James Buchanan's view in *The Limits of Liberty* that individual freedom should become the overriding objective of social policy.

As a University of Leeds linguist, Sampson carefully distinguishes his position from David Friedman's anarchocapitalism or Murray Rothbard's concern about encroaching statism so strongly that he looks at children as free agents. Sampson rejects Friedmanland and Rothbardland; the tastes of individual anarchists, as Leon Baradat would refer to them, are not his cup of tea.

One must read William Galston's "Defending Liberalism" to put Sampson's classical liberal, capitalist stance into perspective; individual responsibility does not characterize libertarian ideas alone. If "the questions make you human," Sampson has done a provocative job. Should he now consider moving to California to experience the quintessential libertarian state?

CHARLES T. BARBER
University of Southern Indiana
Evansville

VAN DYKE, VERNON. *Human Rights, Ethnicity and Discrimination*. Pp. xii, 259. Westport, CT: Greenwood Press, 1985. $35.00.

Human Rights, Ethnicity and Discrimination is obviously the work of a mature and seasoned scholar. In this book, Vernon Van Dyke, professor emeritus of political science at the University of Iowa, has attempted to deal with one of the knottiest problems in American society—how to maintain individual rights while at the same time providing compensatory help to those who have been historically discriminated against in this country. Van Dyke's approach is unique in that he only comes to this problem after having analyzed other societies divided by race, religion, or language such as Belgium, India, Fiji, Malaysia, and South Africa. He demonstrates convincingly that many nations, deeply divided by questions of ethnicity or language, have, in effect, given differential and preferential treatment to minority groups within their societies. Van Dyke feels that such policies are justified if the net effect is to promote the equal enjoyment of human rights throughout the society. Van Dyke ranges in depth over many of these problems, and it is a delight to see an intelligent and informed mind, steeped in the literature, grapple with the problems that beset so many societies today. And he takes care to present carefully the case of those who disagree with him.

The two best chapters in the book deal with the United States and South Africa. Having earlier examined other societies, Van Dyke has managed to place the ethnic divisions of the United States and South Africa into historical and cultural context. In the American chapter, Van Dyke challenges neoconservative views on affirmative action and instead argues that a one-tracked insistence on individualism and majority rule means that the larger community—whites, that is—will be able to make the government their tool and use it to oppress and exploit blacks. Certainly, this was historically the case in the United States. The chapter on American society also contains good discussions of the *Bakke* and *Weber* cases. The discussion on South Africa is likewise well done and informative.

The book is a bit overlong, and at times it is repetitive. And one wonders why Van Dyke left his brilliant analysis of traditional liberal thought to the last chapter when it would have made a fine introduction. These are minor objections, however. The book is well worth reading for anyone interested in an informed and broad survey of the problems involved in balancing the rights of majorities and ethnic minorities in modern societies.

ALLEN BALLARD
City College of New York
New York City

AFRICA, ASIA, AND LATIN AMERICA

BANERJEE, SANJOY. *Dominant Classes and the State in Development: Theory and the Case of India*. Pp. xi, 116. Boulder, CO: Westview Press, 1984. $13.95.

BENNER, JEFFREY. *The Indian Foreign Policy Bureaucracy*. Pp. xiv, 305. Boulder, CO: Westview Press, 1985. $19.50.

The first of these two books, each published in the Westview Replica Edition series, is one in which excessive behaviorism is blended with quite good descriptions, first, of the emphasis in planning during Nehru's administration on the heavy industry sector of India's economy and, second, of the switch under Shastri to the agricultural sector. Banerjee's theoretical base accompanied by his requisite review of the literature—as this is a published version of a Ph.D. dissertation—is overly jargonistic and of little value to the reader familiar with India. When he purges himself, not entirely, of this liturgical display of his diligence, he describes with improving clarity the coalitions that supported the basic industry approach of India's first prime minister. He notes the enormous growth, for example, of the public sector corporations (see the chart on page 62) at the expense of private sector enterprises. He adds that the support group included the brains of the Planning Commission, who were in general agreement with Nehru and followed his lead while opponents, such as the later prime minister, Charan Singh, who favored agricultural development, had no political clout at the time. The support shifted to agriculture under Lal Bahadur Shastri as his entry into the head-of-government role coincided with the most dismal period of food production in India's post-independence history. If one can take the jargon that dominates the first part of the book and permeates the remainder, there is much of value in this work for those who wish to learn more of India's economic development. As a last comment, Westview should avoid the typescript used here in future works; it is difficult to read with i and l appearing as the same letter.

The Benner work also shuttles between jargon and description, although the latter tends to be pedestrian and is often confusing as Benner jumps back and forth between time periods. There is a valuable historical introduction that explains the pre-independence role of the government of India in foreign and political affairs and the reliance by Nehru after independence on Indian Civil Service officers such as Bajpai and Menon. The closing chapter is a well-integrated discussion of the relationship between the prime ministers and foreign ministers and the career officers of the Ministry of External Affairs (MEA). In between are chapters devoted to the structure of the ministry and of the functional parts of MEA, none of which will add significantly to the knowledge of those who have worked with that ministry. All of this is done within the framework of neo-reductionism, developed by Benner and explained in an appendix. Benner appears to be one who is devoted to his model but who has little familiarity with the Indian scene about which he writes. For example, the Soviets will be surprised to learn that they supplied aircraft to the Pakistanis; Uma Shankar Bajpai to be separated from his father, G.S., and brother, K. S.; and B. K. Nehru to find that he was chief minister—rather than governor—of Jammu and Kashmir. Nonetheless, the book is valuable and adds insights to the study of Indian foreign policy however much it suffers from an excess of jargon and the resultant poor style.

CRAIG BAXTER

Juniata College
Huntingdon
Pennsylvania

CALLAGHY, THOMAS M. *The State-Society Struggle: Zaire in Comparative Perspective.* Pp. xviii, 515. New York: Columbia University Press, 1984. $45.00.

This work focuses on issues that are the source of considerable scholarly contention, namely, the issues raised by the response of the state in Africa to the demands of groups and classes within the society encompassed by its geographical boundaries. In this instance, Zaire under Mobutu Sese Seko forms the material for a case study, and on the whole Thomas Callaghy does a creditable job. An assistant professor of political science at Columbia University, Callaghy is the editor of two previous books on the complex issues confronting contemporary Africa, and in the present study he demonstrates a firm grasp on both the methodology and the sources germane to his subject.

The State-Society Struggle is a complex, lengthy book, but it is one no serious student of modern Africa can afford to ignore. Combining careful field research with a solid grounding in the printed sources and employing comparative approaches connected with such disparate disciplines as history, sociology, and political theory, Callaghy provides a convincing picture of the problems confronting Mobutu's Zaire. Here we see the work of an authoritarian regime set in sharp relief against the competing demands of local interests, class considerations, and external pressures. Also, there are interesting sidelights on what Zaire has to tell us about similar problems currently existing or likely to emerge elsewhere in Africa and the rest of the world.

Although the publisher's blurb on the dust jacket would have us believe that the work would be "valuable as a textbook for undergraduate and graduate courses in comparative and African politics," this can be readily ignored as a woefully misguided sales pitch. For graduate courses it might form significant outside reading, but the book's real audience, as I suspect Callaghy would agree, will be Africanists who specialize in one of the fields or disciplines touched on in this wide-ranging book. A revision of Callaghy's doctoral thesis, which won the American Political Science Association's Gabriel Almond Award in 1981, this study forms a significant contribution to the ongoing debate concerning the formation of new states and the special problems that African circumstances pose for such political entities. The volume should include a map, and at times it makes for somewhat difficult reading, but these are minor quibbles. The book belongs in every serious African-studies collection.

JAMES A. CASADA

Winthrop College
Rock Hill
South Carolina

DAVIS, NATHANIEL. *The Last Two Years of Salvador Allende.* Pp. xv, 480. Ithaca, NY: Cornell University Press, 1985. $24.95.

Insurrection is a dangerous game. It involves bloodshed, terror, and, almost inevitably, dictatorship. Spain and Chile illustrate, each in its own fashion, the price of insurrection in the twentieth century. Nathaniel Davis's study is limited to the game that was played out in Chile from 1970 to 1973; it deals with the dangers only in passing.

The Last Two Years of Salvador Allende is an honest book and comprehensive within its deliberately limited scope. It relates an oft-told tale that does not pretend to entertain but that grasps the reader, at least up until the actual demise of the former president. It is an interesting book in that it unfolds on a split level; it covers events that took place within Chile and the role of the United States in those same events. More than a contribution of new insights, it accurately synthesizes old and new material available to Davis, who was the American ambassador to Santiago between 1971 and 1973. It is not, fortunately, a self-serving memoir; Davis does not attempt to justify. More important, he goes beyond the raw material and raises questions, explicitly and implicitly.

"Did the United States want to preserve a democratic system or destroy a democratically elected government?" asks Davis in his treatment of efforts to "destabilize" Allende. How does a democratically elected socialist act during a crisis that threatens his regime from two sides? "Assassination or Suicide?" is the title of the chapter dealing with Allende's death. Assassination or suicide of Chile? it might well be asked with respect to the insurrection itself.

Davis aptly describes the atmosphere during the first week of September 1973 as "crackling with electricity." He refers to the choice of the military: "They could not stand on a safe shore, as there was none, nor find refuge in the swamp of indecision." He suggests, perhaps for the first time, that Pinochet was reluctant to participate in the overthrow of Allende. He correctly emphasizes Allende's own vacillations.

The final chapter expresses the fear that President Pinochet's actions against democratic forces will create a wasteland. Yet Davis ends on a hopeful note. And so he should; there will be no wasteland because democracy does not die.

DAVID M. BILLIKOPF
Santiago
Chile

HUSSAIN, ASAF. *Islamic Iran: Revolution and Counter-Revolution*. Pp. ix, 225. New York: St. Martin's Press, 1985. $27.50.

MARR, PHEBE. *The Modern History of Iraq*. Pp. xvii, 382. Boulder, CO: Westview Press; London: Longman, 1985. $38.50.

The Iran-Iraq war, among other recent events, has brought Iran and Iraq into prominent public focus. An explosion of publications has followed, with uneven results, as might well be expected. The two books under review here are written from radically different perspectives; their usefulness to readers will likewise vary.

Asaf Hussain, a social scientist based in both Pakistan and England, presents what is just short of an insider's account of the Iranian revolution. His work consists of six chapters treating the political context—with a very uneven and certainly controversial historical account—the political system, the Islamic opposition, the revolutionary struggle, the Islamic republic, and "counter-revolutionary postures." Probably the best chapters are the third, fourth, and fifth, which reveal Hussain's deep study of the revolution from within, his personal acquaintance with many of the principal actors and with a broad spectrum of the Iranian public, which was gained through travel, residence, interviews, and access to documents, and those aims of the revolution with which Hussain clearly sympathizes: refusal to be part of the East-West conflict, rejection of the shah's imperial system, and protest against social and economic injustice. Readers will gain most from seeing the Iranian experience from the perspective of a committed Muslim activist struggling to define the revolution in terms derived from a passionate search for an authentic Islam.

Phebe Marr, a historian at the University of Tennessee, Knoxville, has written a synthesis of Iraqi history concentrating almost exclusively on the twentieth century. A brief, but useful, chapter treats the land, people, and civilizations of the past. Nine chapters, of which two concentrate on economic and social change, cover the British mandate (1920-32), the interwar and war years (1932-45), the old regime (1946-58), the revolutionary regimes since 1958, and the Iran-Iraq war to mid-1984. Readers will appreciate the lucid prose, the clear analyses, and the balanced treatment of complex aspects of Iraq's recent past. Particularly useful is the annotated bibliography of works in both Arabic and Western languages. Marr has written an authoritative work that meets a great need: an up-to-date, readable, and comprehensive treatment of recent Iraqi history.

KARL K. BARBIR

Siena College
Loudonville
New York

TEVETH, SHABTAI. *Ben Gurion and the Palestinian Arabs: From Peace to War.* Pp. x, 234. New York: Oxford University Press, 1985. $17.95.

REICH, WALTER. *A Stranger in My House: Jews and Arabs in the West Bank.* Pp. 134. New York: Holt, Rinehart and Winston, 1984. $12.95.

The main subject of the two books under review is the relationship between Zionists and the Palestinian Arabs. The first volume, written by Shabtai Teveth, is an Israeli account of Ben Gurion's perceptions and policies toward the Arabs. Teveth depicts Ben Gurion as a man who did not have many direct contacts with Arabs and who derived his policies from his Zionist ideals. Thus for Ben Gurion, the Arab person, as distinct from the abstract, remained an unknown, a failing that led to errors of judgment, such as his belief that the Arabs would easily accept a "Jewish state within an Arab federation of states."

In addition to its main theme, the book gives an interesting account of the conflicts and divisions among the socialists in the Zionist movement during the twenties and thirties.

On the whole, the first half of the book is rather confusing with a wealth of unstructured detail that tends to leave the reader disoriented. It is only in the second part, more rooted in specific events, that we get a clearer picture of Ben Gurion. That portrait displays a pragmatist, who not only plans his next step carefully, but who is even willing to sacrifice his socialist and humanitarian beliefs in the service of his Zionist ideals.

The second book, *A Stranger in My House,* is the narrative of an American psychiatrist who traveled to the West Bank in order to talk to a variety of people on both sides of the controversy and thus to assess the problem of Jewish West Bank settlements and the possibilities of a future Palestinian homeland. The people he interviewed ranged from Jewish extremists who virtually denied the existence of Palestinians to Palestinian Arabs who predicted that one day the Jewish state would disappear as a result of an Arab victory, and most others in between. The book generally reveals an author who was patient, aggressive, and able to play the devil's advocate when necessary.

In the end Reich comes to the conclusion that the Israelis are increasing in numbers and settlements on the West Bank and that the Arabs had better compromise, and soon, if they are to establish an Arab state there. He also advises West Bank Palestinians to take their distance from the Palestine Liberation Organization, in order to win concessions from Israel, and to elect independent West Bank personalities to conduct negotiations. This advice, however, flies in the face of the main trend among the Palestinians, whether inside or outside the West Bank, who see the Palestine Liberation Organization as the symbol of their national movement.

Many of the interpretations in the introduction to the book, a sketchy history of the Arab-Israeli conflict, would be contested by Arab historians. While Mr. Teveth's book is likely to be of more interest to the Middle Eastern specialist, that of Mr. Reich is likely to appeal more to the general reader less well informed on the Arab-Israeli problem.

LOUAY BAHRY

University of Tennessee
Knoxville

EUROPE

SNYDER, LOUIS L. *Diplomacy in Iron: The Life of Herbert von Bismarck.* Pp. xii, 235. Melbourne, FL: Robert E. Krieger, 1985. $16.50.

Snyder's biography studies the great Bismarck's eldest son, Herbert. Although interesting, it displays some weaknesses as biography. In the beginning, when the reader would like to know something of Herbert's appearance, such as the color of his eyes, or his height and weight—simple traits that bring an adult to life—Snyder offers little. One eventually learns that Herbert grew into a "giant," but that, too, tells little to a reader living in an age when professional basketball centers often stand at seven feet or better.

Snyder points out that Herbert aped his father's mannerisms and political attitudes, but took them to extremes. His father might respect, even if he disliked, a political enemy, while Herbert only hated and despised foes. Bismarck could combine charm and irritation in equal measure, while Herbert greatly favored irritation. Bismarck drank heavily, but Herbert approached the alcoholic. The illustrations in this biography of Herbert are all of his father, from newspaper or magazine cartoons.

After performing heroically as a soldier in the Franco-Prussian War, Herbert became his father's secretary and went on to become secretary of state for foreign affairs in 1886. Snyder details Herbert's hard work as a diplomat: the maneuvering to gain for Germany southwest Africa; the efforts to secure a settlement satisfactory to Britain, the United States, and Germany relative to Samoa; the German-British settlement of differences in Africa; and the German acquisition of Helgoland. These achievements, while not insignificant, pale in comparison to the great Bismarck's role in first building a united Germany. In any event, Herbert worked mainly to carry out his father's policies, which he made his own. The only time the son acted relatively independently was when he served as a deputy in the Reichstag. But, as Snyder notes, the Reichstag was a relatively impotent legislative body when compared, for example, to the British Parliament.

Herbert died a frustrated man in 1904. Groomed to follow his revered father, Herbert, a fierce defender of his father's policies, could not continue the Bismarck political dynasty because of the enmity of Emperor William II.

Overall in this work the writing is solid, the examples pertinent, and the story clear. But one wonders if the subject was worth the effort Snyder devoted to him. Far more interesting than Herbert Bismarck to me were Snyder's descriptions of political infighting in imperial Germany during the late nineteenth century.

FRANKLIN B. WICKWIRE
University of Massachusetts
Amherst

UNITED STATES

KREISBERG, PAUL H. et al. *American Hostages in Iran: The Conduct of a Crisis.* Pp. xiv, 443. New Haven, CT: Yale University Press, 1985. $25.00.

The hostage crisis in Iran was an unusual event and this is an unusual book. The burdens carried by the delivery system of the U.S. government during those fateful 444 days while our embassy personnel languished in Tehran often appeared to be overwhelming. The very duration of this episode rendered it a crisis prolonged for an eternity to those caught in its dynamics.

American Hostages In Iran: The Conduct of a Crisis recounts these events from the perspective of policymakers directly involved in extricating our embassy staff from the clutches of the Khomeini regime. Warren Christopher, deputy secretary of state responsible for negotiating the release with the Iranian government, introduces the collection. Also included are selections by Harold H. Saunders, former assistant secretary of state for Near Eastern and South Asian affairs, who coordinated State Department policy during the crisis; Gary Sick, National Security Council staff member and the president's personal representative in matters pertaining to the crisis; Robert Carswell and Richard D. Davis, former officials in the Department of the Treasury responsible for applying economic pressures on the government of Iran; and John E. Hoffman, Jr., who reveals the existence of "the banker's channel," an informal avenue for "confidential contacts and negotiations between U.S. bank lawyers and Iranian representatives."

Oscar Schachter, a Columbia University professor of international law, and former U.S. Senator Abraham Ribicoff conclude the volume by evaluating the long-range implications of the lessons outlined by the practitioners. These assessments are developed in terms of international law, the dynamics of domestic politics, and U.S. foreign policy formulation.

Only those crises of greatest magnitude tend to attract such multifaceted treatments as that which emerges here. Thus the overriding virtue of this book is its pellucid view of the U.S. policymaking process in times of stress and exigency. Our government was neither woefully lacking nor especially strong. But a careful reading of this book reveals the inadequacy of intragovernmental coordination linking political, military, economic, and intelligence organizations. This was not merely a bilateral crisis; it was an interagency one as well. Students of U.S. foreign policy formulation, third-party mediation, congressional-executive relations, the organization of government to conduct foreign policy, and influence stand to benefit from this study.

EDWARD WEISBAND
State University of New York
Binghamton

LAMBRIGHT, W. HENRY. *Presidential Management of Science and Technology.* Pp. xii, 224. Austin: University of Texas Press, 1985. $25.00.

W. Henry Lambright is a well-known authority on public policy dealing with science and technology. Lambright takes 24 cases during the Johnson presidency, from the New York City blackout to defoliation in Vietnam, to describe "the policy system of the science and technology presidency, the top management of the executive branch as it relates to this specific policy area." Access to material in the Lyndon B. Johnson Library and the rich variety of issues during the Johnson presidency provide a solid and broad spectrum of information for Lambright to organize. And organize it he does. The book is literally a framework, a descriptive map of every conceivable influence on science and technology policy. He analyzes the "dispersion" of authority, the "sequence" of decision making, the "integration" of management in the subpresidency, and the "strategic" efforts to bring policy coherence. Lambright calls these the "central issues." He identifies the decision-making actors as the "president" and "subpresidency"; the latter includes the "principals" close to the president, the "budgeteers," the "professionals" with some kind of special knowledge, and the "administrators."

Besides applying the aforementioned variables to the 24 cases, Lambright also uses the cases to illustrate the stages of the policymaking process. He calls these stages "critical decisions" because they are concerned with "agenda setting," "adoption," "implementation," and "curtailment."

A selection from the chapter on agenda setting reveals both the strengths and weaknesses of this work.

Every presidency must establish an agenda [or agendas]. What it puts on its agenda may or may not be new to the government. Indeed, there are initiating and continuing presidential agendas. Issues on the initiating agenda are those with which the presidency concerns itself as a potential adopter. These are policies that are new to a particular presidency. Issues on the continuing agenda are those with which a presidency is concerned as an implementer. These are issues that relate to the administration of policies established by previous adoptions. The adoptions may be a given presidency's own or they may be those of a predecessor, in which case the presidency is placed in a position of implementing policies adopted by a predecessor. Thus, a distinction may be made between the initiating and continuing White House agenda.

A sensitivity to and awareness of the many ways a variable can vary bring descriptive breadth to this study. The reader sees case studies fitting "the temporary agenda," "the emergent agenda," or "the priority agenda." For adoption, there are cases that illustrate presidential "acquiescence," "partnership," "arbitration," and "preemption." Precise categorizing is also applied to each of the other policymaking stages. Truly, this work is a *tour d'horizon*.

The book's breadth, however, leaves little room for hypotheses and hypothesis testing. Theoretical conceptualizations are scarce. Perhaps this is inevitable in an administrative history of a particular policy area in a particular presidency. In addition, the paucity of studies on presidential policy management makes a broad, descriptive study a necessary foundation for future analyses.

NICHOLAS O. BERRY
Ursinus College
Collegeville
Pennsylvania

McCOY, DONALD R. *The Presidency of Harry S. Truman.* Pp. xii, 351. Lawrence: University Press of Kansas, 1984. $25.00. Paperbound, $14.95.

Donald R. McCoy's *Presidency of Harry S. Truman* is a comprehensive, informative, and well-written study on Truman and his administration, its achievements, and the issues it faced. This volume, which is the thirteenth to be published in the American Presidency Series, succeeds in the aim of the series, which is, to quote the foreword, "to present to historians and the general reading public . . . interesting, scholarly assessments of the various presidential administrations."

Selected by the towering and charismatic Franklin D. Roosevelt in 1944 to be his running mate and vice-president, Truman became president—in a sense, accidentally—when Roosevelt died on 12 April 1945. Such a beginning was hardly an advantage to Truman, for the reverence that Roosevelt had received was not extended to him. All presidents face the problems of comparison with other presidents, but for Truman this was to be especially painful. Preceded by the legendary Roosevelt, when Truman left office in 1953 he was followed by the triumphant General Dwight D. Eisenhower, whose very name was synonymous with the Allied victory in Europe. As William E. Leuchtenburg so well develops in his book, *In the Shadow of FDR: From Harry Truman to Ronald Reagan,* Truman was the president most burdened by the Roosevelt legacy.

Yet, Truman managed to turn his disadvantage to an asset, and it may be suggested that what Truman came to play on so successfully was the status of being an underdog. Paradoxically, it is this quality that attracted so much attention to Truman. His being an underdog, so pronounced in the election of 1948, is what made Truman so appealing, distinctive, and unique; it was a role that the common citizen could understand and could identify with and that enabled him to triumph over the apparently favored Thomas Dewey. Although McCoy does not stress this particular argument, a critical reading of the narrative lends itself to such a view. This feature, of the man struggling against great odds, has become Truman's legacy and has been frequently invoked by subsequent presidential candidates, irrespective of party, up to our recent elections.

As McCoy shows, the years of Truman's administration were marked by momentous developments and critical issues that outlined and presaged American diplomatic and domestic policies in the post-World War II period and that last to the present day. It was Truman's awesome decision to drop atomic bombs on Japan in 1945. That same year, the United Nations Charter was adopted at the

San Francisco Conference. In 1946, Winston Churchill delivered his celebrated iron-curtain speech in Missouri, which became a declaration recognizing that East and West were locked in a cold war. In 1949, Truman was the first international statesman to recognize the newly created State of Israel.

At the conclusion of World War II, American prestige and influence had acquired global proportions, its panoply of worldwide power unmatched. Henceforth, this was going to be the American Century. But only five years after World War II, North Korea and the new Communist regime in China defiantly challenged American power in Korea. In response, Truman committed American troops to repel the North Korean invasion of South Korea. The Korean War was the forerunner of many undeclared wars. In addition, it led to such a grave civil-military conflict that Truman relieved General Douglas MacArthur of his command in Korea. Although Truman had widespread support for this decision, it was a costly political act. A disconcerting question had been raised: who best represents the interests of the American people—the military commander or the civilian leader? And to round out the growing national crisis, the antidemocratic phenomenon known as McCarthyism made its appearance. It was also during Truman's administration that the civil rights movement, an issue with a long history in American life, burst forth.

Despite the many conflicts that Truman faced, it must be noted, too, that his administration ushered in unprecedented economic growth and prosperity. The mass consumption, urbanization, and technology introduced during his administration became features of the American landscape.

In sum, McCoy's book on Truman is an extensive piece of work, useful as a general reference and helpful for its substantial bibliographical essay. As a work on the Truman presidency it is a landmark.

JACQUES SZALUTA

U.S. Merchant Marine Academy
Kings Point
New York

PERNICK, MARTIN S. *A Calculus of Suffering: Pain, Professionalism, and Anesthesia in Nineteenth-Century America.* Pp. xiii, 421. New York: Columbia University Press, 1985. $35.00.

Surely the introduction of anesthesia was one of the greatest boons humanity has experienced. The pioneers were Georgia's Crawford W. Long, who quietly tried ether as early as 1842, and William T.G. Morton, who demonstrated and publicized it in 1846. When chloroform was used by Sir James Simpson of Edinburgh the next year, the curtain gradually fell on a period in which professionals sawed off limbs and knocked out teeth, inflicting staggering pain, some dared say, for people's good. Pain teaches, disciplines, and may well be God's own punishment!

This marvelous book of research—there are 86 pages of notes, 48 of bibliography—pioneers in redefining professionalism by insisting on the use of historical perspective. Thus, physicians in the 1840s who claimed to be specialists were termed quacks, but American medical journals completely avoided evaluation of new developments. Again, by 1830 all but three states had passed licensing laws, but by the 1850s all but three had none. Professionalism was ever in flux.

Anesthesia dramatically changed the hospital environment and the very lives of professionals. Freed considerably from pitiful moans and outcries, they could concentrate. Freed of patient intervention en route, theirs was now the right of decision. At last the meddlesome clergy had been brushed aside, while nurses and attendants calmed down somewhat. Unfortunately, gangrene had not been defeated, so surgical benefits still had to be weighed against risks. It was conceivable that women and the sensitive could finally enter medicine, for strength to use brute force, and dulled sensitivities, ceased to be absolute prerequisites.

Although Francis Bacon long since had enjoined doctors to mitigate pain, many early nineteenth-century American physicians and dentists were not entirely convinced. Earlier towering figures like Benjamin

Rush and Samuel Thomson—questionable professionals by our standards—only gradually lost their blind following. Before we sneer at leaders of that day, however, we should bear in mind that today the powerful case for legalized euthanasia to end terminal suffering still falls on too many deaf medical, legal, and religious ears.

In the nineteenth century it was believed, quaintly, that sensitivity to pain varied greatly by gender, age, social condition, race, nationality, education, and military status. Here, human beings definitely had not been created equal! Some worried that civilization was bringing a new and ominous delicacy of feeling. Many whites saw Negroes as relatively insensitive to pain, while the ex-slaves preferred to suggest eventual numbness or perhaps reliance on prideful fortitude. Pernick explores such cloudy questions as who received anesthesia; who used it; and what various observers thought.

Here is a profound, thoughtful, original, and timely book that is well within the reading ability of past, present, and future patients. It is also one that many professionals ought to consult. After all, like that age, ours is a time of disputation over the new: organ transplants, exotic and rare equipment, burgeoning alleged miracle drugs, alternatives, and costs. We can and should empathize with the struggling professionals of yesteryear.

            VAUGHN DAVIS BORNET
Southern Oregon State College
Ashland

PINCKNEY, ALPHONSO. *The Myth of Black Progress*. Pp. 198. New York: Cambridge University Press, 1984. $17.95.

JONES, JACQUELINE. *Labor of Love, Labor of Sorrow*. Pp. 432. New York: Basic Books, 1985. $25.95.

These two volumes both deal with the history of blacks in America, but in different ways and with completely different results.

The Myth of Black Progress studies the current status of blacks and concludes that, despite the enactment of civil rights laws, the lot of blacks today is still an extremely difficult one. Poverty and prejudice continue to exist and black progress, says Alphonso Pinckney, is indeed a myth. Pinckney, a professor of sociology at Hunter College, presents a mass of statistics to prove his thesis. Unfortunately, the sociologist too frequently gives way to the polemicist. Pinckney has written an angry book, and indeed his anger is justified. But his wrath obscures the reality that there has been progress—not enough, but some. And his anger spills out on other scholars who do not agree with his belief that a massive infusion of government aid is the only cure for the plight of blacks today in America.

Jacqueline Jones is a professor of American history at Wellesley College. She does a superb job in *Labor of Love* in analyzing the role of black women in work and the family from slavery to the present. These women endured the double prejudice of being both black and female, and their lives were in many ways even more harsh than that of black men.

Jones destroys several clichés about slavery in this volume. Most specifically, she convincingly paints a tale of the extremely harsh life that women servants had who worked in a slave owner's home. In light of current interest in the nature of the contemporary black family in America, I hope that Jones would next apply her considerable skills to an examination of this extremely important issue.

            FRED ROTONDARO
National Italian American
  Foundation
Washington, D.C.

WESTON, JACK. *The Real American Cowboy*. Pp. xviii, 267. New York: Schocken Books, 1985. $19.95.

This book is intended as a corrective to the popular myth of the cowboy. In its rhetoric it seems to attack mainly the stereotype of the loyal, professional, and aggressive white male who works steadfastly in the cattle drives and eventually succeeds in acquiring his own ranch and herd, becoming a small landholder himself. Although Weston in his earlier chapters asserts this to be the principal myth of the cowboy, in a later chapter he shows the development of this myth into a variety of patterns; thus, he may be said to expose the myth of the myth. Weston does not attempt to give a complete picture of the cattle industry or of the work of the cowboy under changing conditions; he assumes some knowledge, though distorted, of the principal period to which the myth refers, namely the 30 years after the Civil War. He selects topics in which he can show strong differences between the stereotypes and the particular conditions that he describes. Thus, in different chapters he shows examples of the hardship of the cowboy's work, the control of the cattle industry by large-scale, Eastern-dominated cattle associations, the low chances cowboys have of ever obtaining their own land, cases of labor unrest, the presence of Mexicans and blacks among the cowboys, and the role of women. The instances are frankly selected as counterexamples to the author's picture of the prevailing myth.

The argument leads to discussion of the cowboy myth itself, to which the last chapter is dedicated. As the nature of myth in general is not accuracy to historical fact, but appeal to human emotion and imagination, Weston's narrow interpretation is somewhat beside the point. Weston sees the popularity of the cowboy myth as an escape to a precapitalist paradise, an interpretation that contrasts strongly with that of previous chapters of the myth: chauvinist, sexist, racist, and apologetic for the misdeed of capitalism. The same chapter, however, treats the changes in the myth over the years. Each new feature is described and interpreted as showing some reprehensible aspect in the culture. The early stories, the basic myth, center on the creation of community and are seen as the longing of suppressed desire in a capitalist economy; the later so-called new Westerns, the John Wayne vehicles stressing a male group, are dismissed as fascist fantasies. Could the new myths not also be discussed as representing ideals that are suppressed in today's society? Consonant analysis of both types of cowboy myths may well stand and fall together.

The volume presents a collection of little-known facts about the history of the West in general and of cowboys and cattle drives in particular. The main argument is questionable. One does not correct a myth with a collection of facts. Few readers believe that the cowboy myth is a historical representation, and it is unlikely that many readers care whether it is. A myth appeals to some basic concerns that are treated within an available historic framework; can the Homeric myths be judged as social history of the Doric invasions? The final chapter discussing the myth resolves itself into a list of complaints about the values represented and their relation to trends in American society that go against Weston's grain. The two last paragraphs deal with Clint Roberts, a former Republican congressman from South Dakota, and with Ronald Reagan, ostensibly clinching the argument.

It would seem that Weston wants to substitute his own myth for those he detests. This would be a myth in which cowboys, with their proper quotas of Mexicans, blacks, and women, fight in the vanguard of the working class against the cattle barons and Eastern syndicates.

KURT W. BACK

Duke University
Durham
North Carolina

SOCIOLOGY

ADLER, PATRICIA A. *Wheeling and Dealing: An Ethnography of an Upper-Level*

Drug Dealing and Smuggling Community. Pp. xi, 175. New York: Columbia University Press, 1985. $25.00.

Participant observation research procedures seem easy, but potentially they are a trap for unwary investigators. They may treat their study population as so unique that it is not comparable to others; they may fail to check alternative sources of information that may also be available, actually engage in the criminal behavior of their subjects, write up their results in such an informal style that professional colleagues are repelled, or, finally, they may not spend enough time in the field to study the population or phenomenon under investigation adequately.

Adler manages to avoid these traps. During her five-year study, she observed a shift from an orientation focusing predominantly on marijuana to an emphasis on cocaine, and from relatively loose-knit Central American smuggling relationships to more tightly organized and controlled Colombian ones. She learned, too, that if upper-level dealers and smugglers are to avoid arrest and prosecution, they must live and work within an unstable, small circle of friends or associates; the hope is that the more tightly the circle is drawn, the greater the likelihood of effective concealment. At the extreme, this results in paranoid isolation. Nonetheless, these carefully drawn networks are penetrated; operations are detected and disrupted; and those who are arrested become informers for reduced sentences. The heavy personal use of marijuana and cocaine by these large-scale importers and dealers makes for carelessness and increases their vulnerability. While the financial structure of their business relationships is based on faith and trust, as well as suspicion and fear, their work organization and market pricing practices are rational. In stark contrast, their personal lifestyles are utterly hedonistic.

Adler is blessed with a fine working knowledge of the immediately relevant literature, but she fails to explore some broader implications of her work. She discusses both rational and irrational elements, but apparently fails to appreciate the significance of this inversion of Camus's existentialism: a rational world in apposition to irrational human beings! Nor does she explore the fact that her study population was of the same cohort as the protesters of the sixties and early seventies. In rebellion against middle-class parental norms of drug use, sexual behavior, and child raising, they were involved in their own version of ripping off the system. They suddenly found themselves with incomes beyond their wildest dreams, and a hedonistic subculture rather than Durkheim's anomie was the result. Finally, Adler's data indirectly seem to lend support to the proposition that an unanticipated consequence of the successful suppression of the marijuana and cocaine traffic would be a version of Lasswell's garrison state. That consequence does not seem to be in the immediate offing. Rather, what has actually happened is that, instead of a new approach to drug policy that would resolve some of the contradictions that we have as heirs of the nineteenth-century Moral Reform and the Harrison Act (1914), there is a kind of stalemate in what Lewin would call a field of forces, involving the drug rebels, on the one hand, and the agents of law and order, on the other. What are the implications for political theory?

LEONARD BLUMBERG
Temple University
Philadelphia
Pennsylvania

BECKSTROM, JOHN H. *Sociobiology and the Law: The Biology of Altruism in the Courtroom of the Future.* Pp. 151. Urbana: University of Illinois Press, 1985. $19.95.

This highly speculative work tries to apply insights from sociobiology to selected issues in legal policy concerning family relations—judicial disposition of intestacy, child custody, in-law marriage, and child abuse. While this has the appeal of novelty and the apparent encouragement of the noted sociobiological theorist Edward Wilson, it is nonetheless a peculiarly reasoned work, marked by unexamined ambiguities, an ingenuous approach to the relations between empirical data, theory, and policy, and a rather dubious orientation to the role of law in human society.

The basic theme is the theory of the so-called selfish gene, which asserts that humans are programmed to be disposed to act so as to benefit genetically related humans. Evidence on this issue is both controversial and subject to alternative interpretation, but Beckstrom usually takes it as a given. He then proceeds to compare current legal practices in handling cases of intestacy with the apparent dictates of genetic programming, concluding that the former are typically contrary to the latter and should be altered in the direction of the latter.

There are immediate difficulties with this viewpoint. First, Beckstrom cites the sociobiological contention that culturally induced, countergenetic behavior will not endure for long in human history. If so, why is further policymaking necessary? Second, why should sociobiological patterns be superior to prevailing legal-cultural solutions and to the expressed values and intentions of interviewees on the issue of bequests? Third, Beckstrom also adopts the view that culturally induced behavior "never strays too far or too long from what is called for by biological programming." This suggests that, if left alone, lawmakers and cultural leaders will somehow devise biologically appropriate cultural patterns. In my opinion, this discussion—largely in chapter 1—is a morass of inconsistencies that should have been identified, discussed, and at least partially resolved before publication.

In succeeding chapters, the basic theme is applied to selecting the appropriate parent in child-custody cases. It is concluded that, biologically speaking, the mother is typically more nurturant. Regrettably, cultural grounds for a similar conclusion are ignored, and the general argument is flawed by proclaiming that females are programmed to be discriminating in selecting mates—despite the widespread phenomenon of promiscuity. Likewise, in a discussion of child abuse, the genetically derived argument that abusers would be predominantly step-parents rests on a woefully weak empirical base—a study of 24 households in rural Pennsylvania.

Toward the end of this short book, Beckstrom becomes less assertive. He seems to have less faith in the strength of selfish genes and even admits that biological predispositions can be modified and overcome by cultural influences, including law. Indeed, he begins to question whether sociobiological theory can really help lawmakers, and he concludes that they might be served by empirical research unencumbered by biological theories. Sociologists who are interested in the relevance of sociobiology—its potentials and limitations—will probably find that this work promises much more than it delivers.

ALVIN BOSKOFF

Emory University
Atlanta
Georgia

CARNOY, MARTIN and HENRY M. LEVIN. *Schooling and Work in the Democratic State.* Pp. 307. Stanford, CA: Stanford University Press, 1985. No price.

In *Schooling and Work in the Democratic State,* Martin Carnoy and Henry Levin suggest that "though [American] schools are organized like workplaces, screening and preparing youth for inequality, they are more equal and participatory than offices and factories." This uniformly well-written, often insightful, and always provocative volume proceeds to analyze this paradox in considerable detail, arguing that there exists a continuing dialectical tension between schooling and work that is part of a larger tension between "the imperatives of capitalism and those of democracy in all its forms."

In the first eight chapters, Carnoy and Levin probe both this paradox and its attendant tensions from the perspectives of history, political philosophy, economics, and sociology, among others. The final chapter deals with current American reform efforts and their policy implications. Each of the chapters truly deserves extensive comment, but space limitations dictate that this brief review focus on a handful of the contentions made in this volume.

Carnoy and Levin write that American schools are inherently conservative institutions that "in the absence of external pressures for change... tend to preserve existing social institutions." Suggesting that strong social movements tend to promote a "democratic dynamic" in education, they also suggest that whenever such movements are weak, "schools tend to strengthen their function of reproducing workers for capitalist workplace relations and the unequal division of labor."

Carnoy and Levin see such shifts as part of a continuing dialectical process. In the period from 1900 to the 1930s, for example, big business dominated labor; in the next four decades a series of important social movements shifted the balance of power in the direction of labor, the disadvantaged, racial and linguistic minorities, women, and so forth. Since the late 1970s, however, because of a deteriorating economic situation, the democratic trends of equity, equality, and access in education were reversed, and today American education is blamed for the nation's economic decline. Influential reports, such as *A Nation at Risk,* call for often simplistic reforms to restore America's economic primacy through greater academic rigor.

Following a trenchant discussion of recent structural changes that have transformed America's production system, the reader is presented with a provocative analysis of the Reagan administration's economic and social initiatives as they are reflected in its policy of "using the schools for reproduction of the work force" while deemphasizing the democratic themes that dominated the 1960s. Carnoy and Levin point out, however, that such factors as "the false promises of high technology; high unemployment; neglect of minorities and the poor; and the general trend toward participation in the workplace" contain the seeds of change that will result in the pendulum's swinging back to the "democratic dynamic" in the educational sector.

While I am not convinced by Carnoy and Levin's argument of the inevitability of a dialectic process informing the history of modern American education, I am persuaded that this is an important book deserving a wide audience. Even while finding much with which to disagree, readers will be provoked to reaction and, thus, forced to confront their own assumptions and biases. This is, in brief, a book that will be debated for some time to come.

EDWARD R. BEAUCHAMP
University of Hawaii
Honolulu

GOODIN, ROBERT E. *Protecting the Vulnerable: A Reanalysis of Our Social Responsibilities.* Pp. 235. Chicago: University of Chicago Press, 1985. $25.00.

Robert E. Goodin, of the Department of Political Science, Sussex University, has written the type of lucid, concise exposition of a demanding idea that we expect of British colleagues. His thesis is that the philosophic justification for our obligation to others springs from their vulnerabilities to us rather than any special membership we might share. We owe concern to our children, for example, because of their need of us. For Goodin, needs are not limited to the means for physical survival. A spouse is vulnerable to his or her need for our emotional support.

Considering another widely perceived obligation, Goodin dismisses the prevalent notion of political communities. If they constitute clubs, on what moral basis do we exclude any from membership? The obligations the more internationally powerful have toward the poorer cannot be justified on the basis of past colonial exploitation. What matters is the sensitivity of Third World peoples to our actions. And, Goodin reminds us, the peoples who are vulnerable to our actions include others of future time, who will face an environment insulted or nurtured by us.

Neatly, almost surgically, Goodin leads us through the defenses he has aroused. Our cultural commitment to the contract, actual or implied, is shown neither to explain our current moral positions nor to allow for a wider justification. Support is drawn from sources ranging from American constitutional history to the ongoing discussion of Rawls's *Theory of Justice.* Some readers may also be reminded of Lewis Hart's *The Liberal Tradition.*

How are we to respond to this awesome thesis of obligation? Goodin, like many professional philanthropists, is suspicious of activism achieved through personalizing anguish. He contends that giving to a particular starving child, for example, may actually be negative in effect since it may not address the world within which that individual beneficiary exists. By turning his back on this form of caring, Goodin makes a very large step. Our route should be "to campaign for our governments to organize generous and well integrated multilateral schemes for foreign assistance."

The reader, stranded between disdain for Save the Children and a disheartening injunction to take on the government, may be forgiven a feeling of letdown. Although it is not the philosopher's task to answer the question of how in a democracy one applies these insights, Goodin does not appear to eschew practicality. The child psychiatrist Robert Coles recently reported that the urgent questions children can conceive of are class defined. Those who found nuclear annihilation a problem, for example, tended to be upper middle class. Goodin would certainly respond to the implied question of democratic choice that the fact that others do not act morally does not excuse us from so doing.

Both concern for the implementation of philosophic conclusions and recognition of the daunting nature of the task have been addressed by Robert Payton, president of the Exxon Education Foundation and leader of Columbia University's Seminar on Philanthropy.

The closest we seem to be able to come to the idea of a just world is one in which *only* those with surpluses of material resources *and* with the philosophical and spiritual conviction that philanthropy is necessary are prepared to act generously. Do we propose to reach a point where the goods of the world are owned and controlled in such a way that tragedies of this kind [Ethiopia] would be impossible?

My group membership may be showing, but I regretted that Goodin did not carry us a bit further in considering the policy implications of his luminous view of humankind.

JANET CARTER
Bruner Foundation
New York City

McCLELLAN, JAMES E., III. *Science Reorganized: Scientific Societies in the Eighteenth Century.* Pp. xxix, 413. New York: Columbia University Press, 1985. $45.00.

Science Reorganized presents an account of the growth and some of the activities of scientific societies in Europe and the Americas from 1660 to 1793. Its underlying premises

are that the scientific societies of the eighteenth century constitute a coherent subject important in understanding the development of science since the Scientific Revolution and that only by considering the scientific societies collectively as a single phenomenon can proper perspectives be brought to bear on their impact and history (xiii).

While primarily a work in the history of science—ambitious in its geographic scope, narrow in its institutional focus on scientific societies—the book is informed by and explicitly addresses itself to certain relatively recent issues in science studies and the sociology of the professions. As the principal focus is state-recognized societies, the book also has some pertinence for students of state interventions in nongovernmental spheres. Of special value are appendixes providing information on a virtually complete list of more than 70 official scientific societies from 1660 to 1793 and a second list of 67 "notable" private societies. Information includes, where available, the type of society, political source of formal recognition, dates of activity, sources of support, extent of orientation toward science, size, organization, facilities, publications, and prize and other activities as well as bibliographic sources.

The book's opening chapter introduces scientific societies and their two general forms of organization: societies, modeled after the Royal Society of London, and academies, modeled after the Paris Academy of Science. These differ in organization and in the nature of state support and control. Subsequent chapters cover the growth—roughly exponential—of scientific societies up to 1793; communications between scientific societies; and cooperative projects undertaken by two or more societies. A final chapter deals with the making of the scientist, that is, with the role of scientific societies in the development of science as a profession.

An excellent integrative survey of the nature and distribution of the Enlightenment's most distinctive type of forum for scientific activity, McClellan's book is likely to become a standard work. The book's shortcomings, such as they are, stem primarily from the narrow focus on scientific societies and their dispersion. Missing or very circumscribed are systematic discussions of the relationship of scientific societies to other spheres of scientific activity or to cognitive developments within science. We learn little about society members—especially McClellan's protoprofessionals, the employed academicians—their activities, or their recruitment. The discussions of scientific communication and the professionalization of science are provocative, but probably not wholly satisfactory for specialists in science studies or the professions. Using the appendixes for guidance concerning sources, however, those specialists should be able to find the data necessary to develop their own conclusions.

CARL B. BACKMAN
Buffalo State College
New York

NELSON, BARBARA J. *Making an Issue of Child Abuse: Political Agenda Setting for Social Problems.* Pp. xiv, 169. Chicago: University of Chicago Press, 1984. $17.50.

Nelson has three broad aims in this book: to provide a history of child abuse policymaking over the past three decades, to analyze the process of agenda setting, and to discuss the "advantages and limitations of liberal reform." She traces how child abuse moved from being a marginal concern of charities to a central policy problem, through the media, the legal system, and Congress. Her general conclusion is that liberal reform, treating the problem as one of deviance and out of concern for maintaining family authority, failed to address the root causes of child abuse and neglect. The syllogism that emerges in the course of her book and in her conclusion goes something like this: child abuse is caused by family stress, which is caused by inequality, racism, and patriarchy; liberal reform does not deal with inequality, racism, or poverty—only programs that seek to eliminate these problems can do this. The aims of the book are shaped by the desire to validate this syllogism. In this narrow framework she succeeds in providing a book that is generally clear, concise, and well written.

The major problem is that not only is there little evidence to support the syllogism's assumptions, but there is considerable evidence against them. To start, Nelson herself admits, "No one actually knows the extent of child abuse and neglect, or whether their incidence is increasing or decreasing." Given such a lack of data, how can it be asserted that child abuse and neglect are the result of inequalities of wealth and power between the sexes and races? She does refer to Pelton's essay about the "myth of classlessness" in child abuse and neglect, but this essay is tainted because it provides no original data itself, because it uses secondary sources mostly compiled by child welfare agencies that are bound to have an overrepresentation of the poor among them, and because Pelton deliberately confuses abuse and neglect, two distinct phenomena.

Nelson provides no time-series data that show a positive association between levels of poverty and unemployment, on the one hand, and child abuse, on the other. Without such proof, it is impossible to say unequivocally that there is a relation between inequality and child abuse. Indeed, in the period since 1960 for which she does provide some evidence that reported child abuse has increased, the poverty level of Americans has declined. Measures of racial prejudice in America fell dramatically during the same period, while the percentage of black college graduates rose tremendously. So much for racism. The percentage of, and public acceptance of, married women working outside the home has increased greatly during this period, the proportion of females in college graduating classes is higher than that of males, and the percentage of elective offices held by women has tripled. So much for patriarchy. To be fair, she did not set out to prove this point. What is a serious flaw in the book, though, is that the causal relation between poverty and abuse is assumed, even though it is central to her attack on liberal reform. One simply cannot base an analysis on a relationship that has not been conclusively proved.

An old joke goes, "How many social scientists does it take to change a light bulb?" "They do not change light bulbs. They search for the root causes of why the last one went out." In this case, there is still disagreement about what the root causes are.

WILLIAM R. BEER

Brooklyn College
New York

PFEFFER, LEO. *Religion, State and the Burger Court*. Pp. xiv, 310. Buffalo, NY: Prometheus Books, 1984. $22.95.

This is another good book by the premier participant-observer and chronicler of the constitutional relations of church and state in America. Leo Pfeffer is not uncritical of the decisions of the Burger Court. He pledges both "not . . . to make any effort to exclude [his] own partisan judgment as to the significance and correctness of the decisions discussed in the book" and, for all his Jeffersonian starch on free exercise of religion and the separation of church and state, to be nonpartisan "as far as possible." The pledge is kept. As a result, the book can be enjoyed both for its evenhanded explanation of the setting, stakes, and arguments in religious cases that have been or may yet be before the Supreme Court and for the exposition of a considered position on religious freedom. The chapter on "the free exercise of disfavored religions" is less objective, more argumentative than the rest, but no less valuable.

Pfeffer concludes that the Burger Court has been reasonably faithful to the spirit of the Free Exercise Clause. He explains how the purpose-effect-entanglement test of religious establishment was used most often in the 1970s to strike school-aid laws down, while in the 1980s it has been employed as a rationale for accommodation—though he does not fault the test itself, for its ambiguity. In 1985, after the publication of *Religion, State and the Burger Court,* the Court took another turn: it voided an Alabama law authorizing a moment of silence in public school for meditation or prayer, a Connecticut law giving employees the right to refuse work on their chosen sabbaths, and municipal ordinances putting publicly paid teachers in parochial schools to conduct classes on secular subjects. In all likelihood it will change course again with new appointees.

This is a book aimed at the general reader. It is not deep, but wise and informative. Pfeffer offers an analysis of the support of public aid for religious schools by those on the run from integrated public schools, for example, and of the costs and benefits politicians perceive in taking stands on church-state issues. I recommend it, cover to cover or as a reference for its chapters on tax exemption, even though it ignores the extraordinary games that members of the Universal Life Church play with the tax collector; religion in public places; religion in military, penal, and legislative service; religion in labor law; religion and the family; and other topics.

ROBERT J. SICKELS
University of New Mexico
Albuquerque

ZOLLAR, ANN CREIGHTON. *A Member of the Family: Strategies for Black Family Continuity.* Pp. 174. Chicago: Nelson-Hall, 1985. $22.95.

A Member of the Family is an assessment of the urban black family experience and the role played by extended kinship. Zollar's perspective views the black family as a cultural variant in American society. This perspective emphasizes the distinctive qualities of black families and implies that it is a special black culture that accounts for the observable differences between black and white families. Further, those characteristics of black families that are similar to those in white families have evolved through different processes and styles of interaction. This perspective differs from the cultural-deviant and cultural-equivalent views in that it gives much less emphasis to a definition of the family constrained by the conjugal bond or by reliance on a common residence unit.

Zollar points out that black families may be dispersed over several household units and that one person may have differential family loyalties to a number of households. Quoting from Carol B. Stack's *All Our Kin,* Zollar notes, "'A resident... who eats in one household may sleep in another and contribute resources to yet another. He may consider himself a member of all three households.'" Zollar emphasizes that we must look at factors that determine household composition rather than seeing households as closed units.

This failure to recognize that "household" refers to residence while "family" refers to kinship has led to an overemphasis on the female-headed black family. Indeed, Zollar points out that black families are not necessarily best conceptualized by focusing on the conjugal bond. The economic and social implications of other relationships may be more important than those of the relationship between husband and wife. Her conceptualization of the black family could be captured by Litwak's phrase, "a modified, extended family." The extended kinship network exists in affluent conditions as well as in poverty, in urban conditions as well as in rural ones. Black families "transmit from generation to generation the knowledge that sharing between and among kin constitutes appropriate behavior."

Zollar gives us case studies of four contemporary, urban black families and identifies commonalities and differences among them. In each of the families there was a span of three to four generations spread out over several households. Usually, the core family consisted of a woman and her children and grandchildren with any spouses who were present. These families also kept looser connections with a larger kinship network.

In all the families there was mutual aid and reciprocity of giving among the scattered kin. Most of the exchanges were of a sort Zollar calls "generalized reciprocity." Goods and services were given with no expectation of immediate or necessarily balanced return. Only one of the four families expected immediate and even exchanges. Zollar points out that this family was the poorest of the four and not to repay directly meant that someone in that family would go hungry.

The primary process through which the mutual aid flowed was gifts to the mother from those who were able to give. The mother then parceled out these goods and services to those in need. There was a felt obligation to make contributions when one could and no hesitancy about calling on the mother for aid, even long-term aid, when one was needy.

One of the continuing questions in the literature on the black family is whether or not this mutual aid system is a deterrent to upward economic mobility for family members. Stack and others have suggested that kin who have been upwardly mobile often shut themselves off from other family members who are welfare recipients. Zollar found three patterns of interaction with family members after a couple had achieved a moderate degree of economic success. The most common pattern was to continue to participate in the mutual aid system. The families of these couples identified with their success and accorded them status. Other mobile relatives who were less well off did not contribute to the family, but as long as they kept up regular contact, the families were satisfied with their behavior. A few upwardly mobile couples had cut themselves off from the extended family and did not participate at all in the system of mutual aid even though they were able to do so. These, however, were the minority.

Zollar concludes as McAdoo and others have done before her, that this family helping behavior does not seem to hurt the economic mobility of some of the members. It also occurs at all socioeconomic levels and is not, therefore, an adaptation to urban poverty, but a true cultural attribute of black families in general.

Zollar does an excellent job of integrating historical insights on black families and her own research into a theoretical perspective that gives us a clearer view of the functioning of contemporary, urban black families. Her well-written analysis makes a strong case for the black family as a distinctive, adaptable cultural variant with its own traditions and patterns of behavior.

MARIE RICHMOND-ABBOTT
Eastern Michigan University
Ypsilanti

ECONOMICS

LEAMER, EDWARD E. *Sources of International Comparative Advantage.* Pp. xix, 353. Cambridge, MA: MIT Press, 1984. $45.00.

The generation of econometric evidence to support or dispute a theoretical hypothesis has never been more widespread. Nevertheless, doubt about the validity of that evidence is also at an all-time high. In this book, Edward Leamer demonstrates why this apparent paradox is true. Leamer presents a dazzling menu of tools available to today's econometrician but is careful to emphasize the fragility of inferences drawn with these tools. In this sense, the book is more about econometrics than international trade. In fact, the reader is left with the impression that any theoretical hypothesis for which there were appropriate data could have served as the topic for this book.

As a handbook for application of modern Bayesian econometrics, the book is superb. Leamer is precise and complete in describing the methods he feels are appropriate for generating econometric evidence. Given the careful consideration Leamer applies to the techniques proposed, the reader is led to do the same. More generally, the book represents an expression of how various types of econometric research are supposed to proceed. Leamer starts with an economic theory in chapter 1 and derives testable implications, being sure to emphasize the conditions necessary for a valid test, in chapter 2. He then discusses, in chapters 3 through 5, both the data and their interaction with the econometric methods to be applied. Finally, in chapters 6 and 7, Leamer presents estimates of the empirical model and briefly interprets the results. Even if one does not accept the Bayesian approach, the thoroughness of the empirical work sets an appealing standard.

From an international economist's perspective the book is less appealing. Contrary to the book's title, Leamer makes little effort to present the empirical regularities in the sources of comparative advantage. The reader is left to sort through multitudinous scatter diagrams and plots, which constitute a 90-page appendix, as well as statistical results. This is a formidable effort. Moreover, the brief discussion of results is heavily sprinkled with references to technical issues such as "prior densities" and "orthogonalities." There is, however, a wealth of material presented, and simple examination of the plots provides intuition about shifting comparative advantage.

There is a final caution. In the preface, Leamer states that "understanding everything in this book will be a formidable task for most people." This is an understatement. The book is both technical and difficult, and it is accessible only to those who have had previous econometric training.

MICHAEL D. BRADLEY
George Washington University
Washington, D.C.

MINTZ, BETH and MICHAEL SCHWARTZ. *The Power Structure of American Business.* Pp. xix, 327. Chicago: University of Chicago Press, 1985. No price.

The Power Structure of American Business is a treatise on the preeminence of financial institutions in American business. Beth Mintz and Michael Schwartz argue that financial institutions, predominantly banks, are the most influential institutions in American business. Beyond their immediate impact on business, it is implied that financial institutions' decisions are capable of transcending government policies for change.

Mintz and Schwartz condition their argument by stating that on a day-to-day basis, nonfinancial institutions are left alone to act autonomously, with financials interfering in nonfinancials' decision making to prevent destructive competition, to prevent an unprofitable investment, or to protect the interests of a major borrower. Also, the financials' power is most significant during certain economic conditions: recession; when nonfinancials require capital financing; and when financials can coordinate their actions to act in unison against nonfinancials.

Mintz and Schwartz make these assertions based on the financials' control over capital flow decisions and on leverage over nonfinancials' actions through stocks held in the nonfinancials. Through their decisions, financials change the environment in which nonfinancials and the government function.

As evidence of their argument, Mintz and Schwartz present compelling examples from the business press that illustrate instances where financials have prevailed over nonfinancials. Some examples include the defeat of the manufacture of the airbus in 1976; prevention of the acquisition of Chemical Bank by Leasco, a computer company, in 1968; and the Big Three automakers' yielding of the manufacture of car parts to suppliers when financials refused to support full funding of fuel-efficient cars.

There is no disputing that financial institutions are powerful; however, upon reflection, it is questioned whether Mintz and Schwartz have sufficiently explored the weak side of banks, such as their dependency on nonfinancials as depositors of capital that permit financials to lend money, the government's regulation of bank activities, the vulnerability of banks to failure when they make poor loans, and government rescue of failing banks.

Also questioned is whether Mintz and Schwartz were not unduly influenced by the findings of the Mathematical Analysis of Corporate Networks (MACNET), an earlier research project Mintz and Schwartz conducted to study the division and groupings within American business in an effort to untangle power relations among corporations. Its purpose was to measure the centrality of corporations based on the frequency of companies' representation on various corporate boards of directors and to indicate the linking relationships between companies. MACNET revealed that banks were the most centrally linked institutions in business, either through representation on other companies' boards or through other companies' representation on banks' boards.

From the quantitative research performed under MACNET, Mintz and Schwartz then proceeded to cull through the most widely read business publications to gather evidence to back up the findings of MACNET, to see if the real world of business functioned according to the network that MACNET revealed.

It seems that all that can be inferred from MACNET is an indication of the method of communication between corporations and not of power among corporations. As Mintz and Schwartz themselves point out, corporate representation on boards provides the information necessary to implement control but is not a source of control.

The reason for the frequent representation of financials on corporate boards and for nonfinancials' representation on financials' boards reflects a need to maintain goodwill and to gather information. Nonfinancials invite financials to sit on their boards because the financials are important lenders or major stockholders; and financials invite nonfinancials to sit on their boards to solicit information for making investment decisions and to ensure that the nonfinancials, as the largest depositors, continue to maintain large deposits with them.

Nevertheless, *The Power Structure of American Business* provides an in-depth account of conflicting theories over ownership and control of large corporations and differing viewpoints on corporate behavior. It provides, too, an illustration of the financials' influence and a sense of the ways in which this influence operates at the particular moments it is exercised. It also gives us food for thought in considering which is most powerful in American business: financial institutions, nonfinancial institutions, or the government; or do all three share equally in exerting influence?

JOHN C. BEYER

Robert R. Nathan Associates
Washington, D.C.

TAYLOR, SERGE. *Making Bureaucracies Think: The Environmental Impact Statement Strategy of Administrative Reform.* Pp. x, 410. Stanford, CA: Stanford University Press, 1984. $29.50.

The central concern of this book is the social intelligence that goes into environmental decisions. Taylor evaluates the first ten years of the environmental-impact statement (EIS) process of the 1969 National Environmental Policy Act—in particular, how it has worked inside two federal agencies with important impacts on the environment, the Forest Service and the Army Corps of Engineers. The book grew out of a dissertation done in the political science department at Berkeley and, in Taylor's words, "owes much to what I only later came to realize was a special intellectual culture, one intensely concerned with how knowledge and politics influence each other."

Environmental values are described as "precarious" and as needing the protection of special arrangements. The antidote for this weakness is what sociologists call institutionalization: the vesting of resources in the hands of those committed to a particular value in order to protect and further that value.

As environmental groups grew stronger and richer in expertise, their political clout increased, putting pressure on governmental agencies to mend their ways. In Taylor's convoluted language, "Early legal and political victories by environmentalists on EIS issues . . . probably acted as a selection pressure for them to acquire or augment their research arms in order to participate effectively in a now more analytically intensive kind of politics." An investment in a research capability "increased the pressure on agencies to present more thoroughly researched justifications for their proposed policies."

As some interest groups acquired greater analytical resources, the agencies and other interest groups came under greater pressure to respond in a similar fashion, for groups without an analysis capability had diminished chances of winning once the rules changed. Nor was this simultaneous evolution of politics and policy confined to the interplay of agencies and interest groups; the growth of analytically more sophisticated interest groups undoubtedly encouraged the courts to undertake a more searching review of the factual underpinnings of agency decisions and to elaborate more demanding rules of analysis.

If the reader can cut through the jargon, he or she can conclude that Taylor wants environmental pressure groups to have more power to pressure government agencies into conforming to their views. Many Americans believe that such groups have had a negative effect on the economic development of various industries in this country, particularly the nuclear power industry, at the same time that these industries are flourishing, safely, abroad.

ANTHONY T. BOUSCAREN
Le Moyne College
Syracuse
New York

OTHER BOOKS

ADAMSON, MADELEINE and SETH BORGOS. *This Mighty Dream: Social Protest Movements in the United States.* Pp. 143. Boston: Routledge & Kegan Paul, 1984. $22.95. Paperbound, $9.95.

ALBA, RICHARD D., ed. *Ethnicity and Race in the U.S.A.: Toward the Twenty-First Century.* Pp. iv, 186. Boston: Routledge & Kegan Paul, 1985. $24.95.

ARON, RAYMOND. *On War.* Translated by Terence Kilmartin. Pp. 163. Lanham, MD: University Press of America, 1985. Paperbound, $10.75.

ARON, RAYMOND. *The Great Debate: Theories of Nuclear Strategy.* Pp. ix, 265. Lanham, MD: University Press of America, 1985. Paperbound, $13.50.

ARON, RAYMOND. *The Opium of the Intellectuals.* Translated by Terence Kilmartin. Pp. xix, 324. Lanham, MD: University Press of America, 1985. Paperbound, $14.50.

BARNETT, A. DOAK. *The Making of Foreign Policy in China: Structure and Process.* Pp. xiii, 160. Boulder, CO: Westview Press, 1985. $18.50. Paperbound, $10.95.

BARNETT, FRANK R., B. HUGH TOVAR, and RICHARD H. SCHULTZ, eds. *Special Operations in US Strategy.* Pp. 326. New York: National Strategy Information Center, 1984. Paperbound, $7.95.

BARTKE, WOLFGANG and PETER SCHIER. *China's New Party Leadership.* Pp. 289. Armonk, NY: M. E. Sharpe, 1985. $50.00.

BEETHAM, DAVID. *Marxists in Face of Fascism.* Pp. vii, 381. Totowa, NJ: Barnes & Noble Books, 1985. $29.95.

BENDER, GERALD J., JAMES S. COLEMAN, and RICHARD L. SKLAR, eds. *African Crisis Areas and U.S. Foreign Policy.* Pp. xiv, 373. Berkeley: University of California Press, 1985. $40.00. Paperbound, $9.95.

BERK, STEPHEN M. *Year of Crisis, Year of Hope: Russian Jewry and the Pogroms of 1881-1882.* Pp. xvi, 231. Westport, CT: Greenwood Press, 1985. $39.95.

BEW, PAUL and HENRY PATTERSON. *The British State and the Ulster Crisis.* Pp. 160. London: Verso, 1985. Distributed by Schocken Books, New York, NY. $20.00. Paperbound, $6.95.

BLACKABY, FRANK, JOZEF GOLDBLAT, and SVERRE LODGAARD. *No-First-Use.* Pp. ix, 151. Philadelphia: Taylor and Francis, 1984. Paperbound, no price.

BOGART, LEO. *Polls and the Awareness of Public Opinion.* 2nd ed. Pp. xxxiii, 264. New Brunswick, NJ: Transaction Books, 1985. Paperbound, $14.95.

BOSWORTH, EDMUND and CAROLE HILLENBRAND. *Qajar Iran: Political, Social and Cultural Change 1800-1925.* Pp. xxv, 414. New York: Columbia University Press, 1984. $32.00.

BURCHELL, ROBERT W. et al. *The New Reality of Municipal Finance: The Rise and Fall of the Intergovernmental City.* Pp. xxiii, 433. New Brunswick, NJ: Center for Urban Policy Research, 1984. Paperbound, no price.

CORWIN, EDWARD S. *The President: Office and Powers, 1787-1984.* Pp. xxii, 565. New York: New York University Press, 1984. $45.00. Paperbound, $20.00.

CREWS, KENNETH D. *Edward S. Corwin and the American Constitution: A Bibliographical Analysis.* Pp. xiv, 226. Westport, CT: Greenwood Press, 1985. $35.00.

CROTTY, WILLIAM. *The Party Game.* Pp. x, 212. New York: W. H. Freeman, 1985. $19.95. Paperbound, $11.95.

DASTRUP, BOYD L. *Crusade in Nuremberg: Military Occupation, 1945-1949.* Pp. xi, 159. Westport, CT: Greenwood Press, 1985. $27.50.

DAVIS, MIKE, FRED PFEIL, and MICHAEL SPRINKER, eds. *The Year Left: An American Socialist Yearbook.*

Pp. ix, 358. London: Verso, 1985. Distributed by Schocken Books, New York, NY. $8.95.

EVERTS, Ph.P., ed. *Controversies at Home: Domestic Factors in the Foreign Policy of the Netherlands.* Pp. x, 363. Dordrecht: Kluwer Academic, 1985. Distributed by Kluwer Academic, Hingham, MA. $45.00.

FISHER, FRANKLIN M. et al. *Folded, Spindled, and Mutilated: Economic Analysis and U.S. vs. IBM.* Pp. xvi, 443. Cambridge, MA: MIT Press, 1985. Paperbound, $9.95.

FUSFELD, DANIEL R. *Economics: Principles of Political Economy.* Pp. xix, 777. Glenview, IL: Scott, Foresman, 1985. $27.95.

GASTIL, RAYMOND D. *Freedom in the World: Political Rights and Civil Liberties, 1984-1985.* Pp. x, 438. Westport, CT: Greenwood Press, 1985. $35.00.

GOEHLERT, ROBERT U. and FENTON S. MARTIN. *The Presidency: A Research Guide.* Pp. xxv, 341. Santa Barbara, CA: ABC-Clio Information Services, 1985. No price.

HAZAN, BARUCH A. *The East European Political System.* Pp. xvi, 396. Boulder, CO: Westview Press, 1986. Paperbound, $25.00.

HESS, BETH B. and ELIZABETH W. MARKSON, eds. *Growing Old in America: New Perspectives on Old Age.* 3rd ed. Pp. xv, 582. New Brunswick, NJ: Transaction Books, 1985. Paperbound, $12.95.

HUNTER, ROBERT E. *NATO: The Next Generation.* Pp. x, 272. Boulder, CO: Westview Press, 1985. $34.50.

JACKALL, ROBERT and HENRY M. LEVIN, eds. *Worker Cooperatives in America.* Pp. x, 311. Berkeley: University of California Press, 1985. $24.95.

JASANI, BHUPENDRA and CHRISTOPHER LEE. *Countdown to Space War.* Pp. viii, 104. Philadelphia: Taylor and Francis, 1984. Paperbound, $11.00.

JONES, R.J. BARRY and PETER WILLETTS, eds. *Interdependence on Trial: Studies in the Theory and Reality of Contemporary Interdependence.* Pp. x, 237. New York: St. Martin's Press, 1985. $29.95.

KAHAN, ARCADIUS. *The Plow, the Hammer and the Knout: An Economic History of Eighteenth-Century Russia.* Pp. xi, 399. Chicago: University of Chicago Press, 1985. $65.00.

KAINZ, HOWARD P. *Democracy East and West: A Philosophical Overview.* Pp. vi, 152. New York: St. Martin's Press, 1984. $22.50.

KENNAN, GEORGE F. *American Diplomacy.* Pp. xii, 179. Chicago: University of Chicago Press, 1985. Paperbound, $5.95.

KIRALY, BELA K., BARBARA LATZE, and NANDOR F. DREISZIGER. *The First War between Socialist States: The Hungarian Revolution of 1956 and Its Impact.* Pp. ix, 608. New York: Columbia University Press, 1984. $40.00.

KLEIN, RUDOLF. *The Future of Welfare.* Pp. vi, 253. New York: Basil Blackwell, 1985. $45.00. Paperbound, $19.95.

KNOX, PAUL L. *The Geography of Western Europe: A Socio-Economic Survey.* Pp. xii, 249. Totowa, NJ: Barnes & Noble Books, 1984. $29.50.

KONEV, IVAN. *Year of Victory.* Pp. 248. Moscow: Progress, 1984. Distributed by Imported Publications, Chicago, IL. $7.95.

KOO, YOUNGNOK and SUNG-JOO HAN, eds. *The Foreign Policy of the Republic of Korea.* Pp. xiv, 306. New York: Columbia University Press, 1985. $25.00.

KOSTUNICA, VOJISLAV and KOSTA CAVOSKI. *Party Pluralism or Monism.* Pp. vii, 168. New York: Columbia University Press, 1985. $25.00.

LADD, EVERETT CARL. *The American Policy: The People and Their Government.* Pp. xxv, 678. New York: W. W. Norton, 1985. $23.95.

LAUFFER, ARMAND. *Grantsmanship and Fund-Raising.* Pp. 320. Beverly Hills, CA: Sage, 1984. $25.00.

LEVINE, ANDREW. *Arguing for Socialism: Theoretical Considerations.* Pp. xiv,

241. Boston, MA: Routledge & Kegan Paul, 1984. $23.50.

LEYDEN, W. VON. *Aristotle on Equality and Justice: His Political Argument.* Pp. ix, 145. New York: St. Martin's Press, 1985. $25.00.

LINDOP, EDMUND. *All about Republicans.* Pp. v, 218. Hillside, NJ: Enslow, 1985. $15.95.

LINDOP, EDMUND and JOY CRANE THORNTON. *All about Democrats.* Pp. iv, 220. Hillside, NJ: Enslow, 1985. $15.95.

LONDON, HERBERT I. *Military Doctrine and the American Character: Reflections on AirLand Battle.* Pp. xi, 67. New Brunswick, NJ: Transaction Books, 1984. Paperbound, $4.50.

LUKACS, JOHN. *Historical Consciousness, or the Remembered Past.* Pp. xxxii, 409. New York: Schocken Books, 1985. Paperbound, $13.95.

MACHIN, HOWARD and VINCENT WRIGHT, eds. *Economic Policy and Policy-making under the Mitterrand Presidency 1981-84.* Pp. x, 293. New York: St. Martin's Press, 1985. $27.50.

MAX, STANLEY M. *The United States, Great Britain and the Sovietization of Hungary, 1945-48.* Pp. vii, 195. New York: Columbia University Press, 1985. $20.00.

MILLS, C. WRIGHT. *The Causes of World War Three.* Pp. 187. Armonk, NY: M. E. Sharpe, 1985. Paperbound, $12.95.

MNOOKIN, ROBERT H. *In the Interest of Children: Advocacy Law Reform and Public Policy.* Pp. xii, 572. New York: W. H. Freeman, 1985. Paperbound, no price.

NEEDHAM, RODNEY. *Exemplars.* Pp. xvii, 247. Berkeley: University of California Press, 1985. $19.95.

NORD, DEBORAH EPSTEIN. *The Apprenticeship of Beatrice Webb.* Pp. ix, 294. Amherst: University of Massachusetts Press, 1985. $25.00.

NOVE, ALEC. *The Economics of Feasible Socialism.* Pp. xi, 244. Winchester, MA: George Allen & Unwin, 1983. $29.50. Paperbound, $9.95.

O'HAGAN, TIMOTHY. *The End of Law?* Pp. vi, 183. New York: Basil Blackwell, $29.95. Paperbound, $12.95.

PEARSON, CHARLES S. *Down to Business: Multinational Corporations, the Environment, and Development.* Pp. vii, 107. Washington, DC: World Resources Institute, 1985. Paperbound, $3.50.

PRIZZIA, ROSS. *Thailand in Transition: The Role of Oppositional Forces.* Pp. xii, 124. Honolulu: University of Hawaii Press, 1985. Paperbound, $9.00.

REARDEN, STEVEN L. *The Evolution of American Strategic Doctrine.* Pp. x, 131. Boulder, CO: Westview Press, 1984. Paperbound, $15.00.

RODE, REINHARD and HANNS-D. JACOBSEN, eds. *Economic Warfare or Detente: An Assessment of East-West Economic Relations in the 1980s.* Pp. xii, 301. Boulder, CO: Westview Press, 1986. Paperbound, $25.00.

ROZANOV, HERMAN. *Behind the Scenes of Third Reich Diplomacy.* Pp. 195. Moscow: Progress, 1984. Distributed by Imported Publications, Chicago, IL. $3.95.

SCHULTZE, WILLIAM A. *Urban Politics: A Political Economy Approach.* Pp. xiv, 241. Englewood Cliffs, NJ: Prentice-Hall, 1985. No price.

SCHULZINGER, ROBERT D. *The Wise Men of Foreign Affairs.* Pp. xiii, 342. New York: Columbia University Press, 1984. $27.50.

SCOTT, SAMUEL F. and BARRY ROTHAUS. *Historical Dictionary of the French Revolution, 1789-1799.* Pp. xvii, 1143. Westport, CT: Greenwood Press, 1985. $95.00.

SHAPIRO, SUSAN P. *Wayward Capitalists: Target of the Securities and Exchange Commission.* Pp. xix, 227. New Haven, CT: Yale University Press, 1984. $26.00.

SIMPSON, JOHN and ANTHONY G. McGREW, eds. *The International Nuclear Non-Proliferation System: Challenges and Choices.* Pp. xiii, 209. New York: St. Martin's Press, 1984. $27.95.

STEIN, WILLIAM W. *Peruvian Contexts of Change.* Pp. x, 400. New Brunswick, NJ: Transaction Books, 1985. No price.

STUBBS, WALTER, comp. *Congressional Committees, 1789-1982: A Checklist.* Pp. ix, 210. Westport, CT: Greenwood Press, 1985. $35.00.

TAR, ZOLTAN. *The Frankfurt School: The Critical Theories of Max Harkheimer and Theodore W. Adorno.* Pp. xx, 243. New York: Schocken Books, 1985. Paperbound, $9.95.

TAYLOR, J. A., ed. *Biogeography: Recent Advances and Future Directions.* Pp. xxviii, 404. Totowa, NJ: Barnes & Noble Books, 1984. $36.50.

THOMPSON, JOHN B. *Studies in the Theory of Ideology.* Pp. viii, 347. Berkeley: University of California, 1985. $32.50. Paperbound, $12.95.

THOMSON, DAVID. *Renaissance Paris.* Pp. 214. Berkeley: University of California Press, 1985. $37.50. Paperbound, $15.95.

UNGAR, SANFORD J., ed. *Estrangement: America and the World.* Pp. xii, 347. New York: Oxford University Press, 1985. $19.95.

WHITLAM, NICHOLAS and JOHN STUBBS. *Nest of Traitors: The Petrov Affair.* Pp. xii, 259. St. Lucia: University of Queensland Press, 1985. Paperbound, $9.95.

WIARDA, HOWARD J. *Ethnocentrism in Foreign Policy: Can We Understand the Third World?* Pp. 67. Washington, DC: American Enterprise Institute, 1985. Paperbound, no price.

WIMBUSH, S. ENDERS, ed. *Soviet Nationalities in Strategic Perspective.* Pp. xxviii, 253. New York: St. Martin's Press, 1985. $27.95.

WOOD, JAMES E., Jr., ed. *Religion and the State.* Pp. xi, 596. Waco, TX: Baylor University Press, 1985. $39.95.

WOODWARD, DAVID R. and ROBERT FRANKLIN MADDOX. *America and World War I: A Selected Annotated Bibliography of English-Language Sources.* Pp. xvii, 368. New York: Garland, 1985. $49.00.

YEARNS, W. BUCK. *The Confederate Governors.* Pp. 295. Athens: University of Georgia Press, 1985. $27.50.

INDEX

Adamany, David, 9
ADAMANY, DAVID, The New Faces of American Politics, 12-33
Advertisements, broadcast, 97
see also Television
Advisory opinions, 142, 144-45

Barone, Michael, 11
BARONE, MICHAEL, Campaign Finance: The System We Have, 158-62
Berman, Michael S., 11
BERMAN, MICHAEL S., Living with the FECA: Confessions of a Sometime Campaign Treasurer, 121-31
Bingham, Jonathan, 10
BINGHAM, JONATHAN, Democracy or Plutocracy? The Case for a Constitutional Amendment to Overturn *Buckley* v. *Valeo*, 103-14
Bolling, Richard, 10
BOLLING, RICHARD, Money in Politics, 76-85
Bradley, Tom, 41
Buckley v. *Valeo*, 43, 44, 45, 46, 47, 70-71, 83, 95, 96, 97, 103-14, 117, 135, 138, 161
Buckley, James, 41
Bundling, 100

Cable television, 156
Campaign Communications Reform Act, 147
CAMPAIGN FINANCE REFORM: THE UNFINISHED AGENDA, Fred Wertheimer, 86-102
CAMPAIGN FINANCE: THE SYSTEM WE HAVE, Michael Barone, 158-62
CAN THE PARTIES REGULATE CAMPAIGN FINANCING? Lloyd N. Cutler, 115-20
Carter, Jimmy, 150
Common Cause, 25-26, 87
Congress, public confidence in, 81, 96
Congressional campaigns for office, 64-75, 76-85, 86-102, 107, 109, 111
  alternative funds, 95
  see also House of Representatives, campaign for office; Senate, campaign for office
Cranston, Alan, 66
Cutler, Lloyd N., 11, 109
CUTLER, LLOYD N., Can the Parties Regulate Campaign Financing? 115-20
CUTLER, LLOYD N. and ROGER M. WITTEN, Preface, 9-11

D'Amato, Alfonse, 143

DEMOCRACY OR PLUTOCRACY? THE CASE FOR A CONSTITUTIONAL AMENDMENT TO OVERTURN *BUCKLEY* V. *VALEO*, Jonathan Bingham, 103-14
Democracy, U.S. public's confidence in, 106
Democratic Party of the United States v. *Wisconsin ex. rel. La Follette*, 117
Dole, Robert, 25, 80, 81
Drew, Elizabeth, 106

Eagleton, Thomas, 67, 81, 94, 140
Equality, political, 61-62, 70
  see also Political communication, equality of

Federal Election Campaign Act (FECA), 13, 18-19, 28, 29, 32, 41-42, 45, 70, 82, 104, 121-31, 142
  1974 amendments, 78, 89, 137
Federal Election Commission (FEC), 28, 101, 123 n. 1, 132-45
Federal Election Commission v. *Machinists Non-Partisan Political League (MNPL)*, 143-144
Federal Election Commission v. *National Conservative Political Action Committee*, 145
First Amendment, 35, 36, 38-39, 41, 44-45, 46, 70, 110, 113, 117, 137-38, 152
Foley, Tom, 54
Ford, Gerald, 150
Frank, Barney, 27
Fund-raising, political, 28, 32, 38, 42, 45, 66, 67, 93, 106, 125

Gardner, John, 44, 83
Goldwater, Barry, 67, 94
Grass-roots political activity, 128-29

Harder, Stephen, 10
HARDER, STEPHEN, Political Finance in the Liberal Republic: Representation, Equality, and Deregulation, 49-63
Hart, Gary, 91
Hollings, Ernest, 96
Honoraria, 82, 83
House of Representatives, campaign for office, 13-14

Incumbents, 41, 43-44, 52-53, 69, 74, 84, 92, 96, 118, 153
Independent expenditures, 42-43, 57-59, 70, 72-73, 96-97, 112, 138-41, 152
Interest groups, 77, 78, 79, 152

193

Javits, Jacob, 143

Legislators, influences on, 25-28, 53-56, 78, 79-80, 92-94
Leventhal, Harold, 110
LIVING WITH THE FECA: CONFESSIONS OF A SOMETIME CAMPAIGN TREASURER, Michael S. Berman, 121-31

Mathias, Charles McC., 10, 92
MATHIAS, CHARLES McC., Jr., Should There Be Public Financing of Congressional Campaigns? 64-75
McCarthy, Eugene, 41
McGovern, George, 41
Michigan, public financing of elections, 159
Minow, Newton N., 11
MINOW, NEWTON N. and LEE M. MITCHELL, Putting on the Candidates: The Use of Television in Presidential Elections, 146-57
Mitchell, Lee M., 11
MITCHELL, LEE M., see MINOW, NEWTON N., coauthor
MONEY IN POLITICS, Richard Bolling, 76-85

NEW FACES OF AMERICAN POLITICS, THE, David Adamany, 12-33
New Jersey, public financing of elections, 159
New York Times v. *Sullivan*, 58

Obey, David, 91
OF PHILOSOPHERS, FOXES, AND FINANCES: CAN THE FEDERAL ELECTION COMMISSION EVER DO AN ADEQUATE JOB? William C. Oldaker, 132-45
Oldaker, William, C., 11
OLDAKER, WILLIAM C., Of Philosophers, Foxes, and Finances: Can the Federal Election Commission Ever Do An Adequate Job? 132-45

Political action committees (PACs), 18-23 (and Tables 3, 4, and 5), 24-28, 29-30, 31-32, 47, 69, 77-79, 82, 83, 90-94, 95, 99, 100, 108, 123, 124, 144
Political campaigns
  contributions to, 44-46, 47, 54-55, 74, 82, 83, 95, 100-101, 118, 123-24, 130
  contributors to, 23-25, 27-28, 45, 62, 68-69, 71
  cost of, 67, 77, 94, 105-6
  election results and, 52-53
  expenditure limits for, 70, 82, 95-96, 107-8, 110, 111, 118-19, 126-29
  treasurer of, 130-31
Political candidates' use of personal funds, 68, 95, 107, 109, 111, 118-19

Political change, 40-41, 44, 45, 53
Political communication, 34-48
  equality of, 38-40
POLITICAL FINANCE IN THE LIBERAL REPUBLIC: REPRESENTATION, EQUALITY, AND DEREGULATION, Stephen Harder, 49-63
POLITICAL FINANCING AND THE CONSTITUTION, Ralph K. Winter, 34-48
Political parties, 13-18 (and Table 2), 24, 29, 30, 31, 32, 73-74, 109, 115-20, 155
  delegates to nominating conventions of, 99
  disparity between, 30-31
  expenditures of, 14, 15 (Table 1), 128, 130
  funding of, 29
Presidential campaigns, 14, 78, 82, 83, 89-90, 109, 112, 121-31, 146-57
Presidential candidate foundations, 99-100, 124
Presidential debates, 150-51, 155
Presidential Election Campaign Fund Act, 140, 142
  1976 amendments, 139
Presidential Primary Matching Payment Account Act, 124-25, 127
Public financing of political campaigns, 71-72, 73-74, 78, 82, 83-84, 89-90, 95-96, 107, 123, 124-26, 151, 159-60
PUTTING ON THE CANDIDATES: THE USE OF TELEVISION IN PRESIDENTIAL CAMPAIGNS, Newton N. Minow and Lee M. Mitchell, 146-57

Representation, political, 80
Response time (broadcasting), 97
  see also Television
Rostenkowski, Dan, 54

Senate, campaign for office, 14
Shannon, James, 81
SHOULD THERE BE PUBLIC FINANCING OF CONGRESSIONAL CAMPAIGNS? Charles McC. Mathias, Jr., 64-75
Soft money, 98, 160-61
SunPAC advisory opinion (AO-1975-23), 144-45

Tashjian v. *Republican Party of Connecticut*, 117
Technology in political campaigns, 15, 28, 155-56
Television
  equal-time law, 149-50, 153-54
  political coverage between elections, 157
  use in presidential campaigns, 146-57
  see also Advertisements, broadcast; Response time (broadcasting)

Watergate, 87-88
Wertheimer, Fred, 10

WERTHEIMER, FRED, Campaign Finance Reform: The Unfinished Agenda, 86-102
Winter, Ralph K., 10
WINTER, RALPH K., Political Financing and the Constitution, 34-48
WITTEN, ROGER M., see CUTLER, LLOYD N., coauthor
Wright, J. Skelly, 110

Of Special Interest

UNDERSTANDING BIG GOVERNMENT
The Programme Approach
by RICHARD ROSE, *Centre for the Study of Public Policy, University of Strathclyde, Glasgow*

What grows when government grows? Why? What are the consequences for government's effectiveness and consent? Richard Rose gives clear, concise answers to these questions by developing the program approach to understanding government. It relates what government is—a set of institutions—to what these institutions do. He explains how they mobilize laws, money and employees to produce public programs in education, health, economic development, law and order and defense. Government is big today because major programs make big claims upon society's resources.

Understanding Big Government contains a wealth of ideas and data about the size and dynamics of government in the United States, Britain, Continental Europe and Scandinavian countries. By systematically analyzing the growth of government programs from the 1950s to the 1980s, it provides a firm foundation for identifying trends—and problems—that will be important to us in 1990 and beyond. Clearly written and comprehensive in its scope, **Understanding Big Government** is an essential source book for students and scholars in the fields of comparative politics, political analysis, and public policy.

"This innovative book breathes the first breath of life in many years into the subject of big government. Rose's 'Programme Approach' is broader in concept and deeper in understanding than alternatives. It will spawn a host of new studies that greatly enlarge our understanding."
—Professor Aaron Wildavsky, *University of California*

"A book which will clearly deepen our understanding of the dynamics of that near-universal phenomenon in the 20th century—the growth of governmental activity."
Professor Rudolf Klein, *University of Bath*

"A remarkable achievement.... By its dispelling of many myths... which surround government activities, this book should stand on top of the reading list of any responsible policy maker in OECD countries."
—Bernard Cazes, *Commissariat General du Plan, Paris*

CONTENTS: Acknowledgements / Introduction: Government in the 1980s // I. Taking the Measure of Government / II. Causes and Consequences of Big Government / III. The Use of Laws as A Policy Resource / IV. Raising Tax Revenues / V. The Work of Public Employees / VI. The Organizations of Government / VII. Combining Resources into Programmes / VIII. The Limits of Big Government // References / Index

1984 / 260 pages / $28.00 (h) / $14.00 (p)

SAGE PUBLICATIONS, INC.
275 South Beverly Drive,
Beverly Hills, California 90212

SAGE PUBLICATIONS LTD
28 Banner Street,
London EC1Y 8QE, England

SAGE PUBLICATIONS INDIA PVT LTD
M-32 Market, Greater Kailash I, New Delhi 110 048, India

Industrial & Labor Relations Review

July 1986   **Volume 39, Number 4**

The Effects of Corporate Strategy and Workplace Innovations on Union Representation .... Thomas A. Kochan, Robert B. McKersie, & John Chalykoff

Unions, Pension Wealth, and Age-Compensation Profiles .... Steven G. Allen & Robert L. Clark

Do Retirement Dreams Come True? The Effect of Unanticipated Events on Retirement Plans .... Kathryn A. Anderson, Richard Burkhauser, & Joseph F. Quinn

The Impact of Deregulation on the Employment and Wages of Airline Mechanics .... David Card

Strikes, Strike Penalties, and Arbitration in Six States .... Craig A. Olson

The Effect of the Cost of Strikes on the Volume of Strike Activity .... Dennis R. Maki

The Relative Earnings of Vietnam and Korean-Era Veterans .... Saul Schwartz

Concentration in the Labor Market for Public School Teachers .... James Luizer & Robert Thornton

Feedback and Grievance Resolution .... Thomas K. Knight

For complete coverage of the world of industrial relations, also see our regular features: Book Reviews *and* Research in Progress.

Annual rates, U.S. and Canada: $18 individual; $30 institution.

Foreign, except Canada: $22 individual, $34 institution.

INDUSTRIAL AND LABOR RELATIONS REVIEW
207 Research Building, Cornell University
Ithaca, New York 14853

NEW from Sage!

MONEY, MEDIA, AND THE GRASS ROOTS
State Ballot Issues and the Electoral Process
by BETTY H. ZISK, *Boston University*

A comparative study of campaigns and outcomes on major ballot questions in four states from 1976 to 1982, this volume analyzes spending, grass roots activity, and voting behavior on 72 controversial issues, including taxes, the environment, the nuclear freeze, crime control, smoking, abortion, and parklands development.

Zisk critically evaluates the relation between campaign spending, media coverage and advertising, and voting behavior. Ballot issue campaigns are then evaluated via two models of democracy: the early Progressive goals for direct democracy and the more limited expectations of contemporary pluralists. The central finding of this volume concerns the crucial role of campaign spending. In both modest and massive campaigns, the high-spending side won 78% of the time. As the bulk of campaign funds went to advertising, one can conclude that voters' decisions were not based on an in-depth understanding of the issues. However, an examination of strategies in 16 underdog victories revealed that success for well-organized grass roots efforts and some degree of voter enlightenment are occasionally possible.

This volume makes an important contribution to understanding state politics, public policy, the electoral process, and the role of a diverse set of institutions, including interest groups, movements, parties, and the media.

ABRIDGED CONTENTS: I. Introduction // II. A Historical and Political Profile of Four States // III. An Overview of Fifteen Elections, 1976-1980: Political Context and Issues // IV. Campaign Expenditures // V. The Campaign, I: Media Intensive Campaigns // VI. The Campaign, II: Grass Roots Activity // VII. Voting Behavior: Confusion and Rationality on Ballot Questions // VIII. The 1982 Elections: High Spending, Old Issues Revisited, and the Nuclear Freeze // IX. Conclusion / Notes / References / Index

Sage Library of Social Research, Volume 164
1986 / 320 pages (tent.) / $29.95 (c) / $14.95 (p)

SAGE PUBLICATIONS, INC.
275 South Beverly Drive,
Beverly Hills, California 90212

SAGE PUBLICATIONS, INC.
2111 West Hillcrest Drive,
Newbury Park, California 91320

SAGE PUBLICATIONS LTD
28 Banner Street,
London EC1Y 8QE, England

SAGE PUBLICATIONS INDIA PVT LTD
M-32 Market, Greater Kailash I,
New Delhi 110 048 India

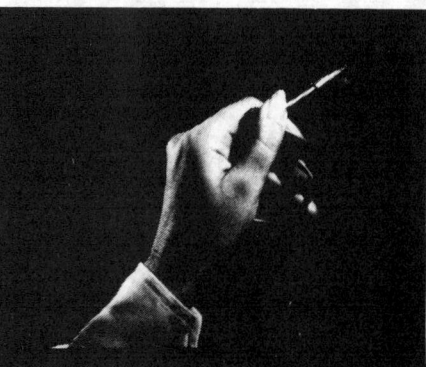

WOMEN GUARDING MEN
Lynn Zimmer
"This book vividly illuminates the legal, structural, and interpersonal dilemmas of women guards in men's prisons, and the various adaptations the women used to overcome these barriers."—Susan E. Martin, author of *"Breaking and Entering": Police Women on Patrol*
Cloth $25.00   288 pages

PROFESSIONAL POWERS
A Study of the Institutionalization of Formal Knowledge
Eliot Freidson
"A new book by Eliot Freidson is an event in sociology. This one will not disappoint. [Freidson] lucidly works his way toward a general sociology of occupations."
—Magali Sarfatti-Larson, Temple University
Cloth $20.00   260 pages

HIGHER EDUCATION AND THE STATE IN LATIN AMERICA
Private Challenges to Public Dominance
Daniel C. Levy
"Levy's work fills a significant void in Latin American studies. It will deservedly become an indispensable source for scholars and practitioners."—Guillermo O'Donnell, University of Notre Dame.
Cloth $27.50   452 pages

THE UNIVERSITY OF CHICAGO PRESS
5801 South Ellis Avenue
Chicago, IL 60637

THE AUTHORITATIVE AND THE AUTHORITARIAN
Joseph Vining
"In this remarkably wide-ranging meditation Professor Vining explores some profound issues of hierarchy, encompassing law, bureaucracy, and theology."—Paul A. Freund, Harvard Law School
Cloth $25.00   288 pages

HEGEMONY AND CULTURE
Politics and Religious Change among the Yoruba
David D. Laitin
Laitin explores the politics of religious change among the Yoruba of Nigeria and develops a theory of hegemony from the work of Antonio Gramsci to explain why this change did not result in political conflict.
Paper $13.95 (est.)   272 pages
Library cloth edition $30.00 (est.)

WRITING FOR SOCIAL SCIENTISTS
How to Start and Finish Your Thesis, Book, or Article
Howard S. Becker
With a Chapter by **Pamela Richards**
Becker offers eminently useful suggestions for ways to make social scientists better and more productive writers. Throughout, Becker's focus is on the elusive work habits that contribute to good writing, not the more easily learned rules of grammar or punctuation.
Paper $6.95   180 pages
Library cloth edition $20.00
Chicago Guides to Writing, Editing, and Publishing

Here's one reason why you need more life insurance...and three reasons why it should be our group insurance.

Family responsibilities increase and change—a new baby, a job change, a new home. Your family could have a lot to lose <u>unless</u> your insurance keeps pace with these changes.

Now here's why you need <u>our</u> group term life insurance.

First, it's low-cost. Unlike everything else, life rates have <u>gone down</u> over the past 20 years. And, because of our buying power, our group rates are low.

Second, you will continue to receive this protection even if you change jobs, as long as you remain a member and pay the premiums when due.

Third, our wide range of coverage allows you to choose the insurance that's right for you. And you can protect yourself and your entire family.

It's insurance as you need it. So check your current insurance portfolio. Then call or write the Administrator for the extra protection you need.

UP TO $240,000 IN TERM LIFE INSURANCE PROTECTION IS AVAILABLE TO AAPSS MEMBERS.
Plus these other group insurance plans:
Excess Major Medical
In-Hospital Insurance
High-Limit Accident Insurance

**Contact Administrator,
AAPSS Group Insurance Program**
Smith-Sternau Organization, Inc
1255 23rd Street, N.W.
Washington, D.C. 20037

800 424-9883 Toll Free
in Washington, D.C. area, 202 296-8030